909.82

The Origins of th

City and Islington Sixth Form College
283-309 Goswell Road
London
EC1
020 7520 0652

...IGTON

The Origins of
the Second World War

Historical Interpretations

Edited by

E. M. ROBERTSON

MACMILLAN

First published 1971 by
THE MACMILLAN PRESS LTD
Houndmills, Basingstoke, Hampshire RG21 2XS
and London
Companies and representatives
throughout the world

ISBN 0-333-11461-2

16   15   14   13   12   11   10   9   8
03   02   01   00   99   98   97   96

Printed in Malaysia

Contents

Acknowledgements

Acknowledgements are due to the editors of the following publications for permission to republish the articles included in this volume: *The Historian*; *Historical Studies (Proceedings of the Irish Historical Conferences)*; *International Affairs*; *Encounter*; *Past and Present*; *The Wiener Library Bulletin*; *The Historical Journal*; *Proceedings of the British Academy*; *The Middle East Journal*; *The Journal of Asian Studies*.

I am greatly indebted to Dr H. W. Koch, who is editing a similar volume to this one on the causes of the First World War, and to Messrs Owen Dudley Edwards and Victor Kiernan for most valuable suggestions; to Mr Colin Davies, Miss A. Jill R. McIntyre and Dr H. Graml for the patient help in the editorial work. I owe a great deal to the stimulus provided by my students, who read as their special subject *The Rome–Berlin Axis and the Destruction of Collective Security*, and to my wife, who has encouraged me throughout.

only expose allied propaganda, but prove that article 231 of the Treaty of Versailles by which Germany and her allies accepted the 'entire' responsibility for causing the war, was vicious. The Germans, under Thimme, worked hard on the publication of these documents, and by 1926 some fifty-four tomes of *Die Grosse Politik* were published.[3] Since the Germans were well ahead with their official publications, most of the early works on war origins were either Germanocentric or pro-German. S. B. Fay's books, which were sympathetic to the Central Powers, were translated into German, but not the more critical writings of Bernadotte Schmitt and later those of L. Albertini.[4] Hence, the historical picture of Germany in the critical years before Hitler came to power was favourable.

For political reasons the publication of the British documents was much slower.[5] Official policy before 1914 had been opposed by the more radical liberals, one of whose leading exponents, the late G. P. Gooch, claimed that the Boer War, which he opposed, forced him to turn from the history of ideas to that of foreign policy. Very courageously he had written a criticism of Grey's foreign policy as early as 1917.[6] After the war, he and Harold Temperley, two men of conflicting political leanings, were commissioned to publish the British documents. But there was much less co-operation between the government and historians in Great Britain than in Germany. Gooch and Temperley constantly had to threaten resignation if their work was tampered with. The final volume of the thirteen that they edited was only published in 1938 by which time interest was focused on more recent events.

Largely as a result of the publications on war origins civil servants and politicians in Britain knew that historians were on their trail. The myth of unanimity of the Cabinet, anonymity of the Civil Service, had to be preserved: hence, a protective cover was found (eventually in the fifty-year rule). There was also, and still is, a tendency in this country not to file important documents but to burn them. One wonders how much material on the Suez Crisis has been allowed to survive.

In the twenties, however, historians could still gain the upper hand of government departments on documents. strictly pertaining to the outbreak of the war. Thus a great number, but approximately only one in ten of the originals, were published. The French government, rather belatedly, followed the lead of others and started to publish its documents. The Italian government and the Vatican kept their archives for the pre-war period closed until much later.[7]

After World War I the documents were published systematically, and the volumes in chronological order. Memoir-writers could only with difficulty find a ready market among uncritical readers and some absurd myths were nipped in the bud. Scholarship, too, was international. For the greater part British, American, German and even French scholars worked on similar assumptions, admirably summed up by G. P. Gooch who, protesting against war propaganda, wrote in 1938: 'The belief that any nation or statesman was an arch-criminal is no longer held by serious students of history. It is part of the tragedy of the World War that every belligerent can make out a case entirely convincing to itself. For tragedy, in Hegel's words, is the conflict not of right versus wrong, but of right with right.'[8] Gooch's words echo some of the phrases used by Abraham Lincoln in his second inaugural, and make strange reading for students of World War II. They can be distorted to mean that the gods were at war with themselves; that questions of right and wrong, which Lord Acton, Gooch's teacher, regarded as the sole criterion for the judgement of men and affairs, are not the business of either the historian or statesman.

The general assumptions held by historians on both wars until very recently were well represented in a work by a Swiss historian, Walter Hofer, translated into English in 1954 with the title *War Pre-Meditated*. Hofer and others maintain that war in 1914 'broke out', or to use Lloyd George's words: 'the nations slithered over the brink into the cauldron of war'. The war of 1939, on the other hand, was 'unleashed' or pre-cipitated. In 1961 both theses were assailed on their flanks. In Germany something of a revolution in historical thinking was caused by the publication of a book, *Griff nach der Weltmacht*, by Professor Fritz Fischer. In some respects Fischer was anticipated by Professor Gordon A. Craig.[9] But Fischer made use of a wealth of unpublished documents from the Reich Central Archives, held in Eastern Germany, and his book reached a wide public. Fischer has discovered few fresh documents of significance for the July crisis of 1914, many but not all of which had already been used in Albertini's exhaustive study, regrettably neglected in Germany.

Fischer's book was translated into English in 1967. His conclusions on the July crisis are significant. He writes: 'As Germany willed and coveted the Austro-Serbian war and, in her confidence in her military superiority, deliberately faced the risk of a conflict with Russia and France, her leaders must bear a substantial share of the historical responsibility for the outbreak of general war in 1914.'[10]

A thesis of Fischer, also very relevant to World War II, is based on a memorandum of 9 September 1914 by Bethmann-Hollweg, from which he claims that it is possible to establish German war aims from the start of the war. They did not, as A. J. P. Taylor and others previously believed, develop as a result of military operations.[11] Fischer and the more extreme members of his school[12] are far less successful in proving that the Kaiser and his government had already formulated their territorial aims before the war broke out. Fischer's chapters dealing with the war years are convincing, and the central theme well substantiated. From the very first day of hostilities William II, not always successfully, made a systematic appeal to the principle of self-determination, above all in so far as it applied to the Islamic subject nationalities of the allies. The Kaiser thereby anticipated Lenin in wanting to convert a war between States into a civil war of liberation, a conclusion which for many of us is surprising and new.

On the whole Fischer's work had been given an ex-

tremely hostile reception in Germany. He has been
accused not only of distorting history but of betraying
his national culture. The basic issue between him and
his opponents revolves not merely round the dangerous distinction (used also in connection with Hitler)
between the words 'tactics' and 'aims'.[13] Fischer has
gone farther than this. He has brought to bear on his
subject a conceptual and methodological approach entirely new to German historiography. He focuses attention, not on the 'world-historical individual' but on the
social and economic structure of late Wilhelmine Germany. The majority of German historians now admit
that there can be no going back to the criteria of Fritz
Fischer's predecessors. Many of us who are in sympathy
with the impetus Fischer has given to modern scholarship are anxious however to know whether in the heat
of controversy he has not, at times, twisted the evidence to fit his central thesis. This subject is to be discussed by Dr H. W. Koch in a companion study of
1914.

There are several reasons why Fischer's writings are
of importance to students of World War II. If he is
right in maintaining that before August 1914 German
policy was already annexationist, then World War II
presents few serious problems. Hitler merely continued
the policy of Bethmann-Hollweg, and the Weimar
Republic, having no roots in German history, was an
awkward interlude. There are strong objections to this
view which will be discussed later.

Our general reaction to the Fischer controversy is to
look self-righteously down our Anglo-Saxon noses and
thank God that 'we are not as other men'. On further
reflection we discover that the question of war guilt,
given a new lease of life by Fischer, affects our own
judgement no less than that of the Germans. In the
first place, controversy on war guilt did not start during the peace negotiations in 1919 but can be traced
back to the very day war broke out. From August 1914
until well into 1915, and again in 1918, the archbishop
of Canterbury, Randall Davidson, kept up an animated correspondence with eminent German theolo-

gians such as Harnack, Dryander and Deissmann on the responsibility for the outbreak of hostilities. Although the exchange of letters was published in 1935, together with violently anti-Serb remarks by Asquith, recorded by Davidson, on 31 July 1914,[14] not a single authority has used these documents. Why was Harnack so desperately keen to vindicate the good name of Germany? Did he, like so many of his compatriots, feel uncomfortable about his country's actions, or did he share the more general view that Germany was subject to a grave injustice? A thorough reappraisal of the evidence is necessary.

After the war the guilt psychosis spread, and Davidson received a stream of irate protests coming, this time, from his own countrymen, one of whom was to be his own distinguished successor, William Temple. The war guilt problem was on the agenda of conferences held by churchmen throughout the twenties and discussion was on a sophisticated level.[15] Political historians have much to learn from what the churchmen had to say in order to understand the 'unspoken assumptions' of the twenties, for it was partly on those assumptions that the policy of both revisionism and appeasement was based.

Despite misgivings about the peace settlement of 1920 there was, in Britain at least, a restrained optimism about the future as a result of which the Royal Institute of International Affairs was established in 1920 and granted a charter in 1923.[16] Its job, according to Grey's opening speech, was to do for the present what historians do for the past. It was to make available a volume of documents and a survey for each year. It has been contended that Sir Arnold Toynbee's *Surveys* will be of practical value long after his *Study of History* is of antiquarian interest.[17]

Toynbee, like so many British historians, had a practical knowledge of affairs, gained largely from the Foreign Office where he worked in the same department as Lewis Namier. Namier, whose insights were also deepened by knowledge of the workings of the Stock Exchange, described his essay 'The Downfall of the Habsburgs' as very much a continuation of what he had been doing during the war.[18] After 1939 he wrote a spate of books on anti-semitism, Nazi Germany and the causes of World War II.[19] Robert W. Seton-Watson tells us that his *Britain and Europe* (1937) largely resulted from war work; in its sequel, *Britain and the Dictators* (1938), he correctly discerned the signs of the times. F. P. Walters gained genuine experience as an official, of the League of Nations on which he subsequently wrote what is still the standard work. E. H. Carr learnt Russian while working as a diplomat in the Baltic states. His intimate knowledge of Central Europe can in part be attributed to the personal role he played in the negotiations over the disputed area of Teschen. Later he may not have hit it off with his chief, Sir Robert Vansittart, who supposedly hated all things German. But it was not personal pique but a careful assessment of power factors that made Carr go over to appeasement, in favour of which he wrote by far the clearest rationale (to be discussed later).[20] Carr, too, never allowed his name to be used for war propaganda, and in 1943 he justified Germany's claims in Upper Silesia.[21] After the war he continued his writings on foreign policy as well as on his masterpiece, the *Bolshevik Revolution*.

Historians in the United States were also interested in public affairs and they may even have exerted a greater influence in shaping policy. Woodrow Wilson, himself a former university professor, took a host of scholars with him to the negotiations at Paris. Wilson has been blamed by Harold Nicolson for putting his men on the wrong jobs: Charles H. Haskins – the 'Duke of Normandy' as he was nicknamed – was not perhaps the right man for expert advice on Finland, but Robert Lord was not a wrong choice for Poland.[22]

No sooner had Wilson and his team returned than the challenge against the peace settlement was taken up by rival scholars. Perhaps no book since the Koran had had greater influence than *The Economic Consequences of the Peace* by J. M. Keynes, published in 1919. The Treaty of Versailles and its supposed author,

Wilson, came under such heavy fire as even to influence a presidential election.

In the United States there was also a revulsion against war propaganda and serious thought given to war origins. But American revisionism was more radical than British. By a roundabout way it prepared the ground for isolationism. Initially the revisionists, such as C. A. Beard, working in universities, tried to persuade their countrymen that the United States should not model itself on the military pattern of European states. Some of their ideas were later taken up by politicians and twisted to mean that the United States should politically, though not economically, stand aloof from the rest of the world.[23]

Historians in the Anglo-Saxon world as a whole, after 1920, regarded such things as the private manufacture of armaments and secret diplomacy, which was then a 'witch' word, with real suspicion. But diplomacy was their subject-matter and diplomatic history held pride of place in the history curricula of many universities. It was believed that the diplomatic documents would somehow lead to the centre of historical reality, a view which, according to Professor Butterfield, was only seriously challenged when Marxism became popular in the late thirties and was used as a criterion to interpret diplomacy.[24]

A whole generation of historians had conscientiously believed that the words exchanged between representatives of different states in some way coincided with what they did. This assumption was not altogether mistaken. Before 1914 there was that bond of understanding between men in high office necessary for the functioning of genuine diplomacy. Many of the crowned heads were blood relatives. A man like King Albert of the Belgians really used his family connections in the interests of peace, a fact often overlooked by those of us who are obsessed by naked power factors. The leading statesmen were of aristocratic or upper-middle-class origin with similar family and educational backgrounds. The foreign policy élite of this country was in some respects an exception. Sir Edward

Grey once remarked: 'These foreigners must be terrible intriguers to suspect us as they do. They should receive education at an English public school.'[25] Yet even Grey could hit it off with Ambassadors Lichnowsky and Cambon.

In the twenties Count von Brockdorff-Rantzau, the German ambassador in Moscow, found a kindred soul in Chicherin, People's Commissar for Foreign Affairs. They were both snobs and enjoyed the same wines.[26] But this was exceptional. Despite a rearguard action put up by certain diplomats, notably Curzon, the twenties witnessed the disintegration of diplomacy, or 'communication', as a means of maintaining relations between states. This process is admirably described in a symposium edited by Professor Gordon A. Craig and Felix Gilbert, *The Diplomats* (1953). With the consolidation of dictatorship in the thirties division hardened: statesmen now addressed each other from behind barriers of closed social systems.[27] We have only to read about the meetings between Eden and Mussolini,[28] Halifax and Hitler, Molotov and Ribbentrop, to realise that the words men said or wrote to each other meant little; the information they believed, or wanted to believe, about each other was paramount. Nothing is more urgently needed today than a book comparable to *The Diplomats* on spies.

After the outbreak of war in 1939 there was a corresponding change in the activities of historians. For a time A. J. P. Taylor worked with the Ministry of Information, Alan Bullock with the B.B.C.; H. R. Trevor-Roper, F. W. Deakin, Geoffrey Barraclough, Hugh Seton-Watson were in one or other of the intelligence departments; W. N. Medlicott in the Ministry of Economic Warfare. By 1945 historians as a rule were intelligence officers, or still worse – it would be embarrassing to mention too many names – Intelligence N.C.O.s in plain clothes.

Many of them were able subsequently to give a first-hand account of the persons and events with which they were only too familiar. Sir John Wheeler-Bennett, whose fluctuating views on Germany have given rise to

recent criticism,[29] was the only Englishman admitted
to the exclusive *Herren Klub* in Berlin where he met
General von Reichenau. He is still one of the leading
authorities on World War II. Miss Elizabeth Wiskemann lived an exciting double life, tutoring students
at Cambridge in term time and travelling extensively
in Europe during the summer vacation where she met
many leading statesmen and men of letters. Like some
of her contemporaries she had no illusion about the
future. She had started writing about the causes of the
war before it broke out, and continued her writings
after doing war work.[30]

A still younger generation of historians, born just
before or after 1939, has already made its debut, and
interest has to some extent switched to new fields, including the social consequences of the wars.[31] There
could be no better time to write about British policy
than the present, for not only has the fifty-year rule been
lowered by twenty years, which means that the Cabinet
papers are accessible until 1940[32] but a large number of
private collections of documents are available.

Soon our knowledge of British policy will no longer
be restricted to memoirs and the Foreign Office publications, in which there are many gaps, and those one-
sided accounts which, as D. C. Watt points out, have
neglected imperial and economic problems will be an-
tiquated.[33] Already Professor Medlicott, using a
wealth of hitherto restricted documents, has buried
some old controversies. He maintains that it is no
longer possible to distinguish between the appeasers
and resisters, 'the hawks and the doves', for both the
Foreign Office officials and their rivals in other departments of state sought some sort of comprehensive agreement with Germany.[34] It is to be hoped that the long-
awaited first volume of *Grand Strategy (The Official
History of the War)* by Professor Norman Gibbs will
soon enable us to see Britain's strategic position between 1919 and 1939 in its true perspective.

Brief mention should be made about the accessi-
bility of documents in other countries. In 1965 State
Department documents were still only open without

check up to 31 December 1932.[35] They are now open until 1939. The French documents are closed. Needless to say, the government of the Soviet Union does not welcome foreign historians with open arms to the archives in Moscow or Leningrad.

Ex-enemy countries provide a better trampling ground for scholars. Mussolini had an efficient intelligence service and came into possession, through more than one channel, of vital British documents.[36] It would be interesting to know more fully how these leakages occurred and whether some interesting things on British policy may not be unearthed in the archives in Rome rather than in the Public Records Office. Moreover, his diplomats were well informed; in many cases their diaries and private papers have been preserved.[37] It is thus possible to give good coverage to Mussolini's policy as well as his sordid private life. Yet the publication of the official Italian diplomatic documents has been slow, though thorough, and there are still wide gaps. In contrast it is impossible to keep Hitler's movements under regular observation. New records of his meetings with his generals and diplomats keep cropping up year by year.[38]

Most of the earlier accounts of World War II were based on the documents of the defeated, not the victorious, powers (see Paper 1). After 1945 the allies seized as much evidence as they could lay their hands on for the celebrated Nuremberg and Tokyo war trials. The documents were assembled hastily, not in their chronological order, and were sometimes badly catalogued. So great was the confusion among the Japanese documents that years later work on them had virtually to start from scratch. But the trials are of historical interest in themselves. The late Mario Toscano described how at first the aim of the Nuremberg trials was to prepare the way for the Tokyo trials, from which the American government hoped to find irrefutable proof of a world-wide Fascist conspiracy for world conquest.[39]

The trials themselves seemed to corroborate the ideas that had been advanced during the war itself; they did

not provoke a fresh inquiry. According to Rohan Butler's *Roots of National Socialism* (1941), German history was a black record which moved with teleological
progression from a remote period in the past to its logical absurdity in Hitler and war. A host of other historians, including A. J. P. Taylor in his earlier
works,[40] and more recently W. L. Shirer in *The Rise
and Fall of the Third Reich* (1962), have also given the
fullest publicity to the view that the German people
were mysteriously endowed with a double dose of
original sin.

The theory of collective war guilt, however, cannot
be dismissed too lightly. Many of us are only too familiar with the way some German historians have been
proclaiming from the house tops that the war of
1939–45 was not a German war but Hitler's war. Professor James Joll is right in pointing out in *Past and
Present* (July 1966) that Hitler and his regime cannot
be seen outside the context of German social life. At
some point before 1939 (Joll does not specify when) the
German public had abdicated political responsibility.

Joll (see Paper 2) and Professor J. S. Conway, survey-
ing the German literature on Hitler's coming to power,
pose challenging questions.[41] Was Hitler the leader
the Germans themselves wanted, or was he the 'evil
magician who misled and deceived them'? While it is
difficult if not impossible to know precisely what the
Germans before 1933 thought of Hitler, more is known
of what Hitler thought of the Germans. In his letter to
Colonel von Reichenau of 4 December 1932 he expressed
contempt for them. They could only be rescued from
their degenerate condition by a process of psychological
rearmament, which included terror. This 'regenerative'
process was to be followed by technical rearmament.

The letter, published by the Institut für Zeitgeschichte in Munich, in one of its celebrated documenta-
tions,[42] has not been translated into English and has
been notoriously neglected in this country. More recently members of the Institute, or those connected
with it, have focused attention not only on Hitler but
on social pressure groups interested in shaping Ger-

man policy. Dr Krausnick has painstakingly analysed the roots of anti-semitism and he demonstrates how it was used by Hitler to further his bellicose aims.[43] Dr H. Graml has compared the aims in foreign policy of Hitler and leaders of the German Resistance. He claims that in one sense the differences between them were not so great as was formerly believed. German Nationalists may have hated Hitler's regime, but they too were annexationists and sought an enlargement of the pre-1914 frontiers of the Reich. They differed from Hitler on one point, which is of such significance that it cannot be dismissed as a matter of mere tactics. They repudiated absolutely resort to war. Professor Trevor-Roper has been taken to task in one of his earlier works for not having taken this into account.[44]

Paradoxically, Goerdeler and Halifax, for very different reasons, held similar ideas on 'peaceful changes' in the status quo. Yet the reasons why Halifax sought an accommodation with Germany through direct approaches to Hitler, and why the German opposition only tried to make contact with the British government late in 1937, when it was too late, have yet to be explained. Very recently the organisation of foreign policy under Hitler and the work of Nationalist societies among racial Germans has been systematically studied by Dr H. A. Jacobsen.[45]

The German historians mentioned above have made good a deficiency in German historiography. They can no longer be accused of concentrating too exclusively on political and constitutional issues. They are working in an environment very different from that of their colleagues in Britain and the United States. The past is so much with them that they cannot be neutral and they are often subject to attack, not only by sections of the press but by certain university teachers. They have almost unanimously rejected the works of A. J. P. Taylor, which supply fuel to those nationalist politicians who bother to read them, not only because of his value judgements but because of his misinterpretation of the evidence. In this country revisionism is already respectable, and has had a longer history than most of us suppose. After 1950 Professor Butterfield, in his comparisons between Hitler and Napoleon and in his strictures on 'the pitfalls of official history', delivered Cassandra-like warnings against placing Hitler in a separate category of humanity.[46] One of his pupils, now Professor T. Desmond Williams, after a fruitful experience of editing the German Foreign Ministry documents, was no longer prepared to accept uncritically Namier's indictment of leading men in the Third Reich and of the appeasers (see Paper 1). In several articles[47] he cautiously put forward certain hypotheses which evidently met with the approval of A. J. P. Taylor, who spoke in praise of the work done in neutral Ireland.[48]

Paradoxically, Taylor adopted in his *Origins of the Second World War*, first published in 1961, precisely the same approach to World War II as that taken by historians to World War I before Fritz Fischer's challenge. The war resulted from faulty political calculations Hitler made of the international situation, not from his megalomania. Hitler made a mistake; he did not commit a crime. There is much in Taylor's book which is instructive. In the early chapters he shows how the debates on World War I prepared the ground for a second conflict. We are well advised to read these chapters carefully. Taylor's account of the reactions in the House of Commons to the Russo-German Non-Aggression Pact of 23 August 1939 is superlative. A first reading of *The Origins of the Second World War* may suggest that Taylor has modified his earlier anti-German prejudices.[49] This is not so. Hitler was just another German who continued the policy of his predecessors, Bethmann-Hollweg and Stresemann. Perhaps Taylor could have explained why there were such wide differences of opinion between Hitler and such men as, for example, Bulow, his State Secretary, who was after all a diplomat of the old school. Had there been full agreement between them Taylor's argument would be more convincing. In trying to prove continuity in German policy he also puts a strained interpretation on Fischer's thesis.

Taylor's ideas no less than Fischer's caused a sensation. But there is a striking difference between their intentions. Whereas Fischer has brought to bear on his subject a weight of documentary evidence, some of which is new, neither Taylor nor his opponents claim to have made substantial new discoveries (see Papers 3–6). Only one instance of a reinterpretation of existing evidence need be cited here, the historical authenticity and importance of the Hossbach Protocol of 5 November 1937 which has been discussed *ad nauseam*. Taylor dismisses the document, and both D. C. Watt and Alan Bullock (see Paper 9) go a long way with him, the latter claiming that it is evidence of a change in Hitler's 'attitude' rather than 'policy'.[50] But suppose the Hossbach Protocol never existed, there is also a directive, signed by Blomberg and approved by Hitler, of 7 December 1937. Taylor, and others, do not lay sufficient stress on this document, perhaps because it was first published in an appendix to one of the volumes of the German documents covering a later period.[51] It makes much stronger reading than Blomberg's directive of 24 June 1937, and some passages in it bear more than an accidental resemblance to Hitler's ideas and Blomberg's reservations in the Hossbach Protocol. It is also argued that Hitler had vented belligerent ideas on ealier occasions, for instance in his memorandum on the Four-Year Plan.[52] But there is all the difference in the world between general statements, such as that 'the German economy must be ready for war in four years', and a military order which names specific enemies and a possible date for action. The evidence on the authenticity of the Hossbach Protocol has been thoroughly reappraised by H. W. Koch (see Paper 8) and W. Bussman.[53]

It is only to be expected that the debate started by Taylor on whether Hitler was an opportunist or a planner will continue, and Bullock's view (see Paper 9) that the one idea does not exclude the other is not entirely convincing.

Foreign policy is less flexible than armament plans. Taylor relied heavily on the conclusions of Burton

Klein, who minimised the degree of German rearmament before 1939 (see Paper 5).[54] Economic historians, who are far from agreement among themselves, have subsequently re-examined the evidence. Alan S. Milward maintains that Hitler planned for a *Blitzkrieg*, and Berenice Carroll in a recent work argues persuasively that the German economy was directed to war even if it was not fully geared to war.[55] But it is not possible from a study of the German war economy alone to determine precisely which enemy Hitler had in mind, at any given time, especially after 1937.

It is the opinion of the editor that Hitler was obsessed, not only by the will to power but also by revenge. Hence the contradictions in his policy and the confusion of historians. At least as early as 28 May 1938 Hitler spoke in all seriousness to his generals about waging war against what he had already described as his 'hate-inspired antagonist', England. He even hinted that there might be a German invasion of the Netherlands.[56] But he could not start on the necessary expansion of the navy for war with Britain, then under discussion with Admiral Raeder, because of the needs of the army, arising from the Czech crisis.[57] In the summer of 1938 Hitler's wrath was still directed against the Czechs, because of 'their rascally trick' in May of having partially mobilised against Germany.

Denied a chance to thrash the Czechs by the Munich Agreement, Hitler's anger was next turned against Churchill, Eden and Duff Cooper. But there were other scapegoats, the pessimists among his own generals and, above all, the Jews. It is more than a coincidence that his famous secret address to the press of 10 November, in which he gloated over the effect of German propaganda 'in wrecking the nerves of the gentlemen of Prague', took place the day after the 'Night of the Broken Glass' (see Paper 8).[58] Hitler also on this occasion attributed German success in the previous summer to the fact that the telephone lines linking Prague with Paris and London, which ran through Geman territory, had been tapped, presumably by

Goering's *Forschungsamt*.[59]

Hitler's thirst for vengeance after 10 November could hardly have been satisfied without an occupation of Prague. What next? For a time Hitler may have been in doubt whether Germany should seek further expansion in the East or, as advocated by Ribbentrop, do a deal with Poland and go to war with the Western Powers.[60] According to his critics he was worried by the prospect of inflation and came round to the view late in 1938 that war was inevitable. Perhaps the intercepts which Goering's office received 'played a part in incensing his animosity against Britain still further'.[61]

Early in 1939 Germany at last started on an ambitious programme of naval expansion.[62] This time it was not to be interfered with by unexpected continental commitments. Even in the directive of 11 April for a campaign against Poland the goal of German armaments still remained war with the West. One very important passage from Hitler's address to his generals of 23 May has been mistranslated in most works in English. Hitler did not say 'there will be war', but 'there will be fighting'. On this occasion he can hardly be accused of monomania, for he spoke confusedly of two quite separate military operations in the East and West, and declared that Germany must not 'slither into war' on account of Poland.[63] Hitler had to reassure his generals that there would not be a war on two fronts but that Germany would have to be prepared to fight one. In his addresses to the generals of 14 and 22 August the stress changed to war with Poland and the necessity of British neutrality.[64] But there was already an element of doubt. On the twenty-third Jodl learnt from Hitler's adjutant, Schmundt, that Hitler was not quite certain whether Britain would not act in earnest this time. But he did not want war with Britain.[65] With Russia neutralised by the Non-Agression Pact of 23 August he knew that if war came it would be a phony war.[66] Thus it certainly cannot be claimed that Hitler 'stumbled' into war. He wanted war with Poland and was prepared for war with the West.

At first Hitler fought a war on two levels: against Poland for the recovery of lost territories; against Britain and France to break a centre of resistance. After the defeat of France he could, at last, plan to fight the war he really wanted, and Bullock dates the real beginning of World War II from Hitler's attack on Russia on 22 June 1941 (see Paper 9). There are those who differ from Bullock about dates. Barraclough argues persuasively that the war started when Japanese armies invaded China in 1937; Haile Selassie dates it from the Italian invasion of his country in 1935.[67] However central was Germany's role under Hitler, the ambitions of other states, notably Italy and Japan, cannot be ignored. It is evident from a study of the Italian and recently published French Foreign Ministry documents that as early as 1932 Mussolini intended by force to topple the Republican government in Spain – the first omen of civil war. Towards the end of that year his own diplomats feared that he might recklessly provoke war with Yugoslavia and France, through the support given by 'private' Italian organisations to Croat terrorists. Conservative diplomats in Rome, the Jesuits and even King Victor Emmanuel, believed that Italy should realise her ambitions in a comparatively 'safe' part of the world, Ethiopia. But they insisted that a military operation against that country could only succeed if Italy were assured that neither Britain nor France would intervene. Late in 1931 and early in 1932 very secret negotiations were held between officials of the French and Italian Foreign Ministries, to the satisfaction of Laval, then premier, but not of Mussolini. For a short time, early in January 1933, Mussolini was persuaded to take up the plan of an invasion of Ethiopia. But he did not believe that an agreement with France was necessary: he expected that the French would merely stand aside in the face of Italian action.[68]

Late in December 1934, after the murder of King Alexander of Jugoslavia and Barthou, Laval's successor, by Croat terrorists, some of whom were sheltered in Italy, Mussolini reversed his policy. Fearing an *An-*

schluss and the resurgence of Germany as a military power, he was now prepared to do a deal with France in return for a verbal promise given by Laval for 'a free hand' in Ethiopia. The meaning of this agreement is open to various interpretations (see Paper 10). The history of the subsequent Rome Agreements has been told admirably in two recent works.[69] There is nothing substantial to add to the sequel, *The Rome–Berlin Axis* (1966) by Miss Elizabeth Wiskemann, except that she might have devoted more space to the exchanges between the two dictators in the year 1933.

Finally, to what extent did Mussolini share responsibility for the outbreak of war? By using terrorism as an instrument of policy and inciting revolt in areas marked out for Italian expansion he had done a good deal of icebreaking for Hitler. By intervening in the war in 1940 he spread the area of operations and thus contributed towards converting a European war into a world war.

It is less easy to establish any direct connection between German and Japanese policy. In recent years a revisionist school of American and Japanese historians have examined the long-term origins of the Pacific war. According to J. B. Crowley the occupation of Manchuria in 1931–2 was not simply provoked by the local army commanders who thereby forced the cabinet in Tokyo to shoulder the consequences of their action (see also Paper 11). Subversion and infiltration, through control of the South Manchurian railway, had been going on with some government approval in the twenties.[70] The Manchurian and Shanghai incidents shattered all hopes of disarmament, and resulted in the Stimson doctrine of non-recognition, but they cannot be regarded by themselves as among the major causes of the war.[71] Nor was there any collusion between Germany and Japan in the year 1933 when both powers left the League of Nations. Although Rosenberg, as a free-lance diplomat, pressed for recognition of Manchukuo, he was overruled by the German Foreign Ministry. Besides, the Japanese abhorred Rosenberg's racial theories. Ribbentrop, far less scrupulous than

Rosenberg, took up the latter's ideas but encountered some difficulties in winning Hitler over to friendship with Japan.[72] On 26 November 1936 the non-committal Anti-Comintern Pact between Germany and Japan was concluded. Thereafter it was hoped in Berlin that Japan would adhere rigidly to an anti-Russian line and co-operate with China.

Unexpectedly, events elsewhere deflected the attention of the Japanese. J. B. Crowley, and others, dismiss the view that the Marco Polo Bridge incident was 'the sequence of a conspiracy by the Japanese military' and a 'repetition of the pattern of aggression identical with the Mukden Incident of 1931' (see Paper 11). Crowley has brought to bear on the subject a wealth of Japanese documentary material. By August 1936 both the Japanese government and most sections of the Army High Command no longer believed that the occupation of North China, except East Hopei, was possible. Instead, they were 'intensely concerned with building a powerful military establishment for a possible war with the Soviet Union'. Indeed, war between Japan and Russia can be described as the inevitable war that never broke out until after Japan's defeat. With their attention fully absorbed by Russia, the Japanese service chiefs were most anxious to avoid serious complications in China and, at first, strove for an immediate local settlement of the dispute. In the confused situation which followed the incident, the government of Nanking sent four divisions into northern China, and later attacked Japanese positions in the Shanghai area. The upshot was an intense wave of chauvinism in both Japan and China, resulting in full-scale war.[73] It has not yet been established what sort of advice Chiang Kai-shek had been given by the pro-Chinese German military mission, which certainly followed a policy at variance with that of the German embassy in Tokyo. At the end of 1937 it encountered opposition from Ribbentrop, who, against the wishes of the German Foreign Ministry, persuaded Hitler to conclude the tripartite anti-Comintern Pact of November 1937 which Ribbentrop intended as a basis for a

tripartite military alliance against the West. He made
his first approach to the Japanese on the prospective
alliance in January 1938.

The bonds which held Germany, Italy and Japan
together were much looser than Chamberlain and his
advisers believed.[74] Although British service chiefs
gave priority to the defence of London against air
attack they could not ignore imperial defence. After
1933 they planned on the assumption of a simultaneous war with Germany and Japan; by July 1937
provision was also made for war with Italy. It is more
than a coincidence that each move to detach Italy from
the Axis that year was accompanied by the dispatch of
reinforcements to the area of the Suez Canal.[75]

The role of India and the Dominions now assumed
capital importance. Palestine, vital for Britain's land
and air communications with India and the Far East,
as well as for oil supplies, was an additional commitment. The Arabs, incited by Italian propaganda from
Radio Bari since 1936, were in full revolt. It is a surprise to many of us to learn that after the Czech crisis
of 1938 Britain deployed more troops in Palestine than
for an expeditionary force to France. Britain too, after
the meeting of the Commonwealth prime ministers in
the summer of 1937, was under constant pressure both
to steer clear of conflicts in Europe and to maintain
adequate naval forces at Singapore (supposedly completed as a naval base in 1937). It has been suggested
that British inactivity during the Czech crisis was in
part due to the pressure of the Dominions and not just
because Chamberlain trusted Hitler.[76]

No better contemporary account of Britain's strategic position can be found than in a lecture delivered
by E. H. Carr late in 1937, which has been surprisingly
neglected. 'We cannot', Carr maintained, 'afford to
pursue a policy which leads straight to a consolidation
of a German–Japanese–Italian bloc confronting the
rest of the world.' There was little chance of a reversal
of Japanese policy, for friendship with Japan 'would
have to be bought at the expense of the United States'.
Britain would either have 'to recognise Italy as the

leading Mediterranean power, or come to terms with Germany in order to reassert her supremacy in the Mediterranean'. In Carr's view the Rome–Berlin Axis presented 'no serious obstacle. It was so brittle that it would snap at a touch.'[77] Carr and others quite understandably failed to perceive that the Japanese and Italians were capable of coming into collision with Britain, not as a result of concerted action with Germany but from fear or jealousy of Germany. Mussolini, for instance, planned his invasion of Albania to forestall complete German domination in the Balkans.

After the Munich Agreement the question facing Chamberlain's Cabinet was no longer whether Britain should confront the Axis Powers but on measures to be taken if confronted by them. There was genuine cause for alarm. According to the diary of Helmut Groscurth, an *Abwehr* officer, who was on bad terms with Hitler, a senior British intelligence officer drew up a report on Hitler's aims at the end of 1938. Its content was described as so accurate as to correspond almost identically with the ideas Hitler expressed at a meeting of officers of all three services on 10 February 1939, no account of which has been found.[78]

In instructions to Lindsay, the British ambassador in Washington, of 24 January 1939, Halifax, with Cabinet approval, described reports emanating from a 'highly placed German' of 'undoubted integrity' who was anxious to prevent Hitler from committing crimes. He maintained that Hitler intended an invasion of the Netherlands and Switzerland and to push Italy into the war. (We now know that the author of the report was Goerdeler.) Action was expected in the middle of February.[79] The Japanese, who were now successful in southern China and resentful because their New Order in East Asia had not been recognised by the Western Powers, might take advantage of Britain's weakness and attack the Dutch East Indies. Halifax felt that 'due account should be paid to possible action by the United States fleet in the event of a war between this country and Japan'.[80]

Soon there was to be a series of crises, different in

character from that envisaged by Halifax, involving
Central Europe, the Mediterranean and the Far East.
As a result of the German occupation of Prague Chamberlain announced his guarantee of Poland of 30
March. On 13 April, after the Italian invasion of Albania, the British and French guarantees to Greece and
Romania were made public.[81] The French, now
alarmed by the prospect of imminent war with Italy,
whose military power was still grossly exaggerated,
started concentrating naval forces in the Mediterranean and insisted that no British forces should be
dispatched to the Far East.[82]

Britain had to consider not only France but the
Dominions, for she had assured Australia that adequate forces should be maintained in the Far East. She
could only meet her commitments if some help was
forthcoming from the United States. Although isolationist opinion in that country was still strong, President Roosevelt and, above all, Cordell Hull were really
suspicious of Japan.[83] Japanese forces had occupied
Hainan early in 1939 and later the Spratly Islands,
from which they could menace the Philippines. It was
believed by Hull that Japan intended not only to conclude a tripartite alliance with Italy and Germany but
to go to war with Britain and perhaps the United
States.[84]

On 11 April Halifax told Kennedy, the American
ambassador, that 'the sooner' the U.S. fleet was sent
from the Atlantic to the Pacific 'the better'.[85] Roosevelt, encouraged by the French, agreed to this 'very
bold step' which duly took effect on 16 April. But
strings were attached. Roosevelt earnestly insisted that
conscription should come into force in Britain before
Hitler's speech of 28 April.[86] It is difficult to assess
fully the result of the fleet movement. Was it intended
as a strategic move, or to put Japan under political
pressure and so deter her from drawing closer to Germany?

Events in another part of the world were soon to
cause the Japanese army leaders, who previously were in
favour of closer relations with Germany, to revise their

attitude. Japanese forces were badly mauled by the Red Army in the frontier incident of Nomonham. Worse was to follow. The Russo-German Non-Agression Pact of 23 August took Tokyo completely by surprise, and the negotiations for a tripartite alliance were temporarily suspended. The defeat of France provided Japan with an opportunity of renewing her advance south, this time into northern Indo-China. In September 1940 a defensive military alliance was concluded by Germany, Italy and Japan: its aim was to deter the United States from armed intervention in Europe or Asia. Instead the alliance hardened the attitude of Roosevelt's administration which, after Japanese forces occupied southern Indo-China in July 1941, took the lead in imposing full-scale sanctions. It was only a matter of time before Japan's economy would be brought to a standstill by lack of oil. Hence, the Japanese had to choose between national humiliation and peace with the United States or a resounding military victory the fruits of which would be the raw materials of East Asia (see Paper 12).[87]

Our knowledge of events in the Far East, despite the excellent work done, is far from complete. Little is known about the policy of Japan's two neighbours, China and the Soviet Union. The latter had to think in terms of the possibility of eventual war with both Japan and Germany, and hence pursued actively the policy of collective security.[88] But Soviet and East European historians are forced to maintain an ominous silence on the reasons why Stalin concluded the Non-Agression Pact with Hitler on 23 August 1939. From Japanese sources G. R. Storry and F. W. Deakin give us penetrating insights into Soviet espionage, but they cannot tell us exactly why Stalin failed to act on accurate information, which Sorge was able to supply him in 1941, about the military intentions of Hitler and General Togo.[89] It is hoped that Professor J. Erickson's sequel to his *Soviet High Command* will enlighten us from Russian sources on why the Soviet armed forces were taken by complete tactical surprise when Hitler attacked on 22 June 1941.

Historical investigation in the United States was also
after 1941 focused on the failure of the armed forces to
draw correct conclusions from accurate information received by the intelligence organisations on the pending
Japanese attack.[90] With the cold war there was a
change. The Americans saw themselves confronted
with a new international threat, this time organised
from Moscow, and it became fashionable for publicists
with Republican leanings to vindicate their past and
to establish firmly an anti-communist line. There were
even attempts to exculpate Mussolini and Hitler.[91]

But revisionism of this sort also won the support of
historians with popular standing. In a symposium *Perpetual War for Perpetual Peace* (ed. H. E. Barnes) the
aim was to prove that in 1941 President Roosevelt
purposely exposed the Pacific fleet at Pearl Harbor and
goaded the Japanese into attacking it, thus bringing
the United States into the war on the side of the Anglo-
Russian allies in Europe. According to one contributor
Roosevelt's 'political ambitions and mendacious
foreign policy' meant that 'some thousand American
boys were quite needlessly butchered ...'. In 1953 a
leading critic of this school, Professor R. H. Ferrell (see
Paper 13) wrote: 'present-day revisionism has joined
itself with a blind partisan hysteria and hatred for the
late President Franklin D. Roosevelt' and the animus
against Roosevelt far extended that against Wilson
after 1919. 'Nevertheless,' Ferrell argued, 'the revisionists have not been able to convince the American
people this time that participation in the Second
World War was a mistake.'

Yet many Americans had not a clear conscience
either about their country's policy towards Japan
under Cordell Hull, or about the conduct of the war in
its concluding phases. Critical scholars with no axe to
grind have taken Roosevelt and his advisers to task for
both negligence and failure to maximise political options; they do not accuse him of 'staging' American
intervention.[92] Moreover, writing mainly from documents produced at the Tokyo war trials, they prove beyond all reasonable doubt that there was no concerted

action between Germany and Japan. Toscano has examined the Italian, and T. Sommer and J. Compton
the German evidence. The two latter have much to say
on the contradictions in Hitler's policy towards both
Japan and the United States, and they have some corrections to make to Toscano's chronology of the negotiations for a tripartite military alliance.[93]

In more recent years Japanese historians themselves
have entered the field (Papers 11 and 12), and the long-
term causes of the Pacific war have been discussed in
joint Japanese–American seminars. The results are
somewhat startling. 'Some American scholars maintain
that the United States was at least partly responsible for
the war.... Some Japanese scholars have insisted that
Japanese militarism, aggression and imperialism were
even worse than they appeared in balanced accounts.'[94]
It is only to be hoped that similar seminars will take
place more regularly among historians of all former
belligerents, including the Soviet Union. By this means
prominence could be given not only to those vital
books and sources which might otherwise be overlooked but to central issues such as the effects of the
world economic crisis of 1930 on international politics.

Notes

[1] *History in a Changing World* (London, 1956) ch.
XIV; *History and the Common Man* (address to the
Historical Association) (London, 1966); *An Introduction to Contemporary History* (Pelican edition, 1968)
pp. 28 and 34–6.

[2] *The Origins of the Second World War* (London,
1963) p. 18.

[3] M. Toscano, *The History of Treaties and International Politics* (Baltimore, 1966) pp. 134–5.

[4] S. B. Fay, *Origins of the World War* (New York,
1928); B. E. Schmitt, *The Coming of the War* (New
York, 1930). According to Professor W. N. Medlicott,
the ideas of L. Albertini in *The Origins of the War of
1914* (London, 1952) are more in line with Schmitt's

than Fay's: see *Contemporary England* (London, 1967) p. 239, n. 7.

⁵ Toscano, *Treaties and International Politics*, pp. 142–3.

⁶ See H. Butterfield, 'Grey in July 1914', *Historical Studies* (Proceedings of the Irish Historical Conferences) 5 (1965).

⁷ Toscano, *Treaties and International Politics*, p. 139.

⁸ *Studies in Diplomacy and State Craft* (London, 1942) p. 104.

⁹ *The Politics of the Prussian Army, 1640–1945* (Princeton, 1955) pp. 287 ff.

¹⁰ *Germany's Aims in the First World War* (London, 1968) p. 88.

¹¹ *The Struggle for the Mastery of Europe* (London, 1954) ch. XXXIII.

¹² Imanuel Geiss, *July 1914: The Outbreak of the First World War – Selected Documents* (London, 1967).

¹³ See J. A Moses, *The War Aims of Imperial Germany: Professor Fritz Fischer and his Critics* (Brisbane, 1968). See also '1914', *Journal of Contemporary History*, 3 (1966).

¹⁴ G. K. A. Bell, *Archbishop Davidson* (London, 1935) pp. 733 ff.

¹⁵ The question of war guilt is discussed extensively in F. A. Iremonger, *William Temple, Archbishop of Canterbury* (London, 1948) esp. p. 382; and in R. C. D. Jasper, *George Bell, Bishop of Chichester* (London, 1967) ch. VI. The efforts of Archbishop Söderblom of Uppsala to bring about an Anglo-German reconciliation, because of the war guilt problem, have until recently been almost totally neglected: see B. Sundkler, *Nathaniel Söderblom: His Life and Work* (London, 1968) chs VI and VII.

¹⁶ See *Contemporary History in Europe*, ed. D. C. Watt, with introduction by Alan Bullock (London, 1969) p. 55.

¹⁷ See R. Pares, *The Historian's Business* (London, 1961) ch. II.

[18] *Vanished Supremacies* (London, 1958) ch. x.

[19] *Conflicts* (London, 1943); *Diplomatic Prelude* (London, 1948); *Europe in Decay* (London, 1950); *In The Nazi Era* (London, 1952).

[20] 'Britain as a Mediterranean Power', *The Gust Lecture* (University College of Nottingham, Nov 1937). Many of the views Carr held before the war can be found in *Ambassadors at Large: A Study of Foreign Policy from Versailles to the Outbreak of War*, with an introduction by Lord Halifax (London, 1940).

[21] *Conditions of Peace* (London, 1943) pp. 47–8 and ch. ix.

[22] *Peacemaking* (London, 1934), and F. M. Powicke, *Modern Historians and the Study of History* (London, 1955) pp. 114–15.

[23] S. Adler, *The Isolationist Impulse: Its Twentieth-Century Reaction* (London, 1957), and M. Jonas, *Isolationism in America 1935–1941* (Ithaca, N.Y., 1966).

[24] *Diplomatic Investigations: Essays in the Theory of International Politics*, ed. H. Butterfield and M. Wight (London, 1956) ch. ix.

[25] G. M. Thompson, *The Twelve Days* (London, 1964) p. 63.

[26] G. Hilger and A. G. Meyer, *The Incompatible Allies: A Memoir History of German–Soviet Relations 1918–1941* (New York, 1953) pp. 94 ff.

[27] For an excellent short account, see G. A. Craig, 'Totalitarian Approaches to Diplomatic Negotiation', in A. O. Sarkissian (ed.), *Studies in Diplomatic History and Historiography in Honour of G. P. Gooch* (London, 1961).

[28] M. Toscano, 'Eden's Mission to Rome on the Eve of the Italo-Ethiopian Conflict', ibid.

[29] See David Astor, 'Why the Revolt against Hitler was Ignored', *Encounter*, xxxii (June 1969).

[30] *The Europe I Saw* (London, 1968); *Czechs and Germans* (London, 1938); *Undeclared War* (London, 1939). See also Bibliography.

[31] E.g., K. Robbins, *Munich 1938* (London, 1968), A. Marwick, *Britain in the Century of Total War* (London, 1968).

[32] Viscount Templewood, in *Nine Troubled Years* (London, 1954) p. 297, describes how Chamberlain took decisions without consulting the Cabinet.

[33] 'Appeasement: The Emergence of a Revisionist School', *Political Quarterly* (April–June 1965).

[34] 'Britain and Germany: The Search for an Agreement 1930–1937', *The Creighton Lecture in History* (London, 1969).

[35] D. C. Watt, *Personalities and Policies: Studies in the Formulation of British Foreign Policy in the Twentieth Century* (London, 1965) p. 214.

[36] Toscano, *Treaties and International Politics*, pp. 28–9. Toscano also describes how the gaps in the Japanese documents can in part be filled because the American intelligence service decoded a large number of telegrams exchanged between Tokyo and several of its major embassies abroad: ibid., p. 335.

[37] Ibid., pp. 454–60.

[38] R. J. O'Neill, *The German Army and the Nazi Party 1933–1939* (London, 1966) p. 127. O'Neill has made extensive use of General von Weich's papers.

[39] Toscano, *Treaties and International Politics*, pp. 164–8 and pp. 335–6. See also E. Davidson, *The Trial of the Germans* (New York, 1966).

[40] *The Course of German History* (London, 1945).

[41] '*Machtergreifung* or due process of History: Historiography of Hitler's rise to power', *Historical Journal*, 3 (1965), and K. F. Werner, *Das nationalsozialistische Geschichtsbild und ie deutsche Wissenschaft* (Stuttgart, 1967); reviewed by F. Graus, *Vierteljahrshefte für Zeitgeschichte*, 1 (1969).

[42] Thilo Vogelsang, 'Hitlers Brief an Reichenau vom 4. Dezember 1933', *Vierteljahrshefte für Zeitgeshichte*, 4 (1959).

[43] See also H. Krausnick's account of the work of the Institutfür Zeitgeschichte in Munich, in *Contemporary History in Europe*, pp. 166–70, and *The Anatomy of the S.S. State*, trans. R. Barry, M. Jackson and D. Long, ed. H. Krausnick *et al.*, with an introduction by Elizabeth Wiskemann (London, 1968).

[44] *Der deutsche Widerstand gegen Hitler*, ed. W.

Schitthenner and H. Buchheim (Cologne, 1966) pp. 22–3.

[45] *Nationalsozialistische Aussenpolitik 1933–1939* (Frankfurt, 1969), reviewed by Miss Elizabeth Wiskemann in *History Today* (April 1969).

[46] *History and Human Relations* (London, 1951) pp. 182 ff. and *Christianity and History* (London, 1950) pp. 44–7.

[47] E.g., 'Negotiations Leading to the Anglo-Polish Alliance', *Irish Historical Studies*, 10 (1956).

[48] *The Origins of the Second World War*, p. 12.

[49] Taylor in the *New York Review* (8 June 1968) wrote: 'Germans were no more wicked in aspiring to dominate Europe, or even the world, than others were in resolving to stop them. The Germans were in a sense less wicked. For their domination of Europe was achieved with little physical destruction and comparatively few casualties, whereas the effort to resist them produced general devastation. However these moral speculations have no relevance for the historical observer.'

[50] Watt, in *Political Quarterly* (April–June 1965). See also *The History of the 20th Century*, ed. A. J. P. Taylor and J. M. Roberts, issue no. 50.

[51] For the text of the conference of 7 Nov 1937, see *Documents on German Foreign Policy*, series D, I, no. 19; for that of the directive of 7 Dec, ibid., VII, app. III k.

[52] *DGFP*, series C, v, no. 490.

[53] 'Zur Entstehung und Überlieferung der Hossbach Niederschrift', *Vierteljahrshefte für Zeitgeschichte*, 4 (1968).

[54] *Germany's Economic Preparations for War* (Harvard, 1959).

[55] *The German War Economy* (London, 1965) and *Design for Total War* (The Hague, 1968) p. 99.

[56] W. Foerster, *General Oberst Ludwig Beck, sein Kampf gegen den Krieg: aus nachgelassenen Papieren des Generalstabschefs* (Munich, 1953) pp. 88–90.

[57] For a discussion of German naval armaments in 1938–9 see D. C. Watt, 'Anglo–German Naval Negotia-

tions on the Eve of the Second World War', *Journal of the Royal United Services Institute* (May–Aug 1958).

[58] W. Treue, 'Hitlers Rede vor der deutschen Presse, 10. November 1938', *Vierteljahrshefte für Zeitgeschichte*, VI (1958).

[59] D. Irving, *Breach of Security: The German Intelligence File on Events Leading to the Second World War*, with an introduction by D. C. Watt (London, 1968).

[60] U. von Hassall, *Diaries* (London, 1948) entry for 20 Dec 1938.

[61] Dr H. Krausnick has very kindly allowed me to see the manuscript of *Helmut Groscurth, Tagebucher eines Abwehroffiziers 1938–1940*, ed. H. Krausnick, H. Deutsch and H. von Kotze. See also D. C. Watt's introduction to Irving, *Breach of Security*, pp. 37–8.

[62] See Hitler's directive to Goering of 27 Jan 1939 *DGFP*, series D, VII, app. III.

[63] *DGFP*, series D, VI, nos 185 and 433.

[64] Ibid., VII, no. 192 and app. I, extracts from the Note Book of Colonel General F. Halder. See also W. Baumgart, 'Zur Ansprache Hitlers vor den Führern der Wehrmacht am 22. August 1939', *Vierteljahrshefte für Zeitgeschichte*, 2 (1968).

[65] See quotation from Jodl's diary in E. M. Robertson's *Hitler's Pre-War Policy and Military Plans* (London, 1963) pp. 181–2.

[66] In August 1939 Goering's *Forschungsamt* had been intercepting messages exchanged between the British and French embassies in Berlin, and their respective governments. On the whole the conclusion to be drawn from these reports suggested that the Allies would take a strong stand against future German aggression but their influence on Hitler is difficult to assess: Irving, *Breach of Security*. Hitler did mention intercepts on 30 August. See *Note Book of Colonel General F. Halder, DGFP*, series D, VII, app. III.

[67] Barraclough, *An Introduction to Contemporary History*, p. 28, and R. Greenfield, *Ethiopia* (London, 1965) p. 188.

[68] Italian plans in Ethiopia in 1932–3 and Franco-

Italian negotiations over Ethiopia are considered in 'Mussolini and Ethiopia: The Pre-History of the Rome Agreements', in *Essays in Diplomatic History, in memory D. B. Horn*, ed. M. S. Anderson and Professor R. Hatton (Longmans).

[69] George W. Baer, *The Coming of the Italian–Ethopian War* (Cambridge, Mass., 1957). Geoffrey Warner, *Pierre Laval and the Eclipse of France* (London, 1968). Unfortunately neither of these authors have used *Documents diplomatiques francais*, 1st series, II, no. 180, which contains interesting material on the Rome Agreements. See also ibid., 2nd series, I, no. 99, a letter from Laval to Mussolini, 23 Jan 1936.

[70] J. B. Crowley, *Japan's Quest for Autonomy, National Security and Foreign Policy* (New Haven, 1963). Cf. G. R. Storry, *The Double Patriots: A Study of Japanese Nationalism* (London, 1957). See also Akira Iriye, *After Imperialism: The Search for a New Order in the Far East* (Cambridge, Mass., 1965).

[71] F. S. Northedge in *The Troubled Giant* (London, 1969) ch. XII gives a full account of the effect of the crisis on British and American policy.

[72] Theo Sommer, *Deutschland und Japan zwichen den Mächten* (Tubingen, 1962) pp. 21 ff.

[73] 'A Reconsideration of the Marco Polo Bridge Incident', *Journal of Asian Studies*, 22 (1962–3) 277–91.

[74] Medlicott, in *Contemporary England* p. 360, quotes a very significant letter by Chamberlain of 26 March 1937 to H. Morgenthau, of the United States Treasury, in which the possibility of war with both Germany and Japan is discussed. Chamberlain suggested that the United States neutrality legislation should be amended and that appeasement should be based on a policy of strength.

[75] I. S. O. Playfair, *History of the Second World War; The Mediterranean and the Middle East* (U.K. series, London, 1965), I, ch. 1.

[76] *Personalities and Policies*, pp. 154 ff.

[77] *The Gust Lecture*, see n. 20 above.

[78] *Helmut Groscurth, Tagebucher eines Abwehroffiziers*, see n. 61 above.

[79] *Documents on British Foreign Policy*, 3rd series, IV, no. 5, see also ibid., nos 27, 39, 87, 88, 113, 129, and *Foreign Relations of the United States 1939* (Washington, 1955–) vol. I 2–6.

[80] *DBFP*, 3rd series, VIII, app. I, pp. 542–50: *Additional Correspondence on the Naval Situation in the Far East.*

[81] C. Thorne, *The Approach of War, 1938–1939* (London, 1967) p. 87 and pp. 130–4.

[82] *DBFP*, 3rd series, V, nos 106, 115.

[83] Ibid., IV, no. 28.

[84] Ibid., nos 122 and 158. See also C. Hull, *Memoirs* (London, 1948) pp. 626–30, and R. J. Butow, *Tojo and the Coming of War* (Princeton, 1961) pp. 188 ff.

[85] *DBFP*, 3rd series, V, no. 130.

[86] Ibid., nos 218 and 227.

[87] See also Akira Iriye, *Across the Pacific* (New York, 1967) pp. 200 ff.

[88] 'The struggle of the U.S.S.R. for Collective Security in Europe during 1933–1935', *International Affairs* (Moscow, 1961). For a full discussion of Soviet historiography and World War II, see articles by A. P. Mendel and D. M. Shapiro in *Contemporary History in Europe*, pp. 263–306.

[89] *The Case of Richard Sorge* (London, 1966).

[90] R. Wohlstetter, *Pearl Harbor: Warning and Decision* (Stanford, 1962).

[91] L. Villari, *Italian Foreign Policy under Mussolini* (New York, 1956), and D. L. Hoggan, *Der erzwungene Krieg. Die Ursachen und Urheber* (Tübingen, 1963). H. Graml, *Hoggan und die Dokumente* (1963), has systematically refuted Hoggan. For the change from an anti-Axis to an anti-Soviet policy in the U.S.A., see Toscano, *Treaties and International Politics*, pp. 224–5.

[92] H. Feis, *The Road to Pearl Harbor* (Princeton, 1950); F. C. Jones, *Japan's New Order in East Asia* (London, 1954); P. Schroeder, *The Axis Alliance and Japanese–American Relations* (Ithaca, N.Y., 1958); Storry, *Double Patriots*, and Butow, *Tojo and the Coming of War.*

[93] *The Origins of the Pact of Steel* (Baltimore, 1967); *Deutschland und Japan zwischen den Mächten* (Tübingen, 1962) pp. 100 ff. *The Swastika and Eagle: Hitler, the United States and the Origins of the Second World War* (London, 1968).

[94] 'Japanese Imperialism and Aggression: Considerations, 1', *Journal of Asian Studies*, 22 (1962–3) 449–72.

1 The Historiography of World War II

T. Desmond Williams

Ten years have now passed since the conclusion of the Second World War, and it is perhaps opportune to consider how far its 'origins' have become a proper subject for historical research. It will, of course, at once be realised that it is at present impossible, and will be for a long time to come very difficult, to reach any definite overall assessment of pre-war diplomacy during the years between 1919 and 1939. This is not because no, or only a small amount of, material is available, or because historians have shirked treatment of the problems involved. On the contrary, a considerable amount of archival material has already been published in book form, or is at the disposal of research students relying on microfilm. In addition, a number of historians have written on various aspects of inter-war diplomacy, some would say too many of them have been writing on the subject. The question arises, however, if their labours have achieved as much as they or their admirers claim, namely if the origins of the war can now be said to have been put in adequate perspective. The archival material available is under present conditions, admittedly, incomplete. And the overwhelming majority of historians concerned with pre-war diplomacy have been – as was only to be expected – inspired by motives which were not exclusively historical. Most, if not all, of these scholars have tended to consider that particular section of the past from the

Reprinted from *Historical Studies*, 1 (papers read before the Second Irish Conference of Historians, 1958) 33–49, by permission of the author. See also Introduction, pp. 12, 15, 20.

viewpoint of present problems, and have rarely been able, and equally rarely willing, to look at it as if it were a 'dead' past. Practical, sociological and political presuppositions have underlain much of the historical analysis of the period, and the historian will also have to ask himself if similar presuppositions have not influenced also the selection of the archival material which has become available.

These, of course, are *ex parte* statements which are made here merely to indicate the nature of the problems set, in the opinion of the present writer, by the historiography of the Second World War, and also some of the conclusions which perhaps will follow from a study of both the analysis and the interpretation, as well as of the actual documentary evidence at the disposal of contemporary historians.

The historiography of the Second World War can, of course, be considered from a variety of viewpoints, and these cannot be exhausted, even in a very general way, in the course of a single paper. However, it is not irrelevant to examine that historiography in relation to the following topics: (1) What is the value of official records, either already published, or potentially available in the future? (2) How useful are the unofficial memoirs of important participants in pre-war diplomacy for either the general historian of the period, or for specialists interested in particular fields? (3) What questions are set in connection with periodisation, that is to say, the choice of particular phases which historians may consider as more important, and more fruitful, than others? This is said without prescinding from the question whether or not there are such useful concepts in history as key points, or turning points. Most historians, in one way or another, have to limit their interests, and they act as if there were such turning points, etc., even if they recognise their use to be only 'practical' and relative, rather than conclusively valid or absolute. (4) What are the particular problems around which controversy has already developed? Why has discussion centred around them, and are the viewpoints expressed in these controversies inspired by a genuine historical interest, or are other presuppositions present? (5) What are the conclusions already drawn, or established, by those historians who have written on this subject? It is not intended to answer these questions either fully or seriatim, but they have to be touched upon.

Finally, has the history of the Second World War – and in this connection we are speaking of its 'origins' – reached what might be called an academic level? Is it possible, or desirable in fact, to include this period in history courses for undergraduates? No interpretation of any period is ever definitive or incapable of revision; but in regard to more remote periods, a certain practical overall picture may often be sketched without the undue danger of young minds being misled either by mistakes of fact or by polemical interpretation of well-established facts.

If we begin with the question of sources, they can be divided into two groups: one which is concerned with government papers, and the second with unofficial memoirs and records. As far as unofficial sources are concerned the situation is at least as satisfactory as one could expect at this interval. This is particularly true as regards the memoirs of diplomatists, soldiers and politicians engaged on the European, the American or the Japanese scene between 1933 and 1939. A great deal has been written by men involved in the making of history of that period, as well as with that of the period between 1919 and 1933. More people have probably written about their part in the 'origins' of the war than was the case after similar intervals in relation to wars in previous centuries. There is an obvious and understandable exception, namely that of Russia, which is, if a very important, certainly also a very special case. In some countries, the influence of Official Secrets Acts is easily detectable, but on the whole, autobiographical studies have given a fairly comprehensive record of the role which most of these writers would like the public to believe they actually played, a role also in which most of them may, however inaccurately, genuinely believe.

The question why certain countries have taken a special interest in the history of the war is, therefore, relevant to a study of the trends of that historiography hitherto visible in historical periodicals. In the immediate post-war period historical studies on the question were monopolised by the victorious countries, and especially by the Anglo-Saxon states. This in part was the result of a state policy which designedly was directed to anticipating the results of any subsequent attempt by historians in vanquished countries to challenge the accepted version of responsibility for the war, which had been laid down at the Nuremberg trials. It is not unnatural to assume that the British, French and American governments, in arranging for the editing of the captured German archives, were determined to get their 'historical' blow in first, so to speak, and thus prevent a situation arising such as occurred after Versailles, in which the defeated countries· were able to reverse the moral judgements imposed by unilateral act in the peace treaties, and later to secure substantial political advantages from the modification brought about in world opinion in regard to the moral issues.

There were also other reasons why the victorious countries should initially monopolise historical treatment of World War II. First of all, they were in occupation of the two main countries, Germany and Japan, and were able to take possession of the invaluable captured documents without which it would be impossible even to start on a definitive treatment. Secondly, and this is particularly true of Germany, the reaction against National Socialism on the part of German scholars was much greater than that which had occurred on the fall of the Second Reich in 1918. Many Germans had an immediate grievance in respect of the so-called war-guilt clause included in the peace treaties of 1919; there were only a few who were immediately prepared to defend Hitler's foreign policy in 1945. Thirdly, the prolongation of the occupation regime in both Germany and Japan, and the rapid assimilation of the new governments in those two countries into the Anglo-American system of alliances, eliminated the

political 'necessity' for a 'historical' attack on Western
policy between 1933 and 1939.

Statesmen in defeated countries, however, have
usually much more reason to write about their past
than have their fellows in the victor states. Because they
have been defeated, and their policies proved unsuccessful, they feel the need to explain either that all was
not as bad as the victors have stated, or that the undoubted faults or wrongs which were committed by
their countries were not the result of their advices or
their actions or those of their political partners or
friends. Since 1947 many memoirs have appeared in
Germany, and for the most part they are the work of
former members of the German diplomatic corps, and
derive from circles which were in opposition to Hitler
from the beginning, or who subsequently resisted his
policy. These works are generally of a purely personal
and apologetical character. It cannot, therefore, be said
that there is as yet any 'scientific' revisionist German
historiography. Certainly, in the memoirs of Erich
Kordt, Dirksen, von Weizsaecker, Rahn, Scmidt, von
Papen, Bluecher, Curtius, Ribbentrop, Hesse or Otto
Dietrich, there are frequent references of a polemical
nature; but they are very often in the form of self-
defence, and are not 'historical' works such as were
speedily produced at the end of the First World War
by Wegerer, Rogge, Thimme, Meinecke or a Mont-
gelas. It may also be noted that these works are
directed as much towards establishing the personal
record of those concerned among the German people, as
to an analysis of German foreign policy or of its relation with the foreign policy of other Powers in the
pre-war period. Most of these writers tend to accept the
broad outline of the judgement passed at Nuremberg,
and supported in the main by Anglo-Saxon historiography, on Hitler's Germany between 1933 and 1939.
As far as they are concerned, they try to point out that
their own policy was or would have been very different
from what everyone seemingly agrees was that of Hitler.

Both army and diplomatic memoirs are affected by

political or personal considerations, and what is true of
Germany applies, doubtless, also to other countries.
There is, however, no unity of front vis-a-vis foreign
public opinion. And instead, the historiography is in
one sense a prolongation of internecine warfare within
the national frontiers. The struggle between Hitler
and the conservative reaction or the Socialist opposition, between 'Vichy' and the French resistance, or
between that resistance and the Communists, or between Italian Fascism and the monarchy and the
Church, or between the two latter forces and the Communists, form the main subjects of contention between
writers from different camps. It is really internal policy
rather than foreign affairs which dominates the historical recollections, as they appear in the very wide
memoir literature – apart from a few significant exceptions.

Finally, in this connection, it must be remarked that
the Nazis and the Fascists have yet to have their say.
Most of their leaders were killed, some are still in
prison, and those who have escaped either one or the
other fate take good care to remain silent until all pas-
sion from those days is spent. However, even if
memoirs from such sources were available, they would
probably not be of much assistance in reconstructing
the origins of the war, but would deal mainly with the
internal feuds which are still being acrimoniously de-
bated in Italy as well as in France and Belgium. Few
writers therefore have been able to rise above the level
of their own contribution to the making of the history
of that period. Some are more skilful than others in the
presentation of their case, either in regard to the
form in which it is presented or in regard to the use of
the documentary material furnished by them. This is
naturally more true of memoirs deriving from British
or French or American sources, because such persons
are able to gain access to the archives of their own
state, or because they possess copies of important documents relating to activities in which they were involved. Memoirs produced by statesmen of the vanquished nations lack this advantage. Either the

archives were destroyed during the war, or were confiscated by the Allied Powers after it. Thus, for example, the memoirs of Sir Winston Churchill or of Lord Templewood, and the biography of Neville Chamberlain offer more concrete material to the researcher than do the autobiographies of men such as von Papen, von Weizsaecker, Rahn, Bluecher, Heusinger, Guderian, Schmidt, Hilger or Dietrich in Germany; or those of Guariglia, Anfuso or Attolico in Italy. These men had to rely for the most part on their memories, and all of them have been hitherto refused access to the archives of their own country, at present located in Washington or at Bletchley. French writers such as Georges Bonnet, Paul Reynaud, General Gamelin, Paul Boncour and, more recently, General de Gaulle, have been able, like their British colleagues, to refer to documentary material either accessible or in their own possession. For this reason, therefore, former statesmen in Western countries possess an advantage over those of the vanquished countries. This advantage is not, however, an important one in the long run, for the selectivity which affects all books of this nature is bound to diminish the influence of and reduce reliance upon these works, as original documentary material is published in due course.

The British government decided as early as 1943 to publish documents from its own Foreign Office relating to the inter-war period, and Mr Woodward and Mr Butler have edited a number of volumes covering the immediate pre-war years. These volumes are enormous in extent, but their value as a guide to the real evolution of policy at the highest level has already been questioned by several American historians of note.

On 26 March 1949, a reviewer in *The Times Literary Supplement* criticised the method of selecting documents employed by the editors, and pointed out that internal minutes by senior members of the Foreign Office were generally omitted. It was afterwards explained that in comparison with minutes written in the period prior to the First World War, notes and memos of the inter-war period were far less numer-

ous and much more brief in substance. This is probably partly true but the fact remains that in the succeeding volumes of the third series (2, 3, 4, 5 and 6)
more internal minutes were in fact published. With
some exceptions, however, those written by the highest
officials such as the permanent under-secretary or his
deputy were referred to only in the form of summaries
contained in footnotes. Mario Toscano, in a review of
the historiography of the Second World War (in his
report delivered to the tenth International Congress of
the C.I.S.H. in Rome, 1955) expresses the view that
these works are now substantially satisfactory in so far
as they give a full account of all the written material
actually available. This, unfortunately, does not appear to be entirely correct, and on numerous occasions,
documents relating to critical decisions between March
1938 and August 1939 are summarised and not reproduced in full. In particular, volume IV, which is
partly concerned with the month of March 1939, and
the British guarantee to Poland given by Neville
Chamberlain on 31 March, offers noteworthy examples
of this method of defective selection.

Letters also published in the appendix of that
volume as well as those of succeeding volumes are
chosen with an apparent view to the discrediting of a
policy of appeasement to which the Foreign Office itself
was opposed. Sir Nevile Henderson's correspondence
is cited at length, but letters from other ambassadors,
in the same period, are usually lacking. It is not explained why his correspondence was published, and
that of others omitted.

There are several occasions, notably the week-ends of
19–21 May 1938, 26–29 March 1939 and 1–4 August
1939, when erroneous intelligence reaching the
Foreign Office was acted upon and important decisions
taken on its basis. There is no possibility of checking
the source of this information or of considering why
the Foreign Office placed reliance on it rather than on
contradictory news sent in by other sources. It is clear
that many permanent officials were inspired by a certain bias which led them to trust advisers who shared

the fundamental anti-German policy of the Foreign Office itself. Furthermore, a few basic memoranda on the general world situation composed at the highest level are reproduced; but all of these are concerned with periods in which decisive decisions had already been taken.

The fact that all internal minutes were omitted in the first volume – and then in later volumes some but not many included (and the overwhelming majority of them merely summarised) – will induce the historian to consider the possibility that the editors may have had 'a guilty conscience'. Otherwise why should they have reversed their original decision, and then only do so in half-hearted fashion?

'Official' history naturally has its traps. The 'official' historian has the advantage of having access to valuable material denied to other historians. And it is not unfair to suggest that those to whom this privilege is given are also people in whom the Foreign Office has special confidence. Why give to some what is denied to the rest? The result is that for any relatively final judgement on the policy of the Foreign Office, its extent and limitations, these volumes are only very provisional in their use. The advantage of internal minutes is, of course, that however brief, they reveal the internal working of the system at its highest level, and that they indicate the considerations which the officials discussed among themselves, and which were not necessarily transmitted either to the public at home or to foreign governments. Dispatches sent out to and received from ambassadors abroad are of much less value for the historian. They often merely reveal what the government wished other governments to know, and what those other governments wished the British government to believe.

There is one noticeable difference for example between the policy of the editors of the captured German documents, and that adopted by the editors of the *Documents on British Foreign Policy*. The former have published documents deriving from every level of the German Foreign Office, and these include not merely internal notes of the state secretaries or of the ministers, but also interdepartmental correspondence of considerable relevance for the development of German policy. What is even more significant is the publication of military and intelligence memos and directives. In fact many high-level documents, whether they derive from the Foreign Ministry itself, the Supreme Command of the *Wehrmacht*, the Economics Ministry or the Chancellery of the Führer, provide a basis upon which a comprehensive understanding of German policy can be formed – at least as far as documentary evidence in the modern age can ever reveal it. To understand the difference between the two publications, it is only necessary to contrast the amount of information and the sources of information provided. As far as Britain is concerned, we have only Foreign Office material, and that usually in abbreviated form as regards the highest level. We have no documents from the Cabinet or from military intelligence; nor is it possible to estimate the attitude of official financial or economic advisers on the pace or direction of British foreign policy.

The English system was more coherent than the German one under the dictatorship of Hitler. Exchange of information at ministerial level was greater, though there were obvious exceptions during Chamberlain's attempts to negotiate a separate agreement with Italy in 1938, as well as during the notorious private conversations exchanged between Sir Horace Wilson and a German economic emissary in July 1939. Because it was more coherent, and because the relations between the premier, foreign secretary and Foreign Office were relatively co-ordinated – despite the clash of policy over Germany – it might have been expected that a greater knowledge of British diplomacy could be gleaned from the archives of the Foreign Office. For one reason or another, this is not the case; and the Woodward series, therefore, is not as interesting or as illuminating as it was once hoped it would be.

There is also a fundamental defect in that the edi-

tors seem to have been working within a limited
framework of ideas. The selection centres around 'appeasement' and the controversy which arose about it.
Sir Nevile Henderson, for example, is made out to be
the villain of the story; reprimands by Sir Orme Sar-
gent, or on odd occasions from Lord Halifax himself,
receive full attention, whereas the mistakes of other
members of the Foreign Office staff are hardly mentioned at all. There is, for example, the mystery of the
News Department of the Foreign Office, which, as is
known, played some part in the moulding of British
press opinion in regard to Germany and Italy. Evidence on the internal working of that particular department and its relations with the permanent under-
secretary and the foreign secretary would have been
very helpful for anyone who wished to examine the day-
to-day evolution of British policy. This is especially
true of the week-end crisis in May 1938, of the false
information given by the Romanian ambassador in
London, Tilea, in March 1939, or of the circumstances
surrounding negotiations prior to the guarantee given
to Poland at the end of the same month. There is, in
addition, a whole series of reports in January and
February 1939 relating to Hitler's assumed plans for
aggression against Western European states. Some of
these reports were sensational, but there does not appear to have been any valid ground for taking them as
seriously as did Lord Halifax, presumably on the advice of the Foreign Office. Who provided these reports?
Why were they accepted? These are questions which
have to be answered in any study of the motives affecting British policy at this time. No answers can be
secured from the Woodward–Butler series.

Within the framework of the anti-appeasement
viewpoint, the Foreign Office comes out well from the
revelations contained in the Woodward series. But by
another interpretation the conclusion has been provided by the Foreign Office itself, confirmed by illogical acceptance of the doctrine *post hoc: ergo propter
hoc*, and by the evidence presented by the particular
documents published. In a sense what we have to deal

with is a circular argument which is difficult to refute unless one either looks at the same facts in a different way, or extends the facts and considers alternative conclusions which might fit them as well. One could say for example that appeasement failed because the Foreign Office was a contributory agent in the moulding of Hitler's plans of aggression. One might suggest also, for example, that the Foreign Office has proved itself right in so far as its own policy was partly responsible for Hitler's decision to go to war over Poland in 1939; or because Hitler's own conception of British policy was to a large extent influenced by news he received from biased party sources as to the attitude of the Foreign Office. All this could be maintained, and yet the fact of Hitler's fundamental intention to upset the balance of power be admitted. But the form which it took, and the precipitation of events *may* have been partly the result of mistakes and prejudices on the part of official British diplomacy.

There are other questions which must have been asked in the Foreign Office in the years 1938 and 1939. They may not have been answered in writing, but we can only be sure that they were not if full access to all top-level internal minutes is made available. Such questions include the following: Did the Foreign Office, or any of its permanent officials, think that war with Germany was inevitable, and therefore to that extent more desirable at one particular point in time rather than another? Did they want war in 1938 or in 1939 or later? What was their attitude to Chamberlain's proposed four-power declaration of 20 March 1939, or to the Polish guarantee? How far did they manoeuvre the premier into a situation which they regarded as desirable, but which he afterwards was to regret? Is it possible that in accepting the unprecedented terms of the Polish guarantee, they, or some of them, foresaw the outbreak of war, which Chamberlain had intended to prevent by subscribing to the same declaration which partly precipitated hostilities in that year? We do not know.

In addition, if one accepts the supposition that war

with Hitler was inevitable because the balance of power in Europe was so drastically upset after 15 March 1939, how far did Foreign Office officials work on the view that it was better soon, rather than later? How far were they guided in this attitude by advices from the chiefs of staff? Or did they really think that acceptance by Poland of the German demands given privately to Beck in March 1939, and published by Hitler on 28 April in his Reichstag speech, seriously endangered the military defence capacity of Poland any more than it had already been weakened by preceding events? Or how far, mistrusting the good faith of Colonel Beck, were they prepared to do anything to bring him in line with the anti-Hitler front, trusting meanwhile in the inevitable participation of Russia in any war which broke out between Germany and the West? Or how far, for example, did they – as Lord Templewood asserts in his recent book, *Nine Troubled Years* – discard Russia as a military factor, and put their faith in the reliability of Poland as an adequate ally against the *Wehrmacht*? How far, in fact, were the preconceptions upon which they based all their policies mistaken in detail, even if the general principles influencing British fear of Hitler were fully correct?

The outcome of the Second World War indicates that many of the premises which may have guided the different actions of Chamberlain and the Foreign Office were mistaken. Men are not necessarily responsible for all the consequences that follow partly from their own actions. But the question of responsibility for blunders can only be decided if there is evidence of what was uppermost in the minds of influential persons at the time. Unfortunately little evidence has been provided on these points in the *Documents on British Foreign Policy*. One is entitled to inquire if any such evidence was available, and if it was rejected for publication by Mr Woodward and Mr Butler as being irrelevant to the 'main issue'. It is certainly possible that the two distinguished editors were in fact working within a certain framework, and that what for them was the 'main issue' is not the only one with which subsequent historians of the period will be concerned.

The other great original source for the historiography of the Second World War is that provided by Professor Chabod in the series edited under his general direction, entitled *The Diplomatic Documents of the Italian Foreign Ministry*. Some volumes have appeared which bear directly on the origins of the Second World War. These are volumes i and ii of series 13 – of a publication in which series i begins with the year 1867. The two volumes mentioned begin on 18 March 1939 and end on 5 September of the same year. In one respect, the comparative paucity of internal minutes included in the records of the Italian Foreign Office gives support to claims made in defence of Mr Woodward and Mr Butler that this type of document no longer plays the same important part in the formation of policy which it played before 1914. Of 880 documents published in full, in volume i of series 13 (from 18 March to 4 August), only 30 come from the hand of the minister, Ciano, and even fewer are written by the equivalent of the permanent under-secretary. The only interesting dispatches are those which are sent in by the Italian ambassadors in Berlin, in Paris and particularly in Moscow. The intelligent and mysterious Signor Grandi remains silent, on the whole, and little light is thrown on Italian policy in London as a result.

There is, however, one important difference between the behaviour one would expect from departmental advisers in a totalitarian, and from those in a democratic, state. With the passage of the years, the Duce's policy deviated more strongly from that of the permanent tradition of the Quirinal, and civil servants in a state where the arbitrary caprice of a dictator met with no obstacle might have been presumed to act and write with greater caution than in the well-established and highly regarded Foreign Office. The act, therefore, that there are few internal minutes to be found in the Italian records does not necessarily imply that they were equally lacking in the British Foreign Office. Furthermore, even if they were equally lacking, the

Italian editors publish their records in full, whereas in
regard to the notable instances mentioned above, summaries are generally provided by the editors of the
Documents on British Foreign Policy.

A source which has been often used by contemporary
historians of Italian policy is the Ciano Diary. This is
not a state document but it can be regarded as ap-
proximating to it. It covers the years from 1937 to the
spring of 1943, and it is a stimulating, and in places
startling, volume. It has been much used by those who
seek to discredit the Duce, and to ridicule the process
by which Italy, as from 1936 onwards, gradually
aligned herself with Germany and Japan under the
Anti-Comintern Pact. It will however always remain
suspect as a *pièce de circonstance,* written by a man
with a view to clearing himself before posterity. It is
probably frank as far as the earlier years are concerned
because there is much in it which tells against Ciano;
and what a man tells against himself is usually, though
by no means always, to be trusted as far as his account
of events is concerned. But diaries are, of their nature,
unsatisfactory because they are egocentric in their terms
of reference, and also because they usually now take a
summarised form. They are useful when, as in this case,
they are written by a person in high authority. But the
character of Ciano makes this particular version more
than usually suspect. He was a vain but intelligent
man; he was no respecter of persons, even of the Duce,
when the shadow of the latter's distrust began to fall
on him. He had supported the general line of the Duce's
policy up to the year of 1940 – with the exception of
the months preceding the outbreak of the war in which
Italy initially remained neutral. He scoffed at the cautious views of his professional advisers who were indirectly warning the minister and the premier against
becoming too firmly committed to the 'Axis'. He was
later to accept their views, but at a time when it was
impossible, or at least very difficult, to reverse the previous policy. He then failed to take into account the
difficulties with which Mussolini was confronted, and
which were partly the natural consequence of Ciano's

own activity in foreign affairs. This was very obviously the case in respect of two events, the first being the invasion of Albania on 7 April 1939, and the attack on Greece on 28 October 1940. He then becomes as unfair to his chief and his policy as he had been unjust earlier on to those who had opposed both.

Ciano is an easy target to hit and he is also exceptionally useful and informative for those concerned to discredit entirely both the old and the new foreign policies of Italy. He is especially vulnerable for those who like to savour their historical analysis with spicy sneers at the expense of personalities involved in the making of policy at that time. Sir Lewis Namier, for example, who is a master of this type of exposition, has drawn much on Ciano. Where it suits him, he ignores the more dull and less exciting evidence provided by official documents. And it cannot be said that Namier is relying on a source favourable to the principles for which he stands.

The memoirs for example of a former Italian diplomat, Raeffelo Guariglia, have not been used to the same extent by historians in either Anglo-Saxon or Latin countries. Guariglia was never a genuine Fascist but was always an Italian, without however being unaware of the prejudices arising from that fact. His comments, therefore, gave the impression of greater independence. He has much to say in criticism of British policy over Abyssinia in the winter of 1935–6, of German pressure and arrogance over the occupation of Austria and Czechoslovakia in 1938 and 1939 and of the inelasticity of French governments in considering Italian claims in the winter of 1938. He is not concerned with showing that he was never a Fascist, nor with attacking Italian policy during those years. For him it was partly right and partly wrong, although the final outcome proved it to be a failure at the end. He appears content with revealing the policy of Italy and of other Powers as it actually evolved, and with reproducing his own views as they were at the time. In contrast with Ciano's Diary, his own recollections include little that is exciting or amusing; personality is not ignored but policy is not considered to revolve entirely around the weaknesses or the virtues of outstanding individuals. It is a serious book, but will never be a best-seller; it will be as useful to objective historians working twent years after the end of the Second World War as some of the contemporary documentation itself. But it has hitherto been ignored because it does not fit easily into the moralistic trend of contemporary historiography.

The sources, official or unofficial, are one problem; the use which historians have made of them is another; and it is the latter which it is now proposed to discuss.

Sir Lewis Namier has tended, in his work on the twentieth century, to interpret historical development very largely in terms of petty vanities and quarrels; and whereas in his eighteenth-century historiography he laid stress – some would say too much stress – on material and institutional forces, he has gone right to the other extreme in his analysis of more contemporary history. The former is good, though perhaps not perfect history; the latter is certainly excellent journalism. Nothing is easier for a man writing with style and shrewdness than to indulge in the play of ridicule. And this Sir Lewis has done in connection with nearly all the personalities on what, for him, was 'the other side of the hill'. Mussolini, Ciano, Ribbentrop, Hitler, Georges Bonnet, Colonel Beck and Neville Chamberlain are all discussed in relation to either their stupidity, their overweening self-confidence, their ambition or in some cases their 'lunacy'. Other influences which may have naturally inspired their policies, such as long-term economic developments or changing political traditions, are lightly dismissed in the series of essays published in book form. The answers he has actually given to the problems of 'responsibility' raised by him in connection with the origins of the Second World War would not be entirely the same if he had looked at events and peoples from a wider viewpoint. Sir Lewis has been the dominating figure in the historiography of the particular problems discussed in this paper. His performance has generally been received with admira-

tion and even those who would like to disagree with
some of his conclusions do so only in the most deferen-
tial manner. His control over source material is uncon-
tested, his familiarity with evidence written in many
languages gives him considerable advantage over many
of his fellow-historians. Furthermore, his access to
official British documents and acquaintance with many
of the major participants in the diplomacy of the pre-
war period enables him to speak with greater authority
than can others. He therefore has been, on the whole,
unchallenged in the interpretations which have flowed
smoothly in the various essays published in three books
during the years 1948–52.

Only one other historian of comparable stature has
written on the same subject, namely Professor W. L.
Langer of Harvard University. Langer has, with the
assistance of Mr Gleason, published two major
volumes; Sir Lewis Namier has produced more than a
score of essays. Professor Langer has chosen mainly one
aspect of the foreign policy of the various Powers,
namely American policy between 1937 and 1941; Sir
Lewis has touched upon many problems covering
many years and many countries. Langer's books are
expensive in price and provided with much of the
panoply of scholarship; Namier has been read by thou-
sands, whereas the former's work has probably been
consulted by scores. And it is therefore Namier who is
cited wherever the Second World War is discussed in
historical terms. He also has the advantage over his
American colleague in that his style is competent, appears light and possesses all the gifts of journalism, to
say the least. And yet the question naturally arises
whether the conclusions which he has drawn, and to a
large extent imposed, are more definitive than the few
which arise out of Langer's research.

Both have approached the subject in fundamentally
different manner. Langer is writing to some extent
from the viewpoint of an American official, engaged
during part of the period which he is discussing in the
execution of some aspect of United States diplomacy.
Where he is interested in the policies of non-American

Powers, he is more or less content to rely on stating the facts as they appear relevant. and does not take up a judicial position. Namier, on the other hand, hovers over almost every field of European diplomacy, and never for once abandons his self-imposed duty of passing judgement on the actors surveyed by him.

Langer's treatment is limited in range but more thorough in depth. From a chronological viewpoint the gradual evolution of American, and particularly of Roosevelt's, policy is outlined in the seventeen hundred pages which have so far appeared in his first two volumes. Namier has, however, concentrated on particular personalities and periods rather than upon the gradual unfolding of a long historical process.

Thus the gaps are as obvious in his treatment as are the peak points of the periods which he regards as relevant. He hops from one person to another, and from one issue to the next. In each of these issues someone appears ridiculous, irresponsible, 'shifty' or 'mad'. An example is provided by the essays on Georges Bonnet's account of the Western Powers' negotiations with Russia, and the inference to be drawn from the facts selected as important by Namier is that the French Foreign Minister was either a fool or a crook. There is the essay on the Ciano Diary, from which it emerges that Ciano was ambitious, vain and intelligent, the Duce corrupt and feeble-minded, Ribbentrop and Weizsaecker timid poltroons and Hitler a dangerous lunatic. There is the article on Munich in which Dr Beneš stands forward as a heroic, far-seeing and betrayed leader of a small 'innocent' country, Neville Chamberlain and Sir Horace Wilson as provincial, arrogant and self-opinionated politicians resisting the objective and correct advices of their official advisers. And in the essay on Anglo-Russian negotiations, Stalin, Molotov and Litvinoff are portrayed as realistic, reasonable and far-seeing nationalists, who were driven into positions which they did not want, but which they could not have been expected to have avoided. Namier has also written a short note on the problem of the German army in which Beck, Goerdeler and Kordt are analysed as pathetic, bungling, narrow-minded, if courageous and honest, German nationalists.

All this, or part of it, may be true; and yet there are different ways of looking at the events and people described and many other facts which he has omitted to stress, because he thought them irrelevant to his main purpose as a contemporary historian. There are also other periods and incidents in them which are ignored in his account of the origins of 'the unnecessary war'. He has his heroes, both as regards persons and institutions. There is rarely a suggestion that the Foreign Office was ever wrong in its assessment of either general trends or particular situations. But he has taken great trouble and shown great skill in describing the defects, moral and intellectual, in the Foreign Ministries and army chiefs of Italy, France and Germany. He does not ask the question (and there is evidence to provide the answer to it) as to what the Foreign Office thought of Dr Beneš's policy between November 1937 and August 1938. He is merely concerned to indicate the great sympathy they had with him when he was defeated in September 1938. He accepts Sir Winston Churchill's judgement on the relative disadvantages of the Munich Agreement for the vital interests of Britain, and for the survival of the democratic principle. He does not mention the existence of evidence already published in the United States which would indicate that the joint chiefs of staff were unanimously in favour of postponing the trial of strength with Hitler in 1938.

In none of these essays, written over several years, has he altered positions taken up in the earlier ones. The 'wicked' men are at least as wicked when more evidence comes to hand as they were at the beginning; and the 'angels' remain as spotless and as intelligent as they always have been. The story in general is the same, and its main outlines are maintained with equal tenacity and unvarying consistency.

Behind Namier's historical approach lie two presuppositions which, accepted, render it intelligible and convincing. They are: firstly, that one side was wrong and bad, and most persons directly or indirectly connected with that side as wrong and as bad as the causes for which they stood. In short, the function of his history is to provide justification for the judicial and the political verdicts passed at Nuremberg in September 1946. The second presupposition arises from the fact that he is as much concerned with the 'might-have-been' of history as he is with what 'actually' happened. This particular presupposition is of course the one held, perhaps validly (but it remains an open, and certainly a 'non-historical', question) that the war would not have occurred if certain people's views had been accepted. He set out essentially to justify the views held by those whom he praises, and to discredit those advocated by people whom he condemns.

Concentration on particular points has made this task easy for him. By so doing, he has avoided asking questions the answers to which might have proved inconvenient for his general conclusions. I say 'might have proved' because as far as he is concerned he does not even ask them. Two or three examples will suffice to indicate what I mean.

He has proved that Hitler wanted war. Nobody would, on the whole, now contest this fact; and it is easy to draw the conclusion that the British Foreign Office was right in supporting the general decision to resist him. Namier does not ask the question as to when Hitler really wanted to go to war, or over *what* issues he would have preferred to take that decision. Namier also has analysed very carefully German policy between 10 and 15 March, in relation to Czechoslovakia; he has very little to say about German policy as revealed in official publications from 15 March to 3 April 1939. By turning his telescope on the first period, he can prove that Hitler had decided on aggression contrary to his promises concerning one country; by avoiding the second period, he eludes asking the question if Hitler wanted to abide by his treaty in relation to a second country. This does not of course affect Hitler's general attitude towards fundamental moral questions of peace and war. But the peace was not broken over Czechoslovakia, and the war was declared over Poland. And if therefore the historian examines the origins of the Second World War, the question of its timing must also arise. War may have been inevitable, sooner or later, after 15 March 1939; but the historian cannot find evidence to establish any conclusion for what did not happen. All he can do is to analyse, on the basis of documentary material, the manner in which 'what did happen' appears to have happened.

Namier does not consider if between 16 March and 3 April mistakes of judgement were not committed by Foreign Office advisers, or if the facts upon which they based their advices did not subsequently prove to be false. Nor does he ask if some of Hitler's own actions were not themselves partly the product of either real or presumed British, French or American policy.

Politicians of the time had to answer two questions: one was whether or not to go to war with Hitler, and the other, when, if the answer to the first was in the affirmative, that war should be started, and upon what issue it should be fought. The answer to the first question does not necessarily give the answer to the second; and those who may have been right as regards the former could have been wrong in regard to the latter. Namier is satisfied with having given the answer to the former question.

Langer's history of American foreign policy from 1937 has been criticised on account of the reliance it places on German White Books published during the war, and whose objective validity therefore is open to question. These White Books, of which there are eight, are, with the exception of the first, concerned with the reproduction of the captured archives of Powers overrun by the German army between 1939 and 1941. They throw some light on French, Belgian, Polish and Yugoslav policy, as documents originating from the Foreign Ministries of these states fell either in part or in entirety into German hands. Accounts of Anglo-French military and diplomatic negotiations in 1939 and 1940 illustrate to some extent the agreed policy of both Britain and France after the outbreak of war.

They do not, however, help very much in an understanding of Anglo-French presuppositions or intentions
before 1 September 1939. It is only the reports of Polish
ambassadors in Paris, Washington and London which
have any real relevance to the attitudes of the anti-German coalition established in March 1939. Langer was
of course mainly interested in the gradual evolution of
American policy from neutrality to 'interventionism'.
But in so far as he necessarily had to take into account
the policies of other Powers, all he could do was to rely
on the reports of American diplomats in the various
European capitals. The original British, French or
Italian sources were not available; and even if the
Americans were kept reasonably well informed by the
British and the French, they must have been kept in
the dark as far as Germany and Italy were concerned.
He is inclined to rely a great deal on German revelations published in White Books for British and French
policies in key periods such as March 1939 or April and
May 1940. It may have been necessary for him to discuss the attitudes of non-American Powers; it was unfortunate however that he had to rely on an incomplete, and necessarily suspect, version put out by the
Germans for purposes which were obviously non-historical. His general interpretation of personalities and
events strikes the reader, however, as being more objective and less partial than have been the interpretations
of British and French historians. But if he wanted to
write a definitive interpretation of American diplomacy, and at the same time refer to the diplomacy of
other Powers, he would have done better to have postponed publication until further series of the Italian,
British and German documents had appeared. His
overall judgements may be correct, but they are obviously questionable; and they have in fact been questioned by those who disagree with his interpretation.
Langer also is in the difficult position that he was an
official of the Department of State, whose actions are
the subject of his work; and he has therefore been
accused of being an apologist, even if his ability in that

field, and his scholarship in many other fields, is widely accepted.

A source which has been very widely used is the file covering evidence, written and oral, at the trials of major German and Japanese war criminals. The Nuremberg records are generally accessible, because both the evidence given in court, and the documentary material submitted to it, have been translated into English, especially as far as the first trial is concerned. The Far Eastern trial is, however, only available to a restricted number of research workers. It has not yet been published generally, and only people with access to the Foreign Offices in Britain and France and the Library of Congress in Washington have been in a position to consult them. In addition, interest in Japanese policy is mainly confined to American scholars; and few Europeans have as yet turned their eyes from the European to the Asiatic scene.

The difficulties in using the Nuremberg and the Tokyo material are twofold. Firstly, the nature of the trial and the rules governing the admission of evidence restrict its value as a complete and impartial source for contemporary history. Lord Justice Lawrence stated that what the court was concerned with was ascertaining the culpable responsibility of the defendants in violating defined rules of international law, and not with the wider historical circumstances under which those violations took place. At a later stage he rejected evidence in relation to the foreign policies of Britain and France between 1933 and 1940 on the ground that if invasion by Germany was admitted the question of planning by the Western Powers of other invasions at the same time was not relevant to the issue confronting the court. The function of the court was judicial; it was not called upon to explain the circumstances under which prima facie punishable actions took place. The plaintiffs were also in a favourable position vis-a-vis the defendants in the provision of documentary evidence. All the property of the former German state was in their hands. The defence were entitled to call for documents relevant to their case, but only

on provision that the date and signature of individual documents was specified by them. They
were not given the right to search for documents in
general. Whereas the prosecution enjoyed the power of
chasing for relevant material throughout all the captured archives, and were under no obligation to hand
over voluntarily material which would run against the
line of prosecution's case. The result of this was that
the balance of documents used at the trial, and subsequently published in its records, is heavily weighted
against the German defendants. We therefore have a
considerable and scattered amount of documents deriving from German military and diplomatic sources. It
is, however, in the main selective and extremely incomplete; and the basis on which it was chosen,
whether by the prosecution for the most part, or to a
lesser extent by the defence, has no satisfactory relation
to history.

Secondly, there is the factor of the time at which the
trial took place. It was within a very short period after
the conclusion of hostilities, and many of the most important archives had either been destroyed or secreted
by interested parties. Such was the case, for example,
with Hitler's private papers, which were entrusted to
Julius Schaub, his secretary, from the year 1924. He has
stated that he burnt them; but how can we have conclusive evidence on this issue at a time when it is still
inadvisable for him to admit to the contrary – if in
fact they still remain intact? We have, in abundance,
the records of the German Foreign Ministry, and most
of these were used in the two main trials at Nuremberg. But Hitler did not rely very much on either the
advices or the information received from official diplomats; of the unofficial, personal and semi-official
sources on which he relied, we have almost nothing.
And yet it is upon the official documents of the Foreign
Ministry that most of the evidence concerning German
diplomacy at these trials is based.

Apart from Germany and the United States, the
foreign policies of France, Britain, Italy, Austria, Belgium and Holland have largely been ignored by most

writers. A certain amount of work has been devoted in a very broad and journalistic fashion to the impact of changing world conditions upon each of these countries; but for one reason or another, detailed study is almost completely missing. This is certainly understandable in view of the paucity of primary source material. In recent years, the *Documents on British Foreign Policy* have covered certain aspects of the years 1919–22 and 1931–4. Here again, however, the framework within which the documents have been selected is in most, though not in all cases, narrowly circumscribed. The Versailles treaty and its immediate consequences dominate the first series; and disarmament and the rise of Hitler feature very prominently in the volumes belonging to the second series. Intelligence and Cabinet papers, on which the Foreign Office presumably based some of its assessments, are no more considered in the first two than they are in the third series; and the historian cannot really get very far, as long as these conditions continue.

The fact is that the whole prospective of World War II has been dominated by what might be called a war mentality. Selection and commentary is for the most part of the 'for' and 'against' type; and very few attempts have been made to get beyond a contemporary vision. Perhaps this is natural, in view of the contemporary nature of the study; but the result is, I think, incontestable. There are many ways of looking at the events of those years, and perhaps the most difficult one is that of trying to view persons and events as if the observer in fact were detached from them. But it is almost inevitable that those who have written about those years, or who have selected documents relating to them, should do so as if they were *engagés*, because after all, most of them have been thus 'involved'. Men will now write about the Reformation in a very different manner from that employed by their predecessors between the sixteenth and the nineteenth centuries. And it is to be assumed, one hopes, that historical writing on that point is nearer to perfection – perhaps not very far, but still some of the way – in 1955 than it was

previously. It is impossible, however, to discuss recent
events according to the strictest canons of historical
objectivity; but professional historians may be expected to be aware of the limitations which necessarily
confront them, and accordingly to be less dogmatic in
their conclusions.

As another contributor to this Conference has said
in his inaugural address, concern with either the practical or the scientific part is not the function of the
historian. If this be true, a great deal of what has
already appeared as history in relation to World War II
cannot be in any way regarded, either in its purpose, or
even to a large extent in its performance, as 'historical'
writing, properly called. How the war broke out, how
what happened in 1939 and earlier years appeared to
happen according to available historical evidence, is a
task which very few historians, either in major works or
in learned essays, have been able, or even apparently
have desired, to perform. Most of the writers concerned, whether reminiscing or apologetic statesmen,
or professional historians, have been interested in the
past mainly from the viewpoint of the present, or they
have wished to deduce, in so-called scientific fashion,
rules and methods of statecraft from the past, with a
view to assimilating it to the present, or to the future as
they conceive it should be.

It may be argued also – admittedly on a level below
the analytical plane on which Professor Oakeshott has
considered the subject of historical presuppositions –
that contemporary history is an even more inadequate
form than is the 'practical' interpretation of more remote periods. There are obvious technical grounds, as
well as philosophical ones, which would serve to deter
all historians from concerning themselves with contemporary, or near-contemporary, history. What is insufficient, according to a philosophical presupposition,
shows itself also inadequate in the face of the merely
technical requirements judged as necessary by all historians, whether or not they have become familiar with
the particular distinctions drawn by Professor Oakeshott. And if other periods of the past are open to the

same danger of being assimilated to the present, then assuredly contemporary history, which is conceived of by so many in terms of revolution and ideological struggle, is even more so.

In this context, abstraction and practice do not contradict each other, and those who reason out from first principles and those who work on the basis of technical data will assuredly find themselves in agreement. The one may adduce different reasons from the other; the conclusions are the same. The former surveys from the heights of general reason; the latter peeps up from the lowlands of empirical experience. But they meet eventually, and will not disagree.

The tragedy – or comedy, as one choose to look at it – is that what was once obvious to working historians, and not merely to them, but also to school examiners and teachers, has now to be established; and what was once known by instinct requires ratiocination. It is certainly true that the avoidance of the subject of the Second World War (which is frequently allowed to bedevil even the study of the period prior to the First World War) offers no necessary guarantee against a non-historical interpretation of what may happen to be under survey – no more than the concentration on other ages has ever offered.

Some of those who scorn – either as a matter of course, or out of academic snobbery (an affectation, needless to say, by no means uncommon) – contemporary history on account of the inadequacy of material, lack of available evidence or difficulties in connection with 'objectivity', and all the other obstacles which beset this type of history at every point – some of these, I suggest, have found it difficult to resist drawing practical lessons or scientific conclusions in the handling of remoter periods. And interest in, or occupation with, pre-contemporary history provides no necessary or indefeatable insurance against the dangers which confront historians engaged in the most modern periods.

But – and here is the main point which, I suggest to you, analysis of recent historiography of the Second

World War establishes – contemporary history exposes in more dramatic and self-evident fashion the limitations of an approach which, though applied by historians of aptitude, fame and industry, is speedily shown to be spurious when tested by the narrow but equally exacting rules of thumb to which all historians, at least formally, subscribe.

2 The Conquest of the Past:

Some Recent German Books on the Third Reich

James Joll

The first Germans born after the end of the Third
Reich are now growing up, and those who played an
active part in Hitler's rise to power or in the running
of his regime are now elderly or dead. Yet the memory
of the Nazi period is still very much alive: during the
last two years, first the Eichmann trial and now the
trial of the Auschwitz guards have brought vivid and
horrifying reminders of the atrocities committed in the
Third Reich and of the part played in them by seemingly ordinary Germans. Although the investigations
leading up to the trials of ex-Nazis are often disagreeable and unpopular – it was recently reported that the
police conducting them had asked to be transferred to
other jobs – it cannot be said that the Germans are
being allowed to forget. Again and again in articles
and discussions the phrase 'the unconquered past' (*die
unbewaltigte Vergangenheit*) recurs, and nineteen
years after Hitler's death and the collapse of his Reich,
the analysis of its origins and the search for an explanation are being pursued more vigorously than ever
before.

In some ways, indeed, it is easier for the Germans to
face the past now than it was ten years ago. Then, it
was natural that they should have found it hard to
look at the recent past, since this inevitably involved a
personal examination of conscience and an agonising

Reprinted from *Encounter* xvi (July 1961), by permission of the author and *International Affairs*. See
also Introduction, pp. 2, 13–15.

confrontation with the actions and attitudes of each individual. Now, although there is much that must still be almost unbearably painful, the basis is being laid for a searching and dispassionate study of the origins and nature of National Socialism. This has become possible partly because of the revival of political self-confidence in Germany and partly because of a feeling that, whatever the defects of politics and society in the Federal Republic, they have nothing in common with the weaknesses of the Weimar Republic, let alone with the wickedness of the Third Reich. Although an occasional voice is raised against the assumption that 'Bonn is not Weimar', such as that of that highly intelligent publicist Mr Harry Pross in, for example, his *Vor und Nach Hitler*, the general assumption is that German society and politics are now in a healthier state than at any time in this century – even though some disturbing parallels can occasionally be drawn between Adenauer's, or Erhard's, Germany and the Reich of William II. In general, however, confidence in the present makes it easier to face the recent past.

Then, too, the younger generation has only a hazy idea of what the Third Reich was really like and does not feel the emotional involvement which their parents did, so that they can read about National Socialism with something approaching dispassionate curiosity. Indeed, the problem of what schoolchildren should be expected to know about the Nazi period is an enormously difficult one. Complaints are often heard that schoolteachers are not teaching anything about the Third Reich; and it may be that the older generation of teachers have been too ashamed of their own acquiescence in Hitler's triumphs to do so. But even if impartial textbooks or introductory histories are becoming available the problem remains a human one as much as a historiographical one. The horrors, for example, of Hitler's policy of racial extermination are almost too great for children to grasp, and a regular recital of the sins of the fathers may not necessarily have the desired effect on the children.

Nevertheless, sooner or later the school textbooks

will reflect the immense amount of scholarly work now being done in Germany on the origins and development of the Third Reich. The credit for this must largely go to the Institut für Zeitgeschichte in Munich, though the work done in this country by the late Alfred Wiener and the Wiener Library in London has also played an important part. The Institute has painstakingly assembled a large amount of documentary material; it publishes an important journal of contemporary history, the *Vierteljahrshefte für Zeitgeschichte,* in which both the results of research at the Institute as well as documentary material and the work of foreign scholars appear. The members of the Institute have produced elaborate detailed studies – of which Dr Thilo Vogelsang's *Reichswehr, Staat und NSDAP* is the most recent – as well as shorter general studies such as Dr Martin Broszat's *Der Nationalsozialismus,*[1] a penetrating essay on the nature of National Socialism, which deserves translating into English.

There have been times when the work of the scholars connected with the Munich Institute has seemed almost too cold and dispassionate, and when it has seemed to treat the recent past as if it were the Middle Ages, so that the actions of people who are still alive seem remote and colourless. In fact, however, this deliberate playing down of the drama and horror of twentieth-century Germany has, in the long run, been worth while. Like a surgeon anaesthetising a patient before performing a painful operation, the best German academic historians have, so to speak, anaesthetised the past, preliminary to dissecting it for analysis. The result has been a restoration, especially abroad, of confidence in German standards of historical objectivity and in the disinterestedness of German scholarship. Moreover, this highly scholarly and professional approach to themes so charged with emotion has effectively prevented the emergence of myths about National Socialism. Every legend is examined and the authenticity of documents tested, so that it is difficult for any tendentious account of the Nazi period to go unchallenged in Germany.

The example of the Munich Institute has been followed on a local basis elsewhere. Thus, for example, an Institute for the study of National Socialism in Hamburg in 1960 produced its first publication – the text of a speech made by Hitler in 1926 to the National Club in Hamburg, with an introduction by Werner Jochmann which throws much light' on the Nationalist party and their relations with the Nazis.[2] The intentions behind such projects are admirable: as Senator Landahl writes of the Hamburg Institute, 'Only the truth can free us from the toils of the past.'

Most recent scholarly writing about contemporary history has tended to centre round the question 'How could it happen?' That is to say, it is anxiously preoccupied with the fall of the Weimar Republic and the stages by which the Nazis succeeded in coming to power. In this field, Professor Karl Dietrich Bracher has produced a massive, learned and definitive – if not easily digestible – work on the last stages of the political crisis of the Republic,[3] and, with two colleagues, has gone on to analyse the early stages in the Nazi party's assumption of control over all aspects of German life.[4] The Institute for the study of Parliament in Bonn, which has also published valuable material on the history of the German Revolution of 1918, has sponsored a study of the end of the republican parties.[5]

We now have, therefore, not only source books based on contemporary documents, such as Albert Wucher's *Die Fahne Hoch*, but also, what is more important, a detailed political analysis of the end of the Weimar Republic. What happened is now clear, even if there is still much room for discussion about why it happened. Some of the leading German experts on contemporary history recently tried to give their answers to this question in a series of talks on the West German Radio, and these have now been published in English, and provide an interesting indication of the kind of answer that is being given, as well as suggesting the various factors, both particular and general, which are being held responsible for the collapse of the Republic. Some of the contributions look beyond the immediate past in order to find their answers. Thus two leading political scientists, Professor Theodor Eschenburg and Professor Ernst Fraenkel, both look to the German political tradition for an explanation. Professor Eschenburg is not surprised at the collapse of democracy in Germany, and points out that it was not a unique phenomenon: in the other states which tried democracy for the first time after 1918, it was not a success either, and, indeed, it was only in countries where parliamentary democracy was firmly established before 1914 that it survived the strains of the post-war world. This is true as far as it goes, but it does not attempt to explain why anti-democratic thought and practice were so much more extreme and virulent in Germany than elsewhere. It is illustrative, too, of a trend that can be found elsewhere in German analyses of National Socialism, which account for what happened in Germany by treating the Nazis simply as an extreme symptom of a disease that was affecting all Europe. Professor Fraenkel, on the other hand, perhaps influenced by long exposure to Anglo-Saxon political thought while working for the U.S. government, points out the deeply anti-democratic nature of the German tradition in political thought and shows how the Hegelian myth of the living state, whose personality is more than, and independent of, the individuals who compose it, and the longing for a *Volksgemeinschaft*, a community in which the individual is submerged in the whole, both militate against producing the attitude of mind which takes readily to the tolerance and compromise on which successful parliamentary government must be based.

Some historians, looking for an explanation in the field of the history of ideas, are more specific. Dr Kurt Sontheimer, for example, both in his contribution to the broadcast symposium and in his *Antidemokratisches Denken in der Weimarer Republik,*[6] traces the links between the right-wing nationalist thought of the twenties and the rise of National Socialism. Certainly this is part of the explanation of Hitler's success. There was much in the mish-mash of second-hand ideas which passed for Nazi ideology that was derived from and appealed to the followers of the various '*völkisch*' and authoritarian sects of the twenties. Equally, two recent studies of Hitler's early days in Munich show how many of his first followers came from the esoteric nationalist groups which sprang up in Munich after 1918. Gunther Schubert, in his *Anfänge Nationalsozialistischer Aussepolitik*, has shown, among other things, how much Alfred Rosenberg, the dilettante architectural student from the German colony in Riga, contributed to Hitler's ideology by his extreme racial feelings, characteristic of the right-wing Germans of the *Baltikum*, by his ill-founded reputation as an expert on Bolshevism and, above all, by his fanatical belief in the authenticity of the Protocols of the Elders of Zion, that disastrous source-book of anti-semitism, to which he introduced Hitler. Still, many of the nationalists who supported Hitler, or who thought he could bring them the mass support they lacked, ended up in disillusionment and sometimes in actual opposition to the Nazis. While nationalist and anti-democratic tradition in Germany is one of the threads which help to lead us to Hitler, it is only one among many, and an explanation of his emergence and success which relies only on ideological factors is bound to be inadequate.

In contrast to those historians and political scientists who stress the role of ideas in the failure of the Republic, most of the historians contributing to the broadcast symposium rely on purely political explanations. Thus Professor Bracher again emphasises, as he does in his books, Hitler's own political skill, by which he contrived to give the impression that he was conducting a 'national revolution' while at the same time using seemingly legal and constitutional means to achieve his ends. When faced with the combination of popular appeal, ability to intrigue and power of intimidation which Hitler and his followers showed during 1931 and 1932, the other parties appear fumbling and helpless, and attempts have been made to fix the blame for the final collapse on each in turn – on the Social Democrats, fettered by their own concept of republican legality and unwilling and unable to resist the expulsion of the legitimate government in Prussia in July 1932, the last chance they had, as Professor Erich Matthias suggests,[7] of saving the Republic; on the Centre, who meekly voted full powers to Hitler in March 1933 and accepted their own dissolution without a murmur; on the Communists, who persisted, even after the Nazi persecution of their party had started, in maintaining that the Social Democrats were still the main enemy and that the National Socialist dictatorship was shortly due to collapse and give way to the triumph of the Communists.

The merit of this type of political explanation is that it stresses how far the Nazi assumption of power was from being the inevitable popular triumph the Nazis in their own propaganda (and especially in their films) made it out to be. Throughout 1932 the Nazi triumph was by no means unavoidable – though whether the Republic could have been saved or whether the only alternative to Hitler was some sort of authoritarian conservative state based on the army is another question. Even in the elections of 1933, as the Germans today never tire of pointing out, held under the eyes and truncheons of the S.A., the Nazis themselves only secured some 45 per cent of the votes, so that without the support of the Nationalists and the acquiescence of the Centre, they would not have been able to maintain the fiction of a legal assumption of power. On the other hand, any account in purely political terms will not be of much use to those who are concerned to unravel deeper causes, or to those who are looking for lessons for the future. If Hitler's success was due less to the popular upsurge of the German people but rather to the skill with which he was able to exploit the stupidity and weakness of his opponents, then these seem to be factors which are likely to recur in any future situation where one politician is cleverer than the others, and there is very little than can be done about it. *Mit der Dummheit kämpfen Gotter selbst vergebens.*

There are other ways of looking at the rise of Hitler, however, which, if they can be sustained, might allow the events of 1931–3 to be set in a wider framework and to form the basis of generalisations applicable to the future. One is to look at the constitutional machinery and political institutions in Germany and to try to see why the Weimar Republic did not work. It is easy to point out the weaknesses – the reliance on the presidential power of government by decree, the failure of the electoral system to produce a majority and the consequent necessity for government by coalition. Deeper and more important than these, however, was the total rejection of the Republic by important sections of the German people. There could be no 'loyal opposition' because the opposition, both on the Right and on the Left, was opposition to the whole existing system and not just opposition to a particular programme or government, so that in these circumstances every governmental crisis tended to become a crisis of the regime. At the same time, the officer corps and many civil servants and judges never really accepted the constitution they were supposed to be serving. The history of 'political justice', the trials and sentences for political crimes, including assassination, in the Weimar Republic has yet to be fully investigated, although Professor Emil J. Gumbel, an eminent mathematician who has also long been concerned with the failure to respect human rights in Germany, has looked at some of the more notorious examples in his short study *Vom Fememord zur Reichskanzlei.* This feeling that, in many cases, the scales of justice were weighted against the Republic because many members of the judiciary were opposed to it accounts, incidentally, for the extreme sensitivity of left-wing opinion in Germany today to any suspicion that there may still be Nazi judges in office; and although this fear is often hysterically expressed and used for irrelevant propaganda purposes, it is based on a sound lesson from the past.

If the inner rejection of the Republic by many who were supposed to be its servants contributed much to the ease with which Hitler was able to take over the whole German administrative machinery, there were other opponents of democracy whose hostility was more directly and openly expressed. In the early days of the Republic, the Free Corps and the various other armed bodies which disturbed the peace showed how weak the power of the Republican government was to maintain order. Of these groups the one which in the long run was to assume the greatest importance was the S.A., and a former member of it, Herr Heinrich Bennecke, who, like many of its early adherents, later quarrelled with Hitler, has published an interesting and valuable account of the way in which Hitler was able to take over this group of adventurers and thugs and use them for his own political purposes, finally in 1934 murdering those who, like Roehm, still thought that they were, as before 1923, in a position where their own policies and goals were the same as those of Hitler.

Bertholt Brecht, in his *Lied vom S.A.-Mann*, suggests the mood in which many people joined the S.A.:

> Als mir die Magen knurrte, schlief ich
> Vor Hunger ein.
> Da hort' ich sie ins Ohr mir
> Deutschland erwache! schrein.
> Da sah ich viele marschieren
> Sie sagten: ins Dritte Reich,
> Ich hatte nichts zu verlieren
> Und lief mit, wohin war mir gleich.[8]

This is indeed the essence of one way of accounting for Hitler's success. Many writers have rejected the political or constitutional explanations, and have tried to show that it was purely economic factors which brought Hitler to power. 'Hitler was no accident', to quote the title of a book by an Austrian Marxist writer, Josef Hindels. On this view, Hitler was himself the product of the decadent society in which he passed his formative years before 1914, and his subsequent success was due

both to the support which he won from the industrialists anxious to preserve their position and increase
their gains, and from the unemployed, the victims of a
system which they erroneously thought Hitler was attacking. The subject is a difficult one. While the support given to Hitler by certain industrialists, especially
Fritz Thyssen, is well known, as is the fact that he was
able to get help at a critical moment early in 1932 from
certain members of the Industrie-Klub in Dusseldorf,
much research remains to be done as to both the extent
and nature of the support which Hitler received, and,
still more, on the subsequent fortunes of the industrialists who had placed their hopes in him. Mr George
W. F. Hallgarten, who is well known for his studies of
the economic aspects of the origins of the First World
War, has published some suggestive and stimulating
essays on the relations between Hitler, the army and
he industrialists, in which he throws light both on
the role of industry in influencing German foreign
policy in 1922–4 and on the differing economic interests which led some sections of finance and industry
to support Hitler while others remained more sceptical
towards him.[9]

Most of the new work in the field of recent German
history has tended to concentrate on the Weimar Republic and on Hitler's rise to power. This is natural
enough, especially if it is, rightly or wrongly, assumed
that we can learn from the past how to avoid mistakes
in the future. Yet in addition to the question of how
Hitler won power, the question of how he kept it is
even more interesting. Most books on the Third Reich
limit themselves to an account of Hitler's foreign
policy and of his conduct of the war. Little research has
yet been done about how National Socialist Germany
was actually administered, how its ecomomy was run,
how labour relations worked or how the educational or
judicial systems functioned. A few younger scholars,
mainly British and American, are starting to fill the
gap, and it is perhaps understandable that the Germans are reluctant to do work which once again brings

them up against personal questions of conscience or of individual responsibility for making the Nazi system work, and which might possibly even lead them to the unwelcome and unpopular conclusion that, after all, in certain fields such as agriculture, for instance, or labour relations, there might be something to praise in the Nazi system. An investigation of the actual working of National Socialism would throw light both on totalitarian government in general as well as on the psychological, sociological and economic grounds which led the Germans to follow Hitler, or at least to tolerate him, even when he was embarking on policies such as the extermination of the Jews from which after the end of the war the Germans made every effort to dissociate themselves. As the youth leader, Baldur von Schirach, put it: 'My guilt lies in organising the youth of our people for a man who as Führer and head of state seemed for many years irreproachable. And this man was a murderer millions of times over.'

An autobiography by a woman who was an official in Schirach's youth movement and who ended the war cooking and washing for a group of S.S. men in hiding from the Allies in a remote Alpine valley might be expected to throw some light on these questions. But all Melita Maschmann's rather dreary and repellent book *Fazit* shows is how easy it was for ordinary people to fall into a routine in which the most appalling things could happen without being questioned or even noticed, and to confirm what Kurt von Stutterheim has written in another connection: 'This indifference to the sufferings of others is not a pleasant trait in the character of the Germans, who nevertheless are so slow to forget the injustices done to themselves.'

However, one aspect of the Third Reich has been given perhaps exaggerated attention by German writers simply because it does counteract this impression of complicity with evil or indifference to suffering. The German resistance to Hitler achieved very few practical results in Hitler's lifetime, but it has provided the Germans since with a symbol of enormous importance for their self-respect. It is easily understandable that German writers make as much as they can of every kind of resistance, though foreigners may find it hard to agree with the view sometimes expressed that Germany was the first country to be occupied by the Nazis. As Professor Hans Rothfels, himself one of the leading historians of the Resistance in Germany, has remarked, 'Rape has seldom been accompanied by such frantic rejoicing on the part of the victims.'[10] Statistics are quoted by, for example, the writer Gunter Weisenborn in his popular chronicle of the Resistance *Der lautlose Aufstand*[11] to suggest that every occupant of a concentration camp was necessarily part of the resistance. Nevertheless, there are enough examples of courage and independence to make an impressive record. In fact, in many ways it is not always the resisters who actually took part in the political conspiracy and the plot to murder Hitler who are the most impressive: disinterested figures like Hans and Sophie Scholl, the Munich students who could bear what was going on no longer and refused to keep silent, or Count Albrecht Bernstorff (now commemorated in a short and moving essay by his friend and contemporary Kurt von Stutterheim), openly and consistently expressing his disapproval in frank and reckless terms, are more sympathetic figures than ex-Nazis like Helldorf who suffered a last-minute change of heart and tried to get rid of Hitler when it was already too late.

The Resistance has become a subject on which it is difficult to touch without offending German susceptibilities. Just how touchy it is, is shown by the controversy which was aroused by the publication in 1961 of the reports which Kaltenbrunner, the chief of the security services, prepared for Bormann and Hitler to tell them the results of his investigations into the plot against Hitler's life and the conspiracy to form a new government. This volume has been criticised as being damaging to the memory of the conspirators, and the editor has been sharply attacked for not providing an adequate commentary or introduction. It is true that the editor and publishers would seem to have intended

the volume as an attack on the myth of the resistance:
'Neither the conspirators nor those who remained true
to their oath [of allegiance to Hitler],' the editor
writes, 'were able to save the Reich.... The martyrdom
of the rebels on the gallows is no less but also no more
than the death in battle of those who remained loyal'
(p. vi). This is indeed a wretched attempt to have the
best of both worlds and a once cast doubt on the intentions of the publication. However, the documents
themselves in fact do little to discredit the conspirators,
and in many cases one is struck even more forcibly
than before by the dignity and intelligence with which
many of them behaved in a situation which was both
desperate and humiliating. Kaltenbrunner's reports
add much to our knowledge of the plot and of the
intentions of the conspirators. They also throw some
light on the internal stresses in the Nazi party, and one
cannot escape the impression, for instance, that
Kaltenbrunner was using his prisoners to voice his own
views when he stresses that one of the reasons that
turned some of them who were originally sympathetic
to the regime against it was the vulgarity and ostenta-
tion of Nazi bosses like Goering or Ley.

Many of the conspirators were German nationalists
whose views, especially about foreign policy, were not
very different from those of the Nazis in the 1930s.
Some of them hoped, for example, to make peace on
the basis of the retention by Germany of Austria and
the Sudetenland. One of the biggest psychological
obstacles in assessing the history of the Nazi movement
is the unwillingness to admit that much of what Hitler
did was what many of his predecessors had wanted to
do. (This helps to account for the outcry that has
greeted the publication of Professor Fritz Fischer's re-
searches into German war aims in the First World
War,[12] when men like Bethmann-Hollweg, who are
generally thought of as 'moderates', entertained plans
which had a striking resemblance to Hitler's New
Order in Europe.) It is this difficulty of where to draw
the line in condemning Hitler that made so many
Germans unwilling to resist him until it was too late;

and it is the problem of dealing with Hitler's personality and of fitting him into German history that is
the hardest task for the historian, whether German or
foreign. For some years, indeed (although there is a
biography of Hitler by Walter Gorlitz and Herbert A.
Quint),[13] the Germans wrote little about Hitler himself, and the German translation of Mr Alan Bullock's
Hitler is still a standard work that has not been superseded.

It has often seemed easiest to dismiss Hitler as a
lunatic or a devil or a kind of natural calamity which
descended on Germany leaving disaster behind him,
rather than to consider him as a figure with any roots
in German history and society itself. As Professor
Freund puts it: 'The Germans did not really want this
Reich of Adolf Hitler, they did not want it in the form
Hitler thought of it with his secret and devilish
goals.'[14] Hitler was the evil magician who had deceived and misled the Germans, a scarcely human force
which had bewitched them. This view has made it hard
to study Hitler's own ideas and methods, for there has
been a strong reluctance to accept the concept of Hitler
as a rational and consistent figure, cleverly and skilfully pursuing his own clearly worked-out and openly
stated diabolical aims. Nevertheless, an understanding
of Hitler himself remains essential for an understanding not only of the Third Reich but also of German
history in the twentieth century. As Dr Max Domarus,
who with a large-scale scholarly publication of Hitler's
speeches and proclamations is making a major contribution to the subject, writes: 'Perhaps in our re-
searches into the history of the Third Reich we have
up to now seen things in too complicated a way. The
initiator and motive force of everything that happened
was Adolf Hitler.' Hitler is the most repulsive of the
great men who have changed the face of Europe, and as
a result he tends to be under-estimated now, just as
he was over-estimated by the Germans thirty years
ago.

The latest attempt to analyse this baffling figure – so
intelligent and so commonplace, so terrifyingly mad in

his long-term goals and basic assumptions, so astute and skilful in his diplomacy and politics – is a long biography by Herr Hans Bernd Gisevius, a man who not only lived through the whole of the Hitler period but who was also involved in the conspiracy against Hitler, of which he has already published his own controversial account. He therefore brings many qualifications to his task; and it may well be that a contemporary of Hitler who experienced at first hand the impact of one of the great demagogues of all time is better equipped to deal with him than a younger scholar for whom Hitler is already a legendary figure to be disinterred from the archives. Herr Gisevius asks whether it is too soon for a German to write about Hitler, and answers: 'Hitler was and remains a German phenomenon.... We not only suffered the phenomenon of Hitler. We helped to create it' (pp. 6–7). The result of Gisevius's work is certainly a very German book, immensely long, involved and rhetorical, much of which it would be very hard indeed to translate into acceptable or convincing English. Still, the book is a considerable achievement. Herr Gisevius has made use of the mass of detailed research which has been done by others on Hitler's early years and rise to power; he has produced a series of vivid portraits of Hitler at the various stages of his life; but above all, he is concerned to combat legends and explode myths. His Hitler remains a monster – there is a terrifying description of the sick and listless Hitler of the last months casually disinterested in the extermination of the Jews which Himmler and his subordinates were carrying out so faithfully in execution of Hitler's wishes – but he is also a rational political leader endowed with great instinctive intelligence and cunning. Above all, as the author pauses to assess the importance of each stage, he stresses again and again that the Third Reich was not an inevitable phenomenon imposed on the Germans by ineluctable laws of historical development, but the product of human will – Hitler's own and that of the Germans who voted for him or who served him.

Herr Gisevius's book will start many controversies

and discussions in Germany. What is important is that the work of men like Professor Bracher and of Dr Krausnick and his colleagues at the Munich Institute of Contemporary History, and many others, has now made it possible for this discussion to be an informed one, so that prejudice and myth can be confronted with sober fact. That this is indeed possible is not the least of the achievements of the Germans since 1945. The problem of the *unbewaltigte Vergangenheit* is not easily solved. The past can never be wholly overcome, and it is impossible to forget or to obliterate from the record the years of the Third Reich when we are still suffering from its shattering effects; but it is by facing the obscure forces within us and the unpleasant truths about ourselves that nations, like individuals, can cope with the world around them and face the future.

The recent books to which Mr Joll refers are:

Vor und Nach Hitler: Zur deutschen Sozialpathologie, by Harry Pross (Olten, Freiburg im Breisgau: Walter-Verlag, 1962) 267 pp. Index. Sw. frs 8.80.

Das Dritte Reich 1933–1939, by Michael Freund (Gütersloh: C. Bertelsmann Verlag, 1963) 190 pp. Index. (Bücherei 'Bildung und Wissen'.) D.M. 5.80.

Reichswehr, Staat und NSDAP: Beitrage zur deutschen Geschichte 1930–1932, by Thilo Vogelsang (Stuttgart: Deutsche Verlags-Anstalt, 1962) 507 pp. Bibliog. Index. ('Quellen und Darstellungen zur Zeitgeschichte', Band II.)

Die Fahne Hoch: Das Ende der Republik und Hitlers Machtubernahme, by Albert Wucher (Munich: Süddeutscher Verlag, 1963) 254 pp. Illus. Tables. DM. 14.80.

The Road to Dictatorship: Germany 1918–1933, by T. Eschenburg *et al.*, trans. Lawrence Wilson (London: Wolff, 1964) 174 pp. 25s.

Anfänge Nationalsozialistische Aussenpolitik, by Günter Schubert (Cologne: Verlag Wissenschaft und Politik, 1963) 254 pp. Bibliog. DM. 26.50.

Vom Fememord zur Reichskanzlei, by Emil J. Gumbel,

with foreword by Dr Walter Fabian (Heidelberg:
Verlag Lambert Schneider, 1962) 90 pp. Tables.
Bibliog. DM. 4.40.
Hitler und die S.A., by Heinrich Bennecke (Munich,
Vienna: Günter Olzog Verlag, 1962) 264 pp. Maps.
Tables. Bibliog. DM. 19.80.
*Hitler war kein Zufall: Ein Beitrag zur Soziologie der
Nazibarbarei*, by Josef Hindels, with foreword by
Peter Blachstein (Vienna, Frankfurt am Main,
Zürich: Europa Verlag, 1962) 198 pp. ('Europäische
Perspektiven'.) Sch. 68. DM. 10.50. Sw. frs 10.50.
Fazit: Kein Rechtfertigungsversuch, by Melita Masch-
mann, with foreword by Ida Friederike Görres (Stutt-
gart: Deutsche Verlags-Anstalt, 1963) 224 pp. DM.
7.80.
*Die Majestät des Gewissens. In Memoriam, Albrecht
Bernstorff*, by Kurt von Stuterheim, with foreword
by Theodor Heuss (Hamburg: Hans Christians Verlag, 1962) 100 pp. Illus. Bibliog. DM. 9.80.
*Spiegelbild einer Verschwörung: Die Kaltenbrunner-
Berichte an Bormann und Hitler über das Attentat
vom 20. Juli 1944. Geheime Dokumente aus dem
ehemaligen Reichssicherheitshauptamt*, with preface
by Karl Heinrich Peter (Stuttgart: Seewald Verlag
für Archiv Peter für historische und zeitgeschicht-
liche Dokumentation, 1961) 587 pp. Tables. Dia-
gram. Index. DM. 38.
*Hitler: Reden und Proklamationen. 1932–1945. Kom-
mentiert von einem deutschen Zeitgenossen*, Band
1: *Triumph (1932–1938)*. Ed. Max Domarus (Würzburg: Dr Max Domarus, 1962) 987 pp. Illus.
Adolf Hitler: Versuch einer Deutung, by Hans Bernd
Gisevius (Munich: Rutten & Loening, 1963) 565 pp.
Illus. Bibliog. Index. DM. 28.

Notes

[1] Stuttgart: Deutsche Verlags-Anstalt, 1961.
[2] *Im Kampf um die Macht: Hitlers Rede vor dem
Hamburger Nationalklub von 1919*, by Werner Joch-

mann (Frankfurt am Main: Europäische Verlags-Anstalt, 1960).

[3] *Die Auflösung der Weimarer Republik* (Stuttgart: Ring Verlag, 1955), reviewed in *International Affairs* (Jan 1956) 101.

[4] *Die nationalsozialistische Machtergreifung*, by K. D. Bracher, G. Schulz and W. Sauer (Cologne: Westdeutscher Verlag, 1960), reviewed in *International Affairs* (April 1961) 235.

[5] *Das Ende der Parteien 1933*, by E. Matthias and R. Morsey (Düsseldorf: Droste Verlag, 1960).

[6] Munich: Nymphenburger Verlagshandlung, 1962.

[7] Erich Matthias, 'Social Democracy and the Power of the State', in *The Road to Dictatorship: Germany 1918–1933*, pp. 57–73.

[8]   From hunger I grew drowsy
                    Dulled by my belly's ache
                    Then someone shouted in my ear:
                    Germany, awake!
                    Then I saw many marching
                    Towards the Third Reich, they said.
                    Since I had nought to lose
                    I followed where they led.
Translation from Bertholt Brecht's Selected Poems: trans. and intro. H. R. Hays (London: Evergreen Books).

[9] *Hitler, Reichswehr und Industrie: Zur Geschichte der Jahre 1918–1933* (Frankfurt am Main: Europäische Verlags-Anstalt, 1955; paperback ed. 1962).

[10] Hans Rothfels, 'Resistance Begins', in *The Road to Dictatorship*, p. 146.

[11] Hamburg: Rowohlt, 1953; paperback ed. 1962.

[12] *Griff nach der Weltmacht* (Düsseldorf: Droste Verlag, 1961), reviewed in *International Affairs* (Jan 1963) 77.

[13] *Adolf Hitler* (Stuttgart: Steingrüben-Verlag, 1952), reviewed in *International Affairs* (July 1953) 370.

[14] *Das Dritte Reich 1933–1939*, p. 9.

H. R. Trevor-Roper

It is over twenty years since the war began. A generation has grown up which never knew the 1930s, never
shared its passions and doubts, was never excited by
the Spanish civil war, never boiled with indignation
against the 'appeasers', never lived in suspense from
Nuremberg rally to Nuremberg rally, awaiting the
next hysterical outburst, the next clatter of arms, from
the megalomaniac in Berlin. Those of us who knew
those days and who try to teach this new generation are
constantly made aware of this great gulf between us.
How can we communicate across such a gulf the emotional content of those years, the mounting indignation which finally convinced even the 'appeasers' themselves that there could be no peace with Hitler, and
caused the British people, united in pacifism in 1936,
to go, in 1939, united into war? For it was not the
differing shades of justice in Germany's claims upon
the Rhineland, Austria, the Sudetenland, Prague and
Danzig which caused men who had swallowed the first
of these annexations to be increasingly exasperated by
those which followed and take up arms against the
last. It was a changing mood, a growing conviction that
all such claims were but pretexts under which Hitler
pursued not justice or self-determination for Germany
but world conquest, and that, now or never, he must be
stopped. And even across the gulf such a mood must be
conveyed by those who teach history to those who learn
it: for it is an element in history no less important
than the mere facts.

Reprinted from *Encounter*, XVII (July 1961), by permission of the author and *Encounter*. See also Introduction, p.16.

Or is it? Mr A. J. P. Taylor, it seems, does not think
so (*The Origins of the Second world War*: Hamish
Hamilton, 25*s*). He sees the gulf all right, and he wishes
to speak to those on the other side of it; but in order to
do so, he has decided to lighten the weight he must
carry with him. Stripping himself of all personal
memories, and thus making himself, in this respect, as
naked as they are, he has jumped nimbly across the
gulf and now presents himself to them as the first enlightened historian of the future, capable of interpreting the politics of the 1920s and 1930s without any
reference to the emotions they engendered, even in
himself. Their sole guide, he tells them, must be the
documents, which he will select and interpret for
them; and indeed, by selection and interpretation, he
presents them with a new thesis, illustrated (we need
hardly say) with all his old resources of learning, paradox and *gaminerie*.

The thesis is perfectly clear. According to Mr Taylor,
Hitler was an ordinary German statesman in the tradition of Stresemann and Bruning, differing from them
not in methods (he was made chancellor for 'solidly
democratic reasons') nor in ideas (he had no ideas) but
only in the greater patience and stronger nerves with
which he took advantage of the objective situation in
Europe. His policy, in so far as he had a policy, was no
different from that of his predecessors. He sought
neither war nor annexation of territory. He merely
sought to restore Germany's 'natural' position in
Europe, which had been artificially altered by the
Treaty of Versailles: a treaty which, for that reason,
'lacked moral validity from the start'. Such a restoration might involve the recovery of lost German territory like Danzig, but it did not entail the direct
government even of Austria or the Sudetenland, let
alone Bohemia. Ideally, all that Hitler required was
that Austria, Czechoslovakia and other small Central
European states, while remaining independent,
should become political satellites of Germany.

Of course it did not work out thus. But that, we are

assured, was not Hitler's fault. For Hitler, according to
Mr Taylor, never took the initiative in politics. He
'did not make plans – for world conquest or anything
else. He assumed that others would provide opportunities and that he would seize them.' And that is what
happened. The Austrian crisis of March 1938, we are
told, 'was provoked by Schuschnigg, not by Hitler'.
Hitler was positively embarrassed by it: 'he was Austrian enough to find the complete disappearance of
Austria inconceivable until it happened'. Similarly we
learn that the Sudeten crisis of 1938 was created by the
Sudeten Nazis, who 'built up the tension gradually,
without guidance from Hitler': Hitler himself 'merely
took advantage of it'. Having taken advantage of it at
Munich, he had no intention of going on and annexing the Czech lands: 'he merely doubted whether the
settlement would work ... [he] believed, without sinister intention, that independent Czechoslovakia could
not survive when deprived of her natural frontiers and
with Czech prestige broken'. So, within six months,
as 'the unforeseen by-product of developments in
Slovakia', he felt obliged to tear up the settlement and
occupy Prague; but there was 'nothing sinister or premeditated' in that. It was an unfortunate necessity
forced upon him by the unskilful President Hacha.
The Polish crisis of 1939 was similarly forced upon him
by Beck. 'The destruction of Poland,' we are told, 'had
been no part of his original project. On the contrary,
he wished to solve the question of Danzig so that
Germany and Poland could remain on good terms.'
The last thing he wanted was war. The war of nerves
was 'the only war he understood and liked'. Germany
'was not equipped to conquer Europe':

> The state of German rearmament in 1939 gives
> the decisive proof that Hitler was not contemplating
> general war, and probably not contemplating war at
> all.

Even on 23 August 1939, when the Nazi-Soviet Pact
was signed, 'both Hitler and Stalin imagined that they

had prevented war, not brought it on'. What rational person could have supposed that this pact, instead of discouraging the British, would determine them to stand by their commitments? The war, 'far from being premeditated, was a mistake, the result on both sides of diplomatic blunders'.

Hitler's own share of these diplomatic blunders was, it seems, very small. He 'became involved in war', we are told, 'through launching on 29 August a diplomatic manoeuvre which he ought to have launched on 28 August'. The blunders of the Western statesmen were far more fundamental. For what ought the Western statesmen to have done when faced by Hitler's modest demands? According to Mr Taylor, they should have conceded them all. They should not have conceded anything to Mussolini, for Mussolini's demands were essentially different from Hitler's. Mussolini was 'a vain, blustering boaster', whose government, unlike the 'solidly democratic' rule of Hitler, 'lived in a state of illegality', and whose demands, since they did not correspond with 'reality', were 'a fraud'. Western statesmen, says Mr Taylor, lost all claim to respect by recognising such a man. But Hitler was a statesman who merely sought to reassert Germany's 'natural weight', and they would therefore have gained respect by recognising him. Accordingly Mr Taylor's heroes among Western statesmen are those who recognised German claims: Ramsay MacDonald and Neville Chamberlain. Winston Churchill believed in the balance of power and would have maintained frontiers designed on principles of security, not nationality. Intolerable cynicism! How much nobler was that 'triumph for British policy', the Munich Settlement!

It was a triumph for all that was best and most enlightened in British life; a triumph for those who had preached equal justice between peoples; a triumph for those who had courageously denounced the harshness and shortsightedness of Versailles.

Munich, according to Mr Taylor, 'atoned' for all the previous weakness of British policy; it was a victory for 'morality' (which is his word for political realism); and he praises Chamberlain's 'skill and persistence' in bringing 'first the French and then the Czechs to follow the moral line'. If only Chamberlain had not lost his nerve in 1939! If only he had shown equal 'skill and persistence' in enabling Hitler to detach Danzig and the Polish Corridor, how happy we should all be! Germany would have recovered its 'natural' position, 'morality' would have triumphed, and everyone would be happy in the best of possible worlds.

Such, in brief, is Mr Taylor's thesis. It is not surprising that it has been hailed with cries of delight in neo-Nazi or semi-Nazi circles in Germany. It is more surprising that the book has been greeted by the fashionable Grub Street of England as the highest achievement of British historiography. Mr Taylor has been compared with Gibbon and Macaulay; his failure to secure worthy promotion has caused astonishment. The anonymous oracle of *The Times Literary Supplement* has predicted finality for the result of his 'methodical and impeccable logic'. In the *Observer*, Mr Sebastian Haffner (who recently published a panegyric of that 'greatest Roman of them all', Dr Goebbels) has declared the book 'an almost faultless masterpiece' in which 'fairness reigns supreme'; and his cosy, middlebrow colleagues in rival papers, hypnotised by a reputation which they are unqualified to test, have obediently jollied their readers along in harmony with the blurb. However, let us not all be hypnotised. Before hurling ourselves down the Gadarene slope, let us ask of Mr Taylor's thesis, not, Is it brilliant? Is it plausible? but, Is it true? By what rules of evidence, by what philosophy of interpretation is it reached?

Perhaps we may begin by noting Mr Taylor's general philosophy. Mr Taylor, it seems, does not believe that human agents matter much in history. His story is 'a story without heroes, and perhaps even without villains'. 'In my opinion,' he explains, 'statesmen are too absorbed by events to follow a preconceived plan. They take one step and the next follows from it.' If they achieve anything, it is by accident not design: 'all statesmen aim to win: the size of their winnings often surprises them'. The real determinants of history, according to Mr Taylor, are objective situations and human blunders. Objective situations consist of the realities of power; human intelligence is best employed in recognising these realities and allowing events to conform with them; but as human intelligence seldom prevails in politics, the realities generally have to assert themselves, at greater human cost, through the mess caused by human blunders. This doctrine (if I have correctly expressed it) seems remarkably like Mr E. H. Carr's 'realist' doctrine, advanced in his book *The Twenty Years' Crisis* (1938) – see the *first* edition – a book rightly described by Mr Taylor as 'a brilliant argument in favour of appeasement'.

Once we accept this general theory, the next stage is easy. All we have to do is to ask ourselves, at what point do we make our calculation of reality? This then provides us with a datum. Mr Taylor takes as his datum the spring of 1918. At that time Germany was victorious in the West and triumphant in the East. This, he implies, was the 'natural' situation: the Allied victory later in 1918 was artificial – or at least it was made artificial (or, in his words, deprived of 'moral validity') by the failure of the Allies to carve Germany up before making peace. This omission left Germany still potentially the greatest power in Europe, naturally tending to revert to the 'real' position of January 1918. All that intelligent German statesmen had to do, or indeed could do, was to work hand-in-glove with this 'historical necessity' – to their profit. All that Allied statesmen could do was to yield to the same necessity – to their loss. In this sense Hitler and Chamberlain were intelligent statesmen.

But is this general philosophy true? Do statesmen really never make history? Are they, all of them, always 'too absorbed by events to follow a preconceived plan'?

Was this true of Richelieu, of Bismarck, of Lenin? In particular, was it true of Hitler? Was Hitler really just a more violent Mr Micawber sitting in Berlin or Berchtesgaden and waiting for something to turn up: something which, thanks to historic necessity, he could then turn to advantage? Certainly Hitler himself did not think so. He regarded himself as a thinker, a practical philosopher, the demiurge of a new age of history. And since he published a blueprint of the policy which he intended to carry out, ought we not at least to look at this blueprint just in case it had some relevance to his policy? After all, the reason why the majority of the British people reluctantly changed, between 1936 and 1939, from the views of Neville Chamberlain and Mr Taylor to the views of Winston Churchill was their growing conviction that Hitler meant what he said: that he was aiming – *so oder so*, as he used to say – at world conquest. A contemporary conviction that was strong enough to change the mood of a nation from a passionate desire for peace to a resolute determination on war surely deserves some respect from the historian. A historian who totally ignores it because, twenty years later, he can interpret some of the documents in an opposite sense runs the risk of being considered too clever by half.

Let us consider briefly the programme which Hitler laid down for himself. It was a programme of Eastern colonisation, entailing a war of conquest against Russia. If it were successfully carried out, it would leave Germany dominant in Eurasia and able to conquer the West at will. In order to carry it out, Hitler needed a restored German army which, since it must be powerful enough to conquer Russia, must also be powerful enough to conquer the West if that should be necessary. And that might be necessary even before the attack on Russia. For in order to reach Russia, Hitler would need to send his armies through Poland; and in order to do this – whether by the conquest of Poland or in alliance with it – he would need to break the bonds of treaty and interest which bound the new countries

of Eastern Europe, the creatures of Versailles, to their
creators, Britain and France. Hitler might be able to
break those bonds without war against the West, but
he could not be sure of it: it was always possible that a
war with the West would be necessary before he could
march against Russia. And in fact this is what happened.

Now this programme, which Hitler ascribed to himself, and which he actually carried out, is obviously
entirely different from the far more limited programme which is ascribed to him by Mr Taylor, and
which he did not carry out. How then does Mr Taylor
deal with the evidence about it? He deals with it quite
simply, either by ignoring it or by denying it as inconsistent with his own theories about statesmen in general
and Hitler in particular: theories (one must add) for
which he produces no evidence at all.

Take the inconvenient fact of Hitler's avowed programme of a great Eastern land empire. In spite of
some casual admission, Mr Taylor effectively denies
that Hitler had any such programme. Hitler, he says,
'was always the man of daring improvisations: he
made lightning decisions and then presented them as
the result of long-term policy'. Hitler's *Table Talk*, he
says airily (as if this were the only evidence for such a
programme), 'was delivered far in occupied territory
during the campaign against Soviet Russia, and *then*
Hitler dreamed of some fantastic empire which would
rationalise his career of conquest'. (My italics here, and
in all quotations below.) But why does Mr Taylor believe, or rather pretend, that it was only in 1942, after
his Russian conquests, that Hitler dreamed of an
Eastern Empire? His programme had been stated, as
clearly as possible, in 1924, in *Mein Kampf*, and on
numerous other occasions since. Mr Taylor hardly ever
refers to *Mein Kampf* and never to the other occasions.
In 1939, he admits, some people 'attributed' to Hitler
'grandiose plans which *they claimed* to have discovered
by reading *Mein Kampf* in the original (Hitler forbade
its publication in English)'. The implication is that
such plans are not to be found in *Mein Kampf* and

that those who 'claimed to have discovered' them had not really read, or been able to read, an untranslated work. But the fact is that those plans are unmistakably stated in *Mein Kampf* and that all the evidence of the 1930s showed that Hitler still intended to carry them out. I may add (since Mr Taylor includes me among those who have ascribed to Hitler 'preconceived plans' which he never pursued) that I myself read *Mein Kampf* in the original in 1938, and that I read it under the impact of Munich and of the remarkable prophecies of Sir Robert Ensor, who had read it and who insisted that Hitler meant what he said. By absolutely refusing to face this evidence, and contemptuously dismissing those who have faced it, Mr Taylor contrives to reach the preposterous conclusion that men like Ensor, who correctly forecast Hitler's future programme from the evidence, were really wrong, and that men like Chamberlain, who did not read the evidence and were proved totally wrong by events, were really right. His sole justification of this paradox is that he has accepted as an axiom a characterisation of Hitler as a 'traditional' statesman pursuing limited aims. Mr Taylor's Hitler cannot have held such views, and therefore the inconvenient fact that the real Hitler uttered such views with remarkable consistency for twenty years and actually put them into practice is simply puffed aside. When Hitler, in 1941, finally launched that conquest of Russia which, as he himself said, was 'the be-all and end-all of Nazism', Mr Taylor easily explains it away. 'By 1941,' he says, 'Hitler had lost his old gift of patience': he 'gratuitously' deviated from his former course; and at the mere thought of such an unaccountable fall from grace, Mr Taylor promptly ends his book.

Nor is this the only perversion of evidence to which Mr Taylor has to resort, in order to represent Hitler as a 'traditional' statesman. The traditional statesmen *did not seek*, as Hitler did, to incorporate the Sudeten Germans in the Reich. Traditional statesmen demanded the frontiers of 1914; but Hitler, again and again, repudiated the frontiers of 1914 as a contemptible ambition. They looked back, at most, to the war-aims of 1914; he repudiated those war-aims. Even the 'natural' position of January 1918, after the huge gains of Brest-Litovsk, was insufficient for Hitler. The Treaty of Brest-Litovsk gave Germany the Ukraine as a colony of exploitation, a capitalist colony. But Hitler always made it quite clear that he spurned such a colony: he wanted the Ukraine as a colony of settlement. 'I should deem it a crime,' he said, 'if I sacrificed the blood of a quarter of a million men merely for the conquest of natural riches to be exploited in a capitalist way. The goal of the *Ostpolitik* is to open up an area of settlement for a hundred million Germans.' All this is pushed aside by Mr Taylor with the remark,

> when Hitler lamented, 'If only we had a Ukraine...' he seemed to suppose there were no Ukrainians. Did he propose to exploit, or exterminate them? *Apparently he never considered the question.*

As if Hitler had not made his answer perfectly plain! As if he had any scruples about transporting or even exterminating populations! What about the European Jews? But that episode is conveniently forgotten by Mr Taylor. It does not fit the character of a traditional German statesmen who 'in principle and doctrine, was no more wicked and unscrupulous than many other contemporary statesmen'.

If Mr Taylor's cardinal assumptions about Hitler's character and purpose are, to say the least, questionable, what are we to say of his use of evidence to illustrate them? Here he states his method with admirable clarity. 'It is an elementary part of historical discipline,' he says, 'to ask of a document not only what is in it but why it came into existence.' With this maxim we may agree, only adding that since the contents of a document are objective evidence while its purpose may be a matter of private surmise, we must not rashly subject the former to the latter. Sometimes a man may say the truth even in a document called forth by tactical necessity. At all events, we are not entitled, in defence of an already paradoxical general theory, to assume that he is lying simply because it may not be tactically necessary for him, at that moment, to utter nothing but the truth.

Now let us take a few instances. On 5 November 1937 Hitler summoned his war-leaders to the Chancellery and made a speech which, he said, in the event of his death was to be regarded as his 'last will and testament'. That suggests that he was not talking irresponsibly. The official record of this speech is the so-called 'Hossbach Memorandum' which was used at Nuremberg as evidence of Hitler's plans for the gradual conquest of Europe. In it Hitler declared that the aim of German policy must be the conquest of *Lebensraum* in Europe, 'but we will not copy liberal capitalist policies which rely on exploiting colonies. It is not a case of conquering people but of conquering agriculturally useful space.' That seems clear enough. Then Hitler went on to consider the means of making such conquests. 'German politics,' he said, 'must reckon with two hateful enemies, England and France, to whom a strong German colossus in the centre of Europe would be intolerable.' Moreover, he admitted, these two hateful enemies would probably, at some stage, resist him by force: 'the German question can only be solved by way of force and this is never without risk'. He then proceeded to discuss hypothetical possibilities. Since the hypothetical circumstances did not in fact arise, we need not dwell on them. The essential points are that the risk of European war must be faced by 1943–5, for 'after that we can only expect a change for the worse', and that 'our *first* aim' must be, at the first convenient opportunity, 'to conquer Czechoslovakia and Austria simultaneously'. This first conquest he hoped to achieve without war, for 'in all probability England and perhaps also France have already silently written off Czechoslovakia'. It could and should therefore be attempted as soon as circumstances made it possible in order that the later, more real risk could be faced before 1943–5. But there was to be no doubt about the nature of the conquest. It was not to be (as Mr Taylor always maintains) the reduction of Austria and Czechoslovakia to the role of satellites: it was to be, in Hitler's own words, 'the annexation of the two states to Germany, militarily and politically'. The idea of satellite states in Eastern Europe, Hitler said in a secret speech delivered only a fortnight later, was one of the futile notions of 'traditional' German politicians, and he dismissed it as 'idiotic' (*wahnsinnig*). Finally, it is clear that conquered Austria and Czechoslovakia cannot themselves have constituted the *Lebensraum* which was the ultimate objective. Austria and Czechoslovakia were to be stepping-stones, 'in all probability' secured without war, towards larger conquests which would entail a greater risk.

Such was Hitler's 'testament' of November 1937. Its content is clear and logical and it has been taken seriously by all historians – until Mr Taylor comes along and tells us that we have all been hoodwinked. For was not this document produced at Nuremberg? All documents produced at Nuremberg, he says, are 'loaded', and 'anyone who relies on them finds it almost impossible to escape from the load with which they are charged'. So Mr Taylor gives us a sample of his method of using such documents. Why, he asks, was the speech made? 'The historian,' he observes, 'must push through the *cloud of phrases*' (so much for Hitler's perfectly clear statements) 'to the *realities* beneath.' The speech, he notes, was not made to Nazis but to generals and admirals, and its purpose was clearly to demand greater rearmament. With this we can agree. But Mr Taylor does not stop there. In order to persuade these 'conservative' war-leaders of the necessity of further rearmament, Hitler (he says) had to overcome the economic opposition of Dr Schacht. His speech therefore '*had no other purpose*' than 'to isolate Schacht from the other conservatives'; the dates 1943–5 (to which Hitler consistently kept) '*like all such figures, really meant* "this year, next year, sometime ..."'; and the content of a speech which Hitler himself described as his political testament (but Mr Taylor does not quote that description) is dismissed as 'day-dreaming unrelated to what followed in real life'. Why Hitler should be expected to speak more 'realistically' on military matters to Nazis at a froth-blowers' meeting than to hard-headed warleaders who would have to organise and carry out his programme is not clear. Presumably it is 'an elementary part of historical discipline' to assume that.

A second example of Mr Taylor's 'historical discipline' is provided by his treatment of the crisis leading to the outbreak of war in 1939. By now Austria and Czechoslovakia had been 'annexed to Germany, militarily and politically', and Hitler had turned the heat upon Poland. According to Mr Taylor, Hitler really only wanted the German city of Danzig, but since geography prevented him from obtaining it except by the coercion of Poland, he was forced, reluctantly, to apply such coercion and prepare military plans. Of course (according to Mr Taylor) he did not intend to execute these plans. His military plans were 'only intended to reinforce the diplomatic war of nerves'. Unfortunately the British government, misled after Hitler's occupation of Prague into thinking that he aimed at far larger conquests, had imprudently guaranteed Poland and thus threatened Hitler with European war if he sought this next 'natural', 'moral' aim by any but peaceful means. However, Hitler was a match for this. By making his pact with Russia, he effectively countered the British guarantee, and therefore, pushing, like Mr Taylor, 'through the cloud of phrases to the realities beneath', he ignored its empty words and relied, as a rational man, on 'the crumbling of Western nerve'. Unfortunately, in this case, he miscalculated. Britain, quixotically faithful to the 'phrases' of the guarantee, and deluded by the idea that Hitler, if given a free hand, would not stop at Danzig, ignored all the 'realities' of the situation and made war, 'war for Danzig'.

Such is Mr Taylor's version of the Polish crisis. In defence of it he finds it necessary here, too, to charm away some important documents, and once again it is instructive to watch the exorcist at work. On 23 May 1939 Hitler again summoned his war-leaders. He told them, according to Mr Taylor, who quotes no other words of the document, 'there will be war. Our task is to isolate Poland.... It must not come to a simultaneous showdown with the West.' 'This,' comments Mr Taylor, 'seems clear enough'; but he then dismisses even this evidence by saying authoritatively that 'when Hitler talked to his generals, he talked for effect, not to reveal the workings of his mind'. So that is that. Three months later, with the signature of the Nazi–Soviet Pact, Hitler again addressed his generals, and again Mr Taylor is content to quote only one sentence from the speech: 'now the probability is great that the West will not intervene'. Apart from that 'hard core', the rest of the speech, he says, can be ignored, as Hitler 'was talking for effect'. After all, by the Nazi–Soviet Pact, Hitler considered that 'he had prevented war, not brought it on'. So, once again, Hitler's mere 'phrases' dissolve on contact with Mr Taylor's 'realities'.

But why should we suppose, as an axiom, that Hitler, when briefing his generals on the eve of a possible war, talked only for effect? Why should we not suppose that he intended them to be ready (as they were) for the real future? And why should we altogether overlook some very clear statements which he made to them? For if we look at the full texts of these two speeches, we find that Mr Taylor has made certain remarkable omissions.

In the first of these two speeches Hitler began by insisting that the next step towards Germany's goal could not be taken 'without the invasion of foreign states or attacks upon foreign property', and that although bloodless victories had been won in the past, 'further successes cannot be obtained without the shedding of blood'. '*Danzig*,' he went on, in words from which Mr Taylor has firmly averted his eyes, '*is not the subject of the dispute at all*. It is a question of expanding out living-space in the East.' Moreover, he looked clearly forward to the prospect of war with the

West. 'The Polish problem,' he said, 'is inseparable from conflict with the West.' For all that, 'we are left with the decision to attack Poland at the first opportunity. We cannot expect a repetition of the Czech affair.' Of course Hitler hoped to avoid a simultaneous conflict with the West, but he did not rely on any such hope: 'the Fuhrer doubts the possibility of a peaceful settlement with England. We must prepare ourselves for the conflict.' The remaining two-thirds of the document deal with the problems of war with Britain, 'the driving-force against Germany'. All this is totally ignored by Mr Taylor: it cannot have been the 'hard core' of any argument used by *his* Hitler: therefore, he declares, it was mere froth, uttered for 'effect'.

In the second speech Hitler similarly made clear statements which Mr Taylor does not quote. For instance, immediately after the 'hard core', the single sentence which he does quote, about the probability that the West will be frightened out of intervention by the Nazi–Soviet Pact, come the words, '*we must accept the risk with reckless resolution*'; and Hitler then went on to explain how Germany, thanks to Russian supplies, could withstand a Western blockade. His only fear, he said, was that 'at the last moment some *Schweinehund* will make a proposal for mediation': a proposal, perhaps, which might have fobbed him off with Danzig which, as he had admitted, was 'not the subject of the dispute at all'. No: Hitler was now resolved on war, even if the West did come in.

I shall give a propagandist cause for starting the war: never mind if it be plausible or not. The victor shall not be asked afterwards whether he told the truth or not.

As for the West, 'even if war should break out in the West, the destruction of Poland shall be the primary objective'. Which indeed was exactly what happened. By last-minute diplomatic manoeuvres Hitler naturally sought to detach the West, but when that could not be done, he went ahead, with his eyes open, into a

European war which, though larger than he had hoped, he still reckoned on winning.

I have said enough to show why I think Mr Taylor's book utterly erroneous. In spite of his statements about 'historical discipline', he selects, suppresses and arranges evidence on no principle other than the needs of his thesis; and that thesis, that Hitler was a traditional statesman, of limited aims, merely responding to a given situation, rests on no evidence at all, ignores essential evidence, and is, in my opinion, demonstrably false. This casuistical defence of Hitler's foreign policy will not only do harm by supporting neo-Nazi mythology: it will also do harm, perhaps irreparable harm, to Mr Taylor's reputation as a serious historian.

But why, we may ask, has he written it? Is it, as some have suggested, a gesture of posthumous defiance to his former master, Sir Lewis Namier, in revenge for some imagined slight? If so, it is just as well that it is posthumous: otherwise what devastating justice it would have received! There would have been no nonsense then about 'impeccable logic' in *The Times Literary Supplement*! Or is it, as Mr Taylor's friends prefer to believe, mere characteristic *gaminerie*, the love of firing squibs and laying banana-skins to disconcert the gravity and upset the balance of the orthodox? Or does Mr Taylor perhaps suppose that such a reinterpretation of the past will enable us better to face the problems of the present? Theoretically this should not be his motive, for not only does Mr Taylor, in this book, frequently tell us that the past has never pointed the course of the future, but he has also assured us recently, in the *Sunday Express*, that the study of history can teach nothing, not even general understanding: its sole purpose, he says, is to amuse; and it would therefore seem to have no more right to a place in education than the blowing of soap-bubbles or other forms of innocent recreation. It may therefore be that Mr Taylor merely means to amuse, not to instruct, by his irresponsible antics. Nevertheless, Mr Taylor is not noted for consistency and it may be that, in this instance, he does see a connection between the past and the present, a lesson for our times. At any rate, it may be worth while to point out lessons which might logically be deduced from Mr Taylor's version of history, if it were accepted as uncritically by the public as it has been by their guides, the weekly reviewers.

Basically, the problem is that of the outbreak of world wars. According to Mr Taylor, the Second World War had a double origin: first, it was 'implicit' in the general situation; secondly, it was made explicit by the particular blunders of statesmen in the face of that situation. The general situation was created in 1918 when the victorious Allies did not carve Germany up, and so made the ultimate recovery of its 'natural weight' inevitable. The particular blunders lay in the failure of Western statesmen to draw the logical conclusions and yield to the inevitable. If only they had shown 'realism' and yielded to all Hitler's demands, they would have found them limited and reasonable: it was only war and victory which surprised him by the size of his winnings and made him think of world conquest.

Now let us transfer these doctrines from the 1930s to the 1950s. The inference is clear. First, the victorious Allies in 1945 did (however unintentionally) carve Germany up, and so (if they will only keep it divided) their settlement of the German problem is 'morally valid', and no new German aggression is to be feared. Secondly, in the new circumstances thus created, 'realism' consists in allowing the new great power which has replaced Germany in Europe to assert its 'natural weight'. Mr Khrushchev, we should recognise, has no more ambitions of world-conquest than Hitler. He is a traditional Russian statesman of limited aims, and 'the moral line' consists in letting him have his way more completely than we let Hitler have his: in other words, unilateral disarmament. Perhaps in this one respect Mr Taylor does display 'methodical and impeccable logic'.

4 (a) How to Quote:

Exercises for Beginners – *A. J. P. Taylor*

Trevor-Roper
(*Encounter, July* 1961)

According to Mr Taylor ... Hitler merely sought to restore Germany's natural position in Europe, which had been artificially altered by the Treaty of Versailles.

For what ought the Western statesmen to have done when faced by Hitler's modest demands? According to Mr Taylor, they should have conceded them all.

Winston Churchill believed in the balance of power and would have maintained frontiers designed on principles of security, not nationality. Intolerable cynicism!

Taylor
(*Origins of the Second World War*)

Hitler, too, wanted to free Germany from the restrictions of the peace treaty; to restore a great German army; and then to make Germany the greatest power in Europe from her natural weight.... Maybe his ambitions were genuinely limited to the East; maybe conquest there would have only been the preliminary to conquest in Western Europe or on a world scale. No one can tell.

Wiser counsels were not lacking. Early in July [1939] Count von Schwerin, of the German War Ministry, was in England. He spoke frankly: 'Hitler took no account of words, only of deeds.' ... This advice was disregarded.... The British statesmen were trying to strike a balance between firmness and conciliation; and, being what they were, inevitably struck the wrong one.

It [Churchill's] was a view which shocked most Englishmen and which, by its apparent cynicism, deprived its holders of influence on policy.

Reprinted from *Encounter*, xix (Sept 1961), by permission of the author and *Encounter*. See also Introduction, p.16.

Munich, according to Mr Taylor, 'atoned' for all the previous weaknesses of British policy. He [Taylor] praises Chamberlain's 'skill and persistence' in bringing 'first the French and then the Czechs to follow the moral line'.

If only Chamberlain had not lost his nerve in 1939! If only he had shown equal 'skill and persistence' in enabling Hitler to detach Danzig and the Polish Corridor, how happy we should all be!

The reason why the majority of the British people changed, between 1936 and 1939, from the views of Neville Chamberlain and Mr Taylor to the views of Winston Churchill was their growing conviction that Hitler meant what he said. . . . A contemporary conviction that was strong enough to change the mood of a nation . . . surely deserves some respect from the historian. A historian who ignores it . . . runs the risk of being considered too clever by half.

But what about the European Jews? That episode is conveniently forgotten by Mr Taylor.

Idealists could claim that British policy had been tardy and hesitant. In 1938 it atoned for these failings. With skill and persistence, Chamberlain brought first the French, and then the Czechs, to follow the moral line.

Men will long debate whether this renewed war [of 1939] could have been averted by greater firmness or by greater conciliation; and no answer will be found to these hypothetical speculations. Maybe either would have succeeded, if consistently followed; the mixture of the two, practised by the British government, was the most likely to fail.

There followed an underground explosion of public opinion such as the historian cannot trace in precise terms. . . . All the prophets had said that Hitler would never rest content; he would march from one conquest to another, and could be stopped only by force or the threat of force. Like water dropping on a stone, their voices suddenly broke through the crust of incredulity. They seemed to have been proved right; and the 'appeasers' wrong. . . . Henceforth the appeasers were on the defensive, easily distracted from their work and hardly surprised at their own failure.

Many Germans had qualms as one act of persecution followed another culminating in the unspeakable wickedness of the gas-chambers. But few knew how to protest. Everything which Hitler did against the Jews followed logically from

It does not fit the character of a German statesman who 'in principle and doctrine, was no more wicked and unscrupulous than many other statesmen'.

the racial doctrines in which most Germans vaguely believed.

In principle and doctrine Hitler was no more wicked and unscrupulous than many other contemporary statesmen. In wicked acts he outdid them all.

According to Mr Taylor, Hitler really only wanted the German city of Danzig, but since geography prevented him from obtaining it except by the coercion of Poland, he was forced, reluctantly, to apply such coercion and prepare military plans. Of course (according to Mr Taylor) he did not intend to execute these plans.

Previously Danzig might have been settled without implying any upheaval in international relations. Now it had become the symbol of Polish independence; and, with the Anglo-Polish alliance, of British independence as well. Hitler no longer wished merely to fulfil German national aspirations or to satisfy the inhabitants of Danzig. He aimed to show that he had imposed his will on the British and on the Poles. They, on their side, had to deny him this demonstration.... Of course Hitler's nature and habits played their part. It was easy for him to threaten, and hard for him to conciliate.

It [the book] will do harm, perhaps irreparable harm to Mr Taylor's reputation as a serious historian.

The Regius Professor's methods of quotation might also do harm to his reputation as a serious historian, if he had one.

(b) A Reply

H. R. Trevor-Roper

I am afraid that after examining Mr Taylor's use of German documents, I am not disposed to accept him as a tutor in the art of quotation. Nor do I think that his 'exercises' amount to much. They are calculated to spare him the trouble of argument and to give a lot of trouble (or, more likely, bewilderment) to the reader. They are certainly no answer to the positive points made in my review.

In my review I tried to summarise Mr Taylor's thesis. Of course such a summary is not tied exclusively to single quotations: it is distilled from many; and it is not refuted by single quotations which in no case conflict seriously with it but, at most, may sometimes illustrate only a part of it or vary the emphasis. In view of the bewildering inconsistencies in Mr Taylor's own presentation of his thesis (some, but only some, of which have been shown by correspondence in *The Times Literary Supplement*), such variations are not hard to find.

For instance, my sentence no. 1 is not based only on the passage which Mr Taylor now places opposite it. It is also based on other passages in his book. Thus, on p. 70, he writes, 'Hitler wanted the Allies to accept the verdict of January 1918; to abandon the artificial undoing of this verdict after November 1918; and to acknowledge that Germany had been victorious in the East. This was not a preposterous programme'; and on p. 108: 'whatever his long-term plans (and it is doubtful whether he had any) the mainspring of his immediate policy had been "the destruction of Versailles"'. I cannot see that my summary is unfair.

Similarly, in quotation 9, if Mr Taylor's own words are boiled down, what do they come to? In this single quotation he is saying that in the material world Hitler only wanted Danzig, but that, by now, he wanted to get it by means which would constitute a prestige victory. On p. 248 he explains that, for geographical reasons, Danzig could not be seized without direct coercion of Poland. In other passages, quoted by me, Mr Taylor insists that Hitler did not want war but only a war of nerves backed by military force. My words, which quotation 9 is intended to refute, seem a fair summary of these passages. And the same can be said, I believe, of all the other 'exercises'.

In one 'exercise' (no. 6) Mr Taylor suggests that I have overlooked a paragraph in his book. I have not. I said that 'a contemporary conviction that was strong enough to change the mood of a nation ... surely deserves some respect from the historian'. 'Respect', not 'notice'. By 'respect' I mean that the historian should consider whether such a 'conviction' may have been based on sound reasons. I do not mean that he should merely note the change in mood, dismiss the arguments and pass on.

I could make the same point about 'exercise' no. 7. When I wrote that Mr Taylor conveniently forgot the persecution of the Jews, I meant, of course, that he drew no deductions from a fact central to the evaluation of Hitler's rule and methods and particularly relevant to the question of the disposal of 'inferior' races. I do not regard this serious problem as faced, or my statement as exploded, by a single parenthetical reference in which a crime unique in European history is flicked aside as the logical result of generally shared German ideas.

In 'exercise' no. 8 Mr Taylor suggests that I have deliberately omitted a distinction which he made between Hitler's relatively innocent principles and doctrines and his admittedly wicked acts. But I scrupulously quoted his limiting words 'in principle and doctrine'. And anyway, if his wicked acts are to be dismissed as merely 'following logically' from his innocent 'doctrines', what is the force of the distinction?

If Mr Taylor had been able to convict me of any 'quotation' comparable with his own version of the German documents (a subject on which he is now silent), or if he had shown my summary to be as inconsistent with his thesis as he so often is with himself (an inconsistency on which – see his letter to *The Times Literary Supplement* – he has also refused to comment), I should indeed be ashamed. But if these 'exercises' represent the sum of his answer to my criticism, I am unmoved.

5 Some Origins of the Second World War

T. W. Mason

The fifth impression of Mr A. J. Taylor's *The Origins of the Second World War* contains a new introductory essay entitled 'Second Thoughts', in which he makes explicit some of the important underlying propositions of the book, and deals in greater detail with a number of specific problems. The central issues are now clear beyond dispute.

'I wrote this book in order ... "to understand what happened and why it happened" ... when I speak of morality I refer to the moral feelings at the time I am writing about. I make no moral judgements of my own.'[1] One of the major themes of Mr Taylor's book is the inability of historians writing on the inter-war period to overcome their horror at the atrocities committed by the National Socialist régime; this horror has led them to mistake the general moral responsibility of the Third Reich for the greatest barbarities in the history of western civilisation for an assumed, concrete historical responsibility for the outbreak of the Second World War. There is certainly much truth in this contention,[2] and Mr Taylor has made a greater effort than any previous historian to achieve an emotional and moral detachment from the subject-matter. The importance of making this effort is demonstrated by the brilliance and lucidity of many passages in *The Origins of the Second World War*: the account of the 1920s, the analysis of the international importance of the Italian conquest of Abyssinia and the portrayal of re-

Reprinted from *Past and Present* (Dec 1964), by permission of the author and *Past and Present*. See also Introduction, pp.16–17.

lations between Britain, France and Russia in 1939 present most complex themes with outstanding clarity and objectivity.

It is no coincidence, however, that the best passages in Mr Taylor's book are those which deal with countries other than Germany, countries whose foreign policies were basically pragmatic, and whose statesmen were seeking more or less limited goals with more or less conventional means. It is the basic unspoken postulate of *The Origins of the Second World War* that the foreign policy of the Third Reich was also of this character. In attempting to lift the shadow cast by the Nuremberg tribunals over the historiography of Nazi Germany, Mr Taylor reduces the international relations of the period to the obsolete formula of independent states pursuing intelligible national interests with varying degrees of diplomatic skill. 'What happened' is by this token the story of the complex interaction of these national policies, an interaction so complex and so swiftly changing that no statesman could come near to grasping it in its entirety; and the answer to the question 'why' lies largely in these inevitable shortcomings of the statesmen.

'The Second World War, too, had profound causes; but it also grew out of specific events, and these events are worth detailed examination.'[3] Yet Mr Taylor's formula largely excludes the profound causes from consideration;[4] it seems unable to accommodate political movements and ideologies. National Socialism was perhaps the profoundest cause of the Second World War, but Mr Taylor's book is not informed by any conception of the distinctive character and role of National Socialism in the history of twentieth-century Europe.[5]

Two main reasons are advanced for this partly deliberate omission: firstly, that foreign policies were determined rather by *raison d'état* and the need to respond to contingent international situations, than by internal political or economical pressures – international relations are portrayed as largely autonomous from other spheres of politics; and secondly, that in the period Britain and France dominated the international scene, their policies were decisive.

It will be argued below that these two theses are invalid, and then further reasons will be suggested as to why *The Origins of the Second World War* does not deal satisfactorily with the foreign policy of the Third Reich.

An experienced British observer who visited Germany in 1938 came away with the conviction that 'at that time, the great bulk of the German people (as distinct from the inner ring of leaders) were thinking of anything rather than war, and were inspired by the economic and social changes which they felt were taking place around them and which seemed to hold out such high hopes for the future. Their eyes were turned inwards, not outwards.'[6] This state of affairs was not congenial to a regime in whose very nature it lay to make continuous and total demands on the loyalty and activity of its subjects, to perpetuate an atmosphere of febrile political enthusiasm and tension. Hitler's remark to his military leaders in November 1937 reads almost as a direct response to the perceptive observation of Guillebaud just quoted:

> If, territorially speaking, there existed no political result corresponding to this German racial core, that was a consequence of centuries of historical development, and *in the continuance of these political conditions lay the greatest danger to the preservation of the German race at its present peak.* To arrest the decline of Germanism (*Deutschtum*) in Austria and Czechoslovakia was as little possible as to maintain the present level in Germany itself. Instead of increase, sterility was setting in, and in its train disorders of a social character must arise in course of time, *since political and ideological ideas remain effective only as long as they furnish the basis for the realisation of the essential vital demands of a people.* Germany's future was therefore wholly conditional upon solving the need for space....[7]

Despite its turgid rhetoric, this passage contains a very clear and important judgement – the movement was becoming slack and sated, losing its demonic edge; the Third Reich had either to set itself new tasks by expanding, or to cease from being totalitarian.

Mr Taylor dismisses such considerations: 'The historian must try to push through the cloud of phrases to the realities beneath', and these realities were the attempts of Great Powers 'to maintain their interests and independence'.[8] This view leads to an overwhelming concentration on the sequence of diplomatic events, and a failure to see German foreign policy in the general context of National Socialist politics. The foreign policy of the Third Reich was dynamic in character, limitless in its aims to achieve domination and entirely lacking a conception of an 'ultimate *status quo*'.[9] This expansionist drive was the unique contribution of National Socialism, and the feature which most clearly distinguishes Hitler's foreign policy from that of his predecessors.[10] In concentrating the reader's attention on the detailed circumstances which enabled Germany to make territorial gains prior to the outbreak of war, Mr Taylor omits a satisfactory analysis of the mainsprings of German policy. Expansionism is sometimes taken for granted, sometimes represented merely as the restoration of German power in Europe or as the revision of Versailles,[11] and is sometimes dismissed adverbially;[12] it is never assigned any definite role among the causes of the Second World War.

This weakness is due in part to Mr Taylor's abrupt dismissal of 'the cloud of phrases' which enveloped German policy, his refusal to accept that policy was in any way determined by the ideology or by the internal political structure of the Third Reich. His choice of words is illuminating; in seeking a language to describe the phenomena of National Socialism, he is driven back on the vocabulary of nineteenth-century liberalism: the gas chambers were 'wicked', 'the rhetoric of the dictators was no worse than the "sabre-rattling" of the old monarchs', Hitler differed from other statesmen in that his appetite for success was greater, and his 'habits and nature' played their part in causing the war – 'it was easy for him to threaten and hard for him to conciliate'.[13] The vocabulary and the analogies are simply inadequate. The wickedness of the gas chambers is not at stake; of more importance for the historian is the light which they shed on the mentality of the regime and on the nature of its aims. Similarly, the terms 'rhetoric' and 'sabre-rattling' hardly do justice to a government which systematically militarised all social relations, turned employers and workers into 'leaders and followers',[14] had its youth do rifle-drill with spades,[15] elevated fanaticism to the supreme public virtue[16] and saw all facets of life as *struggles* or *battles* for existence and domination.[17] This is the historical context in which Hitler's personal characteristics must be seen; the facility with which he resorted to force or the threat of force in international affairs, his need to achieve success after success in foreign policy were not minor contingent factors on the European scene, but basic traits of the political movement which he led.

The second thesis seems equally open to question: 'My book really has little to do with Hitler. The vital question, it seems to me, concerns Great Britain and France. They were the victors of the First World War. They had the decision in their hands.'[18] Mr Taylor has clearly shown that in the individual crises which led up to the outbreak of war in 1939, many important initiatives came from Britain and France, but this is insufficient evidence that his general perspective is the right one. In the Europe of the 1930s the Third Reich was the most potent force for change – for change in boundaries no less than for change in political and economic techniques or social and cultural values. Mr Taylor insists that 'the crisis of March 1938 was provoked by Schuschnigg', and that the crisis which culminated in the Munich Settlement was 'of British making', and he lays some emphasis on the fact that President Hacha of Czechoslovakia was not summoned to Berlin in March 1939 but asked to come of his own accord. In doing so he omits to ask why it was possible for these crises to arise at all – why Schuschnigg thought it necessary to call a plebiscite in Austria, why in the late spring of 1938, 'Everyone in Europe felt [that] ... the Czechoslovak round was due to begin',[19] why Hacha saw no alternative but to turn to Hitler. It is a question of perspective; in a longer perspective the initiatives of other governments appear rather as responses to problems raised by Nazi Germany. Crucial decisions were certainly made in all the capitals of Europe, but the Third Reich determined what it was the victor powers had to decide about. The fact that the Sudetenland and Danzig arose at all as *acute, international* problems was due almost exclusively to the hegemony of the National Socialist party within Germany. In rightly insisting that the expansionist aims of the Reich were at no stage formulated into a comprehensive plan, Mr Taylor wrongly conveys the impression that they were of little importance.[20]

This impression is enhanced by the way in which the appeasers are saddled with the full historical responsibility for the results of their actions (whether these results were intended or not), whereas Hitler is deprived of this responsibility; his successes were largely unpremeditated. The results of the British agreement to guarantee the remains of Czechoslovakia on 18 September, and of the German occupation of Bohemia in March 1939 are analysed at quite different levels. By the former Daladier unwittingly secured Britain's future opposition to German expansion in Eastern Europe; by the latter, 'Hitler ... was ... reverting in the most conservative way to the pattern of previous centuries', he was acting 'without design'.[21] The former analysis is rigorous, objective and forward-looking, the latter merely a subjective explanation – Hitler's prestige was threatened if either the Czechs or the Hungarians attacked Slovakia. In order simply to understand what happened and why, more must be said about the regime which could make a basic foreign policy decision on such grounds, and more about the necessary logic in the development of German policy, which was no less marked than that of Anglo-French policy.

Similarly, the outbreak of a European war over Danzig was not just a matter of miscalculation on Hitler's part. Hitler took the very straightforward risk that Britain and France would declare war in the event of a German invasion of Poland. The decision to take this risk launched the Second World War. Clearly Hitler would have preferred Britain and France to remain inactive, but the risk was obvious enough for him to be presumed to have been ready to accept the consequences if they did not. Mr Taylor illuminates the reason why Hitler may have thought the chance worth taking,[22] but this explanation is on a subjective level and the objective importance of the decision is missed.

The fundamental argument of Mr Taylor's book is that it takes two to make a war; more accurately, that it took Britain and France to make a European war. It does not really explain why the Third Reich was willing to risk a European war.

A number of further reasons may be suggested for the inadequate treatment of German foreign policy in *The Origins of the Second World War*,[23] two of these will be discussed below: the limited nature of the source material selected, and the way in which this material is used.

'...''le style c'est l'homme'': a man may speak untruths, but his very being is laid bare in the style of his self-expression'.[24] Mr Taylor's judgements rest very largely upon the diplomatic documents. Some of the consequent disadvantages have already been mentioned above. In addition, these documents were primarily the work of conservative German diplomats, who, in dealing with their specific problems, were able to cover up or ignore the distinctive language and concepts of National Socialism. This helps to nurture the illusion that the foreign policy of the Third Reich was much the same as that of the Weimar Republic, and that it served the same functional purposes as the foreign policies of the other powers.

Neither do the documents give an adequate picture

of the role of the Nazi movements inside Austria and
Czechoslovakia; their movements are portrayed as the
objects of diplomacy, and Mr Taylor tends to reflect
this emphasis.[25] Thus he adduces the existence of a
militant pro-Nazi movement among the Sudeten Germans as further proof that Hitler did not initiate the
crisis over Czechoslovakia. Though the point is illuminating in a sense, it encourages the making of too
radical a distinction between Hitler the German
statseman and Hitler the leader of the Nazi movement.
The persistent and violent disruption of ordered life in
Austria and Czechoslovakia was a crucial contribution
of National Socialism to pre-war international relations. It severely weakened the internal structure of
both states,[26] created an atmosphere of continual
crisis and in the latter case provided Hitler with the
indispensable pretext of self-determination; in Austria
it was Schuschnigg's discovery of plans for a Nazi insur-
rection which brought him to seek the fateful meeting
with Hitler at Berchtesgaden on 12 February 1938. In
short, the National Socialist movement created conditions in which the actual course of events in Central
Europe was made very probable, if not fully predetermined. And the fact that the Austrian and the Sudeten
parties often acted independently of the German
leadership[27] indicates in the first instance the central
role of the movement in the history of the period; Hitler's opportunism is only meaningful within this context. The question 'why' cannot be asked of the diplomatic documents alone.

A further important reason for Mr Taylor's inadequate treatment of National Socialism is that his handling of the material which he does use is sometimes
drawn from evidence of uncertain validity. On the
question of factual accuracy this article will confine
itself to two major problems: the Hossbach Protocol,
and Germany's economic preparations for war.

The so-called Hossbach conference has been investigated with some thoroughness by German historians,[29]
and although Mr Taylor seems to have drawn on their
research[30] his conclusions do not correspond with

theirs. Mr Taylor advances the thesis that Hitler called together Neurath, Goering and his military leaders in November 1937 in order to gain their support in overcoming Schacht's resistance to increased armaments expenditure. No evidence is cited in support of this interpretation and a number of considerations weigh heavily against it. First of all, the conference was called by Blomberg who wished to press home a complaint against Goering: the latter was misusing his powers as plenipotentiary for the Four-Year Plan and controller of raw materials and foreign exchange in order to favour the rearmament programme of the air force (of which was was marshal) at the expense of that of the army.[31] Hitler was thus faced with the embarrassing situation of having to arbitrate an important dispute between two of his chief subordinates; it is plausible that he sought to escape from this dilemma by talking at length of the general aims of German stategy and impressing his listeners with the general political need for accelerating rearmament.[32] Thus the picture of Hitler calling and manipulating the conference for his own ends is, at the very least, overdrawn.[33] Given the immediate problem with which he was faced by the conference, Schacht can hardly have played more than an incidental role in his calculations.

The evidence that the military leadership curtailed rearmament out of respect for Schacht's views on fiscal policy is very slight and fragmentary, and it is not sufficient to bear out Mr Taylor's statement that 'Hitler's manoeuvre had succeeded: henceforward Fritsch, Blomberg and Raeder had no sympathy with Schacht's financial scruples'.[34] There is record of an agreement in March 1937 between Blomberg, Schacht and Krosigk that the military budget should not exceed ten milliard RM. per annum,[35] but it is not clear that the agreement was carried out;[36] Goering almost certainly did not feel himself bound by it, and fiscal control over the military establishment was anyway very weak. In April 1934 the Ministry for the Armed Forces was exempted fron the requirement to submit detailed estimates to the Ministry of Finance, and the Ministry of

Aviation was accorded the same privilege a year later; global estimates were submitted and bargained over; there was no 'Treasury control'.[37] It is also very doubtful whether Schacht's position in the autumn of 1937 was still strong enough to warrant Hitler's taking such drastic measures to undermine it.[38] His power and influence had already been appreciably reduced by the transfer to Goering of competence for raw materials and foreign exchange in April 1936,[39] and by the creation of the Four-Year Plan Office in the autumn of the same year. Schacht could only secure the termination of the Mefo-bill issue by agreeing to an increase of one-third in its size, and the Mefo-bill was immediately replaced (1938–9) by the delivery note and the tax remission certificate; public expenditure was not reduced.[40] Hitler's reluctance to lose Schacht probably derived from the latter's reputation rather than from his power.

Thus the Hossbach Protocol remains of vital interest to the student of German foreign policy, but the importance of the conference must first be demonstrated before valid conclusions can be drawn from the document. Of the practical effects of Hitler's monologue, Mr Taylor writes, 'There was here ... no directive for German policy'; and, 'At the time, no one attached importance to the meeting.'[41] In the middle of December, seven weeks after the conference, the mobilisation orders of the armed forces were changed; the orders of July 1937 envisaged a preventive German invasion of Czechoslovakia in the events of Franco-Russian aggression against the Reich. Those of December postulated (given favourable international circumstances) German aggression against Austria and Czechoslovakia.[42] This change mirrored the new temper and new aims of Hitler's policy as he had expounded it to his military leaders on 5 November. The conference marks the point at which the expansion of the Third Reich ceased to be latent and became explicit. Hitler's prognostications at the conference were faulty, but the new temper of his policy persisted, as Schuschnigg found to his cost on 12 February. The protocol is indeed a 'pledge to violence'.[43]

It is clear that political, strategic and geographical factors were of more importance in the history of Europe in the 1930s than the factor of sheer military strength. In comparison with British foreign policy, French military strategy and the fragmentation of Eastern Europe into a number of rival national states, the precise level of German rearmament was a matter of relative indifference in determining the development of international relations.[44] However, the extent and nature of German rearmament is not only an interesting question in its own right, but can (in principle) also throw light on the aims of German foreign policy. 'Far from wanting war, a general war was the last thing he [Hitler] wanted.... This is not guesswork. It is demonstrated beyond peradventure by the record of German armament before the Second World War or even during it.'[45] The weakness of Mr Taylor's deduction is that it is based upon a very imperfect knowledge of the economic history of the Third Reich.[46] No authoritative study of this immensely complicated subject exists as yet;[47] the source material is enormous in bulk and of dubious quality. Some caution is thus called for, but Mr Taylor, citing the work of the American economist B. H. Klein,[48] makes a number of sweeping general assertions: the 'German recovery was caused by the return of private consumption and non-war types of investment to the prosperity levels of 1928 and 1929. Rearmament had little to do with it'; and, 'Hitler ... was terrified of inflation.'[49]

The title of Mr Klein's book, *Germany's Economic Preparations for War*, is misleading, for the great bulk of it is in fact concerned with the performance of the German economy *in wartime*, a subject which it treats thoroughly and in some detail. The same cannot be said of the chapters of the pre-war period. Mr Klein's book appeared in 1959, but his bibliography indicates that he used only two works in this field published after 1948; he shows no knowledge of the work done by British and German economic historians;[50] he makes firm judgements about Schacht's policies without having read either of the financier's autobiographies; he does not mention the Mefo-bill issue; his statistics (from which Mr Taylor has chosen a few 'at random') are often inscrutable and occasionally contradictory.[51] Mr Klein is no doubt right that contemporary observers exaggerated the predominance of the military sector in the German economy before 1939, but his own study cannot claim to be definitive; it cannot be described as 'the only book which has looked at what happened instead of repeating what Hitler and others said was happening', nor as a 'dispassionate analysis'.[52]

As the following table shows, categorical judgements are unwarranted; the study of the economy of the Third Reich is still in its infancy. One of the many elementary facts which has still to be established is the precise expenditure of the regime on rearmament; the problem is chiefly one of unsatisfactory source material.

Estimates of German Armaments Expenditure 1933–9[*]

	Stuebel	*Klein I*	*Klein II*	*Hillmann*	*Erbe*
1932–3	(0·63)				(0·62)
1933–4	0·75	5	1·9	1·9	0·72
1934–5	4·2		1·9	2·8	3·30
1935–6	5·5	6	4·0	6·2	5·15
1936–7	10·27	10	5·8	10·0	9·0
1937–8	10·96	14	8·2	14·6	10·85
1938–9	17·25	16	18·4	16·0	15·5
Apr–Sept 1939	11·91	4	10·0	—	—
	60·84	55	50·2	[51·5]	[44·52]
	+c. 3·0				
	c. 64·0				

[*] All figures in the table are in *milliards RM.*; the figures for 1932–3 have been inserted in parentheses for purposes of comparison and are not part of the totals; the totals in square brackets refer to the period up to April 1939 only, no estimate having been made for the last five months of peace.

Sources: Stuebel, in *Europa Archiv* (June 1951) col. 4129; his own total of 59·97 mrd RM. seems to be an arithmetical

The totals of Stuebel, Klein I and Hillmann are roughly reconcilable with one another, and that of Klein II could be brought within the same range by the addition of the Mefo-bill issue (12 mrd RM.), but their figures give rather different pictures of the development or armaments expenditure; this is of some importance in judging economic policy, especially in relation to the financial year 1937–8.[53] The most detailed and thorough investigation seems to be that of Stuebel, though his final total may be a little high since not all of the Mefo-bill issue was used for projects of direct military importance.

This element of uncertainty together with the use of different economic concepts gives rise to a second set of statistics with an even wider range of divergence:

---

mistake; an extra *c*.3 mrd RM. are added to cover the rearmament expenditures of civilian ministries.

Klein I – *American Economic Review* (March 1948) 68–9; the figure for April–Sept 1939 is an estimate.

Klein II – *Germany's Economic Preparations for War*. In table 60, p. 264, these figures are given as *budget* expenditure (as in *Die Deutsche Industrie im Kriege* (Berlin, 1954) p. 17). No source is given for the figures, which appear in table 6, p. 16, simply as 'Armament Expenditures'. He does not explain the difference between his estimates of 1948 and 1959.

H. Hillmann, 'The comparative Strength of the Great Powers' in *Survey of International Affairs: The World in March 1939*, pp. 453–4.

R. Erbe, *Die nationalsozialistische Wirtschaftspolitik* (Zürich, 1959) pp. 25 and 100. Erbe quotes Stuebel's figures (p. 39) but uses his own set for calculations.

(Since this article was first published, an important new contribution has been made to the clarification of the problems presented in the above table and in the subsequent paragraphs. Though the work of Berenice A. Carroll, *Design for total War – Arms and Economics in the Third Reich* (The Hague, 1968) pp. 179–90, 262–7, is not definitive on the German gross national product and its components in these years, it has certainly superseded all previous research and calculations. Her estimate of military expenditure 1933–9 (Sept) is slightly higher than that of Stuebel, in *Europa Archiv* (June 1951) 184.)

Klein estimates German military expenditure at 15 per cent of the country's gross national product for the year 1938–9; the corresponding British figure for 1939, at almost 15 per cent.[54] Hillmann's figures are percentages of the net national product for 1938 – Germany 16·6 per cent, Britain and France both 7·9 per cent.[55] Stuebel's estimates of armaments expenditures as proportions of national incomes for the year 1938–9 provide a third series of figures – Germany 21 per cent, France 17 per cent and Britain 12 per cent.[56]

The picture of the strength of German military forces is not much clearer. In 1938 Chilston estimated the front-line strength of the German air force at the time of Munich at 'nearly 3,000 aircraft';[57] Mr Klein gives two different figures for its strength on the outbreak of war – 1000 bombers and 1500 fighters, and 800 bombers and 1450 fighters; Hillmann's estimate for September 1939 is 2400 frontline planes, and the detailed figures of Kesselring give a total of 2975 combat machines.[58]

These statistical uncertainties are a great impediment to any discussion of the German economy in the 1930s; they show very clearly the dangers of making categorical judgements, and for this reason the following brief remarks must remain tentative and general.

The central historiographical question is once again that of perspective. In his concern of refute earlier works which exaggerated the war-orientation of the German economy before 1939, Mr Klein uses the performance of the economy in wartime as a yardstick for comparison; the pre-war effort is thus made to appear slight, and part I of his book is an attempt to explain why it was not greater. This perspective harmonises well with that of Mr Taylor and seems equally open to question. Comparisons should also be made with the performance of the German economy in 1928–9 and 1933, and with that of the British and French economies in the 1930s. If deductions about foreign policy are to be made from the realm of economics these are, in fact, the only legitimate comparisons.

The sole international comparative study of this

question leaves no doubt as to Germany's overwhelming military–economic preponderance in Europe in 1939.[59] From March 1933 to March 1939 the Third Reich spent about half as much again on armaments as Britain and France put together. The steel production of Greater Germany in 1938 was a quarter as much again as that of Britain and France put together, and by far the greater part of it was used domestically. As early as 1937 the capital goods sector[60] of the German economy accounted for an appreciably higher proportion of total manufacturing production than that of the British economy. Throughout the 1930s Germany exported more machine tools than Britain produced, and German mzchine tools were of a multi-purpose type permitting swift conversation from civilian to military production; British rearmament was hampered by a shortage of machine tools. Further, the British capital goods industries were heavily hit by the slump of early 1938; production of iron ore and pig-iron fell considerably and in the latter case was slow to recover. Germany's autarchic economy remained unaffected by the slump. The briefest survey of the British economy in the 1930s yields many similar examples of events which are wholly inconceivable in the context of the Third Reich: in August 1937 the price of shares in the aircraft industry reached its lowest point since the start of rearmament; production was hemmed in by the reluctance of the government to give long-term and large-scale contracts; the structure of the British capital market was such that the announcement in February 1937 of a big increase in the military budget greatly handicapped private investment; and in April 1940 there were still one million unemployed in Britain.[61] War only replaced deterrence as the aim of British rearmament after Munich; military expenditure in 1939 was about twice as high as in 1938.[62] Thus the unadorned statement that in 1938–9 Britain and Germany spent the same proportions of their gross national products on armaments is not only incorrect; it is a highly misleading comparison.[63]

Of equal importance for purposes of comparison are

the structural changes which occurred in the German
economy between 1929 and 1939. The striking of these
was the steadily growing predominance of the heavy
industrial sector. This sector suffered worst in the
slump, enjoyed a swift rate of recovery and maintained
this impetus throughout the 1930s. The figures for
production are perhaps a better guide to this development than the investment statistics.[64] Thus the production of machine tools (measured in weight)
doubled from 1928 to 1938; that of steel-rolling
machinery trebled while that of textile machines fell
by one-third over the same period. Steel production
had already regained its 1929 level by 1936 and rose
steadily thereafter, and the output of electricity increased by one-third 1928–36.[65] All branches of the
engineering industry expanded,[66] and there was a
marked increase in the labour force of the metal-work-
ing and chemical industries, while that of the consumer goods industries tended to remain stable or even
to decline.[67] In 1929 the capital goods sector of the
German economy accounted for 41 per cent of total
manufacturing production; in 1937, 51 per cent.[68]
This trend was present though less pronounced in the
economies of all industrialised countries during the
period; but the sharpness and peculiar form of the
trend in Germany was due largely to the hegemony of
National Socialism. The scale of the rearmament programme was sufficient to all but eliminate the element
of entrepreneurial risk in the heavy industrial sector;[69]
and secondly, a significant expansion of the consumer
goods sector was impeded, partly by limiting demand
through wage-controls and partly by an allocation of
foreign exchange for the purchase of raw materials
which was favourable to heavy industry.[70] Mr Klein
and Mr Taylor give great weight to the fact that gross
consumer expenditure in 1938 was at least as high as in
1929; the fact assumes a somewhat different significance from that which they attach to it,[71] when one
considers that in this decade both the population and
the employed labour force grew larger, the index of
industrial production rose by some 20 per cent and the

gross national product by almost 40 per cent.[72] This
relative oppression of the consumer can be seen even
more clearly from Mr Hillmann's calculation that in
1938 63 per cent of the German net national product
went on personal consumption; only in Japan and
Russia was the proportion lower; in Britain and
France it was *c.* 79 per cent and in the U.S.A. 84·6 per
cent.[73] The consumer in the Third Reich was not getting butter instead of guns.

The second important structural change in the German economy was the trend towards autarchy; international trade generally was very slow to recover after
the slump, but in Germany the trend was deliberately
fostered by the government for strategic reasons.[74]
Domestic production of basic raw materials expanded
significantly in the last three years of peace; the exploitation of metal ore deposits was intensified and re-
fining capacities were increased;[75] production of synthetic rubber rose from almost nil in 1936 to 22,000
tons in 1939, and that of both synthetic and crude oil
was roughly doubled in the same period.[76] The in-
completeness of the programme on the outbreak of
war[77] should not be allowed to detract from these very
considerable changes. The autarchy policy accentuated
the predominance of the big production goods mono-
polies in the German economy;[78] it also illuminates
the political intentions of the regime – a government
not bent on war will not go to such very great lengths
to secure its independence from international trade.
The precise character of the war was not of course
determined by the autarchy policy, though this policy
did make it easier for Hitler to risk conflict with
Britain.

The third structural change, and that on which the
other changes were in large measure dependent, was
the very great increase in public spending. Reich expenditure increased roughly fourfold during the 1930s,
and the government debt two-and-a-half-fold.[79] There
was clearly a revolution in German public finance, and
this fact should dominate discussion of the problem.
Mr Klein thinks that fear of inflation seriously re-

tarded German rearmament, but the evidence which he quotes proves only that the fears existed, not that they exercised a decisive influence on economic policy;[80] in the present state of research, this point can be neither proved nor disproved.[81]

However, as Mr Klein himself remarks, there were various other good reasons why Germany's preparations for war were not more extensive. Chief among these was the inability and/or unwillingness of the government to effect the necessary additional transfer of money and resources from the non-military sector of the economy. After 1936 such a transfer would have raised enormous administrative and political problems,[82] and it was not in fact achieved until the later stages of the war, under the stimulus of imminent defeat.

It was not achieved earlier because the party had to continue erecting its monumental buildings, and the size and cost of the administrative apparatus could not be held in check; more important, *le plebiscite de tours les jours* made a significant peace-time increase in taxation or reduction of consumer expenditure politically impossible.[83] Although the labour market in the key industries (construction, metals and mining) had been strained to breaking point since mid-1937, the government only began introducing maximum wage legislation and restricting the free choice of work in the shadow of the Sudetenland crisis.[84] And then, the inevitable consequences of this over-full employment: failure to meet delivery dates, a wage spiral, the enticement of scarce skilled workers from one firm to another, a very high and economically wasteful mobility of labour and in many cases a drop in *per capita* productivity and a decline in 'work-morale'[85] – these consequences were combated by the government with only very limited and delayed success; for instance, the abolition of paid holidays and of higher rates of pay for overtime on the outbreak of war produced so much bitter discontent and absenteeism in industry during the Polish campaign that the decrees had to be annulled in the winter of 1939–40.[86] The Labour Front, which depended for even the toleration of its twenty-six million compulsory members on the improvement of living standards, used the new balance of social forces brought about by full employment to make a bid for supreme power in the state in February 1938; the bid failed, but so did the counter-attack by the Reich Chamber of Economics, which aimed at reducing the influence of the Labour Front.[87]

Both crises, the economic and the institutional, were acute and insoluble. The Third Reich was the first modern state to face the many new problems raised by permanent full employment, and was totally unfitted to solve them: the Nazi party had been brought to power to end unemployment, and in the later 1930s the government proved unable to make the great reappraisal and reorganisation necessary to cope with its success;[88] secondly, the labour shortage could not be met by economic contradiction since this would have slowed down rearmament; thirdly, the built-in need of the totalitarian regime to obtain the constant loyalty and continuous adulation of those classes of society which had most reason to hate it disabled it from effective intervention in the labour market until internal crisis had made such intervention essential and external crisis had provided the necessary justification.

Organisational problems also played their part in ruling out a further transfer of resources to the military sector in the immediate pre-war years. Behind the endlessly repeated official fiction of the 'organic, harmonious popular community', there existed a jungle of competing and overlapping economic organisations, interest groups and authorities, which was essential for preserving the political power of the Nazi leadership, but which precluded effective economic planning and administration. Goering could not secure the co-operation of the metal industry in exploiting low-grade domestic iron ores; the pre-war system of allocating the available supply of steel was quite unable to fulfil its function,[89] and the three branches of the armed forces competed ruthlessly with one another for priority status.

All these were necessary and immutable consequences of the style and structure of National Socialist government, and for these reasons it must be doubted whether the Third Reich conceivably could have armed to a higher level before 1939.[90] With his acute sense of power politics Hitler saw that the strategic diplomatic position in Europe and recent developments in weaponry might exempt him from the need to face these structural problems; the *Blitzkrieg* strategy was perhaps as much a product of these problems as the consideration which determined the level of rearmament: it cannot seriously be argued that real opportunities to rearm were neglected before 1939 as a result of the decision to adopt this strategy.

The economic, social and political tensions within the Reich became steadily more acute after the summer of 1937; while it seems safe to say that Hitler himself understood very little of their technical content, it can be proved that he was informed of their existence and was aware of their gravity.[91] If the existence in the winter of 1937–8 of a conscious connection in Hitler's mind between this general crisis and the need for a more dynamic foreign policy cannot yet be established,[92] functional relationships between these two aspects may nonetheless be suggested. The chain of international events unleashed by the browbeating of Schuschnigg on 12 February 1938 aggravated the shortages of labour, raw materials and money. *But* at the same time they provided the only conditions under which the government thought it safe to increase the coercion and exploitation of labour, to depart from conservative principles of sound finance and to intensify government control over business – all measures which the survival of the system demanded anyway; and the seriousness of the crisis over the Labour Front was certainly lessened by the fact that it coincided with the *Anschluss*.[93] The only 'solution' open to this regime of the structural tensions and crises produced by dictatorship and rearmament was more dictatorship and more rearmament, then expansion, then war and terror, then plunder and enslavement. The stark, ever-present alternative was collapse and chaos, and so all solutions were temporary, hectic, hand-to-mouth affairs, increasingly barbaric improvisations around a brutal theme. Mr Taylor is perhaps nearer to the truth than he knows in writing that, '... at best the argument was self-consuming. Germany needed the prizes of war solely in order to make war more successfully.'[94] A war for the plunder of manpower and materials lay square in the dreadful logic of German economic development under National Socialist rule. The sequence of international events was not thereby predetermined, but the range of possibilities was severely circumscribed.[95].

It has been wisely remarked that good works of history are informed by a sense of what could not have happened. The judgement, 'it seems from the record that Hitler became involved in war through launching on 29 August a diplomatic manoeuvre which he ought to have launched on 28 August',[96] is, even allowing for a degree of poetic licence, a flat denial of this dictum; neither factually nor logically is it a necessary consequence of the attempt to portray in moral detachment 'what happened and why it happened'; it is, on the contrary, a judgement which destroys much of the point of studying history at all.

Notes

[1] A. J. P. Taylor, *The Origins of the Second World War*, 5th impression (London, 1963), with a new essay entitled 'Second Thoughts'; the essay is not paginated. The main text will be cited hereafter as *Origins*; the essay as 'Second Thoughts'. The quotation above is from 'Second Thoughts'.

[2] See, for example, ch. 1 of W. Hofer's book, *Die Entfesselung des zweiten Weltkrieges*, rev. ed. (Fisher, 1960). Hofer's basic thesis that National Socialism was the major cause of the war (ibid., intro.) *need not* lead to the moral determination which Mr Taylor rightly criticises.

[3] Taylor, *Origins*, p. 103.

[4] The brief discussion of profound causes (ibid., pp. 103–7) is such as to cast doubt on the very notion of a profound cause; cf. the review by F. H. Hinsley, *Historical Journal*, IV (1961) 222–9.

[5] Neither National Socialism nor the National Socialist Party are mentioned in the very full index.

[6] C. W. Guillebaud, *The Social Policy of Nazi Germany* (Cambridge, 1941) p. 108.

[7] The Hossbach Protocol, *Documents on German Foreign Policy*, series D, I, pp. 29–30 (my italics). It is impossible to conceive of any other statesman of the period talking of foreign policy in these terms; for the language of the diplomatic documents, see p. 106 below.

[8] Taylor, *Origins*, p. 107.

[9] Cf. E. M. Robinson, *Hitler's Pre-War Policy* (London, 1963) pp. 2–3.

[10] The view that National Socialist rule changed every aspect of German public life, but not foreign policy, is fundamentally implausible; why was it alone exempt? (See Taylor, *Origins*, p. 68.)

[11] It is questionable whether the latter 'aim' should be considered as more than a useful slogan for securing popular support.

[12] 'Hitler *undoubtedly* wished to "liberate" the Germans of Czechoslovakia' (my italics): Taylor, *Origins*, p. 152.

[13] Ibid., p. 71, and 'Second Thoughts', pp. 103, 106, 216.

[14] Law for the Organisation of National Labour, 20 Jan 1934.

[15] Cf. Erwin Leiser's film, *Mein Kampf*.

[16] V. Klemperer, *LTI – Notizbuch eines Philologen* (Berlin, 1947) p. 65; this book is a brilliant portrayal of National Socialism by a German-Jewish professor of linguistics who stayed and survived.

[17] *Arbeitsschlacht* – the battle to create employment; *Kampf um Rohstoffe* – the fight for raw materials.

[18] Taylor, 'Second Thoughts'.

[19] Taylor, *Origins*, pp. 149, 155, 202, and 'Second Thoughts', and *Origins*, p. 151.

[20] This is one danger of relying largely upon the diplomatic documents; not every foreign service has its Sir Eyre Crowe; see also below, pp. 106 ff.

[21] Taylor, *Origins*, pp. 177, 202–3.

[22] Ibid., pp. 269 ff. There were also many good reasons why it was a bad risk: Chamberlain regarded his written obligations a little more seriously than Hitler did, and the British public much more seriously.

[23] Anti-German prejudice perhaps plays a role; the insistence that there was nothing exceptional about the foreign policy of the Third Reich damns by implication that of the Weimar Republic and perhaps that of the Federal Republic – see the concluding notes by Prof. M. Freund in the German edition of *The Origins of the Second World War*. Mr Taylor writes that 'most Germans vaguely believed' in racial doctrines, and that Hitler's *Lebensraum* aspirations 'echo the conversation of any Austrian cafe or German beerhouse' (*Origins*, pp. 69, 71).

[24] Klemperer, *LTI*, p. 16.

[25] Taylor, *Origins*, p. 152.

[26] The Czech defences in 1938 were manned in part by German-speaking troops. It must remain an open question how long either country could have withstood the economic and psychological pressures of a state of internal siege; for this dimension G. E. R. Gedye's *Fallen Bastions* (London, 1939) is still necessary reading.

[27] Cf. Robértson, *Hitler's Pre-War Policy*, pp. 123, 137; Taylor, *Origins*, p. 140.

[28] Contrast Mr Taylor's statement that the Saar plebiscite was 'unquestionably free' (*Origins*, p. 86) with the eye-witness account of Alexander Werth, *The Destiny of France* (London, 1937) ch. VII. Compare Taylor (*Origins*, p. 166) and Robertson (*Hitler's Pre-War Policy*, p. 135, n. 1) on German military planning against Czechoslovakia in the summer of 1938. See also the painstaking review article by P. A. Reynolds, 'Hitler's War?', *History*, XLVI (1961) 212–17.

[29] See especially G. Meinck, *Hitler und die deutsche Aufrüstung* 1933–7 (Wiesbaden, 1959) pp. 174–84, 236–7; and H. Gackenholz, 'Reichskanzlei den 5. November 1937', in *Forschungen zu Staat und Verfassung – Festgabe für Fritz Hartung* (Berlin, 1958) pp. 460 ff.

[30] There are regrettably few references in *The Origins of the Second World War*. None are given to secondary works for the discussion of the Hossbach Protocol in the main text; it is wrongly stated that the reasons why the conference was held have not been investigated (ibid., p. 133). Some references are given in the further discussion in 'Second Thoughts', where Mr Taylor casts grave doubts on the reliability of the extant text. Drawing upon the work of Meinck (*Hitler und die deutsche Aufrüstung*, pp. 236–7), Mr Taylor notes that several days elapsed before Hossbach wrote up the minutes of the conference and that his manuscript was transcribed twice before being used as evidence at Nuremberg; only this last abbreviated version, which omits the discussion which followed Hitler's monologue, has survived. On the basis of considerable research, however, Meinck comes to the conclusion that Hossbach's original minutes were a reasonably accurate version of what Hitler said, and that the extant version is an accurate rendering of the original as far as it goes; it corresponds with the notes taken at the time by General Beck.

[31] Meinck, *Hitler und die deutsche Aufrüstung*, p. 174; Gackenholz, in *Forschungen zu Staat und Verfassung*, pp. 461–2.

[32] This does not necessarily detract from the importance of what Hitler said.

[33] Taylor, *Origins*, p. 133.

[34] Ibid., p. 134.

[35] Gackenholz, in *Forschungen zu Staat und Verfassung*, p. 460.

[36] See below, n. 81. There are other inconclusive hints that the military leadership did fear inflation: cf. Robertson, *Hitler's Pre-War Policy*, pp. 84–6; H. Schacht, *Account Settled* (London, 1949) p. 90.

[37] H. Stuebel, 'Die Finanzierung der Aufrüstung im Dritten Reich', *Europa Archiv* (June 1951) col. 4131.

[38] Mr Taylor even goes so far as to assert that the *Reichswehr* crisis of February 1938 was staged with the object of covering up Schacht's resignation (*Origins*, p. 141). No sources are quoted; it is very unlikely that any of the Nazi leaders thought that Schacht was a more influential opponent than the generals.

[39] Meinck, *Hitler und die deutsche Aufrüstung*, pp. 159–64.

[40] Stuebel, in *Europa Archiv* (June 1951) cols 4130–1.

[41] Taylor, *Origins*, p. 132, and 'Second Thoughts'.

[42] Gackenholz, in *Forschungen zu Staat und Verfassung*, pp. 467–81. Goering changed the mobilisation orders of the *Luftwaffe* in this sense immediately after the conference without waiting for orders from his superior Blomberg.

[43] The title of Meinck's chapter on the conference.

[44] Cf. Taylor, 'Second Thoughts'.

[45] Taylor, *Origins*, p. 218.

[46] Compare the judgements quoted at the end of the paragraph above with the following 'first thoughts': Full employment 'depended in larger part on the production of armaments' (p. 104); 'A dictatorship like Hitler's could escape the usual consequences of inflation' (p. 119); the judgements that the Third Reich was short of neither raw materials nor markets (pp. 105–6) are highly contentious.

[47] The work of Arthur Schweitzer, *Big Business in the Third Reich* (Indiana U.P., 1964) appeared too late for consideration here.

[48] *Germany's Economic Preparations for War* (Harvard, 1959).

[49] Taylor, 'Second Thoughts'. Contrast the latter statement with Hitler's repeated insistence in his war economy memorandum of 1936, that the cost of putting industry on a war footing was a matter of absolute indifference. The memorandum has been published with a comentary by W. Treue in *Vierteljahrshefte für Zeitgeschichte* (1955).

[50] See the references given below; they do not claim to be exhaustive.

[51] E.g., the figures for government deficits given in tables 8, 45 and 60.

[52] Taylor, 'Second Thoughts'.

[53] See below, n. 81.

[54] Klein, *Germany's Economic Preparations for War*, p. 19. Taylor quotes these figures in 'Second Thoughts' as though they *both* refer to 1938.

[55] Hillman, in *Survey of International Affairs, 1939*, p. 456; quoted by Taylor (*Origins*, p. 116) who does not seem to notice the discrepancy between Klein's and Hillmann's estimates.

[56] Stuebel, in *Europa Archiv* (June 1951) col. 4129; this does not exhaust the list of such estimates.

[57] 'The Rearmament of Britain, France and Germany down to the Munich Agreement of 30 September 1938', in *Survey of International Affairs, 1938*, III 529.

[58] Klein, *Germany's Economic Preparations for War*, pp. 19, 177 – the latter figures are quoted by Taylor in 'Second Thoughts'; Hillmann, in *Survey of International Affairs, 1939*, p. 395; Symposium, *Bilanz des zweiten Weltkrieges* (Oldenburg, 1953) p. 159.

[59] Hillmann, in *Survey of International Affairs, 1939*. This monograph is praised by Taylor (*Origins*, p. 284) but he makes no use of its admirably balanced conclusions.

[60] Hillmann's definition of war-potential industries; for this and subsequent points above, see *Survey of International Affairs, 1939*, pp. 444 ff.

[61] Chilston, in *Survey of International Affairs, 1938*, III 492; ibid., III 485; M. M. Postan, *History of the Second World War: British War Production* (U.K. Civil series, London, 1952) p. 43; Hillmann, in *Survey of International Affairs, 1939*, p. 466; A. J. Youngson, *The British Economy, 1920–57* (London, 1960) p. 145.

[62] Hillmann, in *Survey of International Affairs, 1939*, p. 453; *History of the Second World War: Statistical Digest of the War* (U.K. Civil series, London, 1951) p. 195.

[63] Taylor, 'Second Thoughts'; see n. 54 above.

[64] The official investment statistics from the Third Reich are implausible; investment in armaments plants in 1935 (the year of conscription) is given as 25 per cent lower than that in 1928: Klein, *Germany's Economic Preparations for War*, p. 14. Most writers stress the extent of disinvestment caused by the slump, but the production indices tend to show that this had only slight effects on production levels during the 1930s: cf. ibid., p. 35.

[65] G. Kroll, *Von der Weltwirtschaftskrise zur Staatskonjunktur* (Berlin, 1958) pp. 611, 615; Klein, *Germany's Economic Preparations for War*, p. 41.

[66] Production of motor vehicles increased by 60 per cent 1928–36: Kroll, *Von der Weltwirtschaftskrise zur Staatskonjunktur*, p. 617.

[67] Klein, *Germany's Economic Preparations for War*, p. 74.

[68] Hillmann, in *Survey of International Affairs, 1939*, p. 444; the process was cumulative.

[69] In October 1938 Goering had to use the threat of nationalisation to get industrialists to produce for the more risky export market: Stuebel, in *Europa Archiv* (June 1951) col. 4133.

[70] Shortage of foreign exchange led to a reduction in the import of textile raw materials in 1934, and the introduction of a thirty-six-hour week in many textile mills.

[71] Taylor ('Second Thoughts') goes so far as to say that butter was produced instead of guns.

[72] Guillebaud, *Social Policy of Nazy Germany*, p. 106; Klein, *Germany's Economic Preparations for War*, pp. 72, 10.

[73] Hillmann, in *Survey of International Affairs, 1939*, p. 456.

[74] See Treue, in *Vierteljahrshefte für Zeitgeschichte* (1955).

[75] Klein, *Germany's Economic Preparations for War*, pp. 45–7. His ch. 11 is the best discussion of this whole question, though he stresses the gap between programme and achievement rather than the achievement itself.

[76] Ibid., pp. 45 and 40; *Die Deutsche Industrie im Kriege*, p. 18. Virtually no synthetic rubber was produced in Britain in 1939.

[77] On the outbreak of war Germany was dependent on imports for 80 per cent of her textile raw materials and 65 per cent of her iron and oil: see Klein, *Germany's Economic Preparations for War*, pp. 48–50.

[78] This judgement refers to economic structure; in matters of economic policy the big concerns did not form a monolithic block; the autarchy policy rested on the support of the chemical industries.

[79] For expenditure: Stuebel, in *Europa Archiv* (June 1951) col. 4132; this includes all rearmament expenditure, but not that of the *Länder* or local authorities; for debt: Erbe, *Nationalsozialistische Wirtschaftspolitik*, p. 54.

[80] Klein, *Germany's Economic Preparations for War*, pp. 21–5. He does show, however, that financial considerations limited the scale of the autarchy programmes for iron ore and synthetic oil: pp. 52–3, but see n. 90 below.

[81] This is chiefly due to the unreliability of the statistics; if those of Stuebel for armament expenditure are compared with those of Erbe for the growth of the debt, it seems that there was a reduction in the rate of growth of both in 1937; this could indicate fears of inflation affecting economic policy: Stuebel, in *Europa Archiv* (June 1951) col. 4129; Erbe, *Nationalsozialistische Wirtschaftspolitik*, p. 54.

[82] Klein does not appreciate the scale of these problems, which he discusses at a mathematical level only: *Germany's Economic Preparations for War*, p. 21; contrast Kroll, *Von der Weltwirtschaftskrise zur Staatskonjunktur*, p. 560.

[83] The reports of the Gestapo on the mood of the population constantly make the mundane point that the popularity of the regime was largely dependent upon the standard of living: see B. Vollmer, *Volksopposition im Polizeistaat* (Stuttgart, 1957) esp. p. 371; also the collections of police documents, R 58 and 1010 EAP, in the Bundesarchiv, Koblenz.

[84] 'Verordnung uber die Lohngestaltung', 25 May 1938, *Reichsgesetzblatt*, 1 691. Implementation was left to the Reich Trustees of Labour, and was a delicate and sometimes long-drawn-out task, frequently involving reductions in real wages. Attempts to restrict the free movement of labour began on a small scale at the end of 1936, and became general in scope on 10 March 1939; they were not very effective before the outbreak of war.

[85] – a lame rendering of *Arbeitsfreude*, literally 'work-joy', which was the current term. The source materials on which these assertions are based are the documents of the Reich Ministries of Labour and Economics, now divided up among the Deutsches Zentralarchiv, Potsdam, the Hauptarchiv, West Berlin, and the Bundesarchiv, Koblenz; also the documents of the Reichskanzlei (now in the Bundesarchiv), which contain regular reports on these problems from the Reich Trustees of Labour (R 4311, file 528). The material is vast; the writer is preparing a documentation on all the problems touched on in this paragraph.

[86] Deutsches Zentralarchiv, Potsdam, Reich Ministry of Economics, file 10401.

[87] The Labour Front was technically responsible to the party (Hess) rather than to the government; in fact, it was responsible to neither, since Ley effectively insisted that his dual position as *Reichsorganisationsleiter* of the party and leader of the Labour Front gave him direct assess to Hitler in *both* capacities – strictly speaking, he had direct access only in the former capacity. Material on this crisis can be found in the documents of most departments of the government; basic material in the Bundesarchiv, R 4311, files 530, 530a, 548a, 548b.

[88] Not until 1 Feb 1939 was the Reich Ministry of Labour reorganised to permit the creation of a new Department 5 dealing solely with the direction and allocation of labour, subjects which had until then been handled by a subsection of the department dealing primarily with unemployment. I am grateful to Dr Dienwiebel of the Bundesarchiv for this point.

[89] Klein, *Germany's Economic Preparations for War*, pp. 55, 76–82.

[90] Without a more drastic system of military priorities, increased government spending on armaments would have achieved very little; for this reason, too, it is hard to accept the overriding influence of fiscal policy, as put forward by Klein.

[91] The content of some of the reports of the Reich Trustees of Labour was brought to Hitler's attention by his secretary of state, Lammers. The conflicts surrounding Schacht's resignation at the end of 1937 were repeatedly referred to Hitler (see A. E. Simpson, 'The Struggle for Control of the German Economy 1936–37', *Journal of Modern History*, XXXI (1959)), as was the crisis brought about by the Labour Front, Feb–March 1938.

[92] The only hint of such a conscious connection which the writer has found to date is the passage from the Hossbach Protocol, quoted above, p. 179.

[93] The difficulties of writing about the Third Reich may be illustrated by the fact that it is also true to say that this crisis was caused by the intensity of the rearmament effort – cause, effect and response are almost inextricable.

[94] Taylor, *Origins*, p. 217. This is one of the few occasions when Mr Taylor hints that there may be a further dimension to historical reality, beyond the calculations and miscalculations of statesmen, but the point does not appear to be offered seriously and is not elaborated. Compare the judgement of General Thomas of the Armed Forces War Economy Staff, that Germany's 'economic collapse would have occurred much earlier except for the fact that Hitler's campaigns of conquest yielded the Wehrmacht tremendous booty in the way of raw materials and fuels'. (Quoted in L. P. Lochner, *Tycoons and Tyrant* (Chicago, 1954) p. 210.) Thomas might have added the materials and foodstuffs delivered to Germany under the terms of the Non-Agression Pact with the Soviet Union.

[95] This cautious, negative formula is deliberate; there is no point in reviving obsolete slogans about the

economic causes of war. Economics was not the only circumscribing factor; British public and back-bench opinion greatly limited the freedom of action of the British government. Mr Taylor notes this (pp. 272, 276), but makes no attempt at all to establish a hierarchy of the causes of the war; rather he offers his readers a simplistic narrative, underlying which is the assumption that the debate about historical inevitability is a tiresome anachronism.

[96] Taylor, *Origins*, p. 278.

6 War Origins Again

A. J. P. Taylor

Any author should be grateful for such careful scrutiny as Mr T. W. Mason has given to my book on *The Origins of the Second World War* ('Some Origins of the Second World War', *Past and Present*, no. 29 (Dec 1964) 67–87 (Paper 5)). The informed critic always sees faults which the author has overlooked. I had already found some of them myself. For instance, I was quite wrong in suggesting that the meeting presented in the so-called Hossbach Protocol was designed by Hitler as a move against Schacht. I was overawed by previous writers who all asserted that the meeting was of great importance. When I read the record, itself highly dubious, I discovered that it would not bear the interpretations put upon it – 'a blueprint of German policy' or 'Hitler's last will and testament'. But surely, I thought, the meeting must have had some significance, seeing that everyone takes it so seriously. So I tried to discover one. However I was mistaken. The meeting had no significance. It followed a dispute between Blomberg and Göring over priorities, and Hitler evaded decision by ranting in his usual fashion. I ought not to have mentioned the meeting at all. But every historian is compelled to spend much time wandering down false trails which have been laid by others.

I dare say, too, that I reacted more than I should have done against the previous exaggerations about German rearmament. Nevertheless it still seems to me a point of great historical interest that German rearma-

Reprinted from *Past and Present* (April 1965), by permission of the author and *Past and Present*. See also Introduction, p. 16.

ment was only about half what it was alleged to be
both by Hitler and by foreign critics, such as Churchill.
I suggested that this exaggeration was, on Hitler's part,
a deliberate and characteristic bluff. Mr Mason argues,
if I understand him aright, that Hitler wanted greater
rearmament and was prevented by circumstances from
having it. Probably there is some truth in both views,
though I still prefer mine. Mr Mason even suggests,
towards the end of his article, that Hitler wanted a
more dynamic foreign policy, or even a war, in order to
overcome economic difficulties within Germany. This
is a very speculative view, a reversion to pre-war Marxist interpretations. The evidence for economic or political crisis within Germany between 1937 and 1939 is
very slight, if not non-existent. Hitler cut German
armament plans by 30 per cent after Munich. He cut
them again drastically after the defeat of France and
was reducing them even after the invasion of Russia.
Indeed large-scale rearmament began only in the summer of 1943. Mr Mason says that Hitler could not have
done it earlier. In my opinion, Hitler believed that he
did not need rearmament in depth, given his method of
the Blitz, both in politics and war. Again, there is probably some truth in both views. Or to put it another
way, Hitler adopted a method which was more congenial to him partly because it also saved him trouble.

In any case, I distrust this elaborate theorising about
Hitler's intentions. G. Meinck has these wise words: 'It
makes things too easy to treat as Hitler's real opinion
only those parts of his remarks which make him appear
in an unfavourable light'[1] – or, for that matter, in a
favourable light. Hitler often said that he wanted
peace and international understanding. His visitors to
whom he said such things often believed him. Many of
them were not political innocents; they were experienced men of the world such as Lloyd George. Yet historians are now agreed that Hitler was lying. Hitler
also said that war was inevitable and sometimes that he
was deliberately leading up to it. This time historians
are agreed that he was speaking the truth. Why believe
one set of statements and not the other? Most his-

torians start with the assumption that Hitler was an indescribably wicked man who was set on world war for some reason or other. Then they construct a perfectly plausible book about war origins, based on this assumption. Hoggan started with the opposite assumption that Hitler was a man of peace and that Halifax was the deliberate planner of war. On this basis, he also constructed a perfectly plausible book. I draw the moral that it is better to start without assumptions and try to construct a book based on the political and military events.

Of course this is a counsel of perfection. I cannot get it out of my head that Hitler was an indescribably wicked man. But this is because I belonged to his generation. He was as wicked as he could be. But he was only a beginner. The rulers of the United States and of Soviet Russia are now cheerfully contemplating a hideous death for seventy million or perhaps a hundred and fifty million people in the first week of the next war. What has Hitler to show in comparison with this? I think we had better leave Hitler's immorality alone as long as we go clanking around with nuclear weapons.

My serious disagreement with Mr Mason is over his attitude towards Germany or rather towards the German problem. He seems to imply that Hitler was responsible for National Socialism. He certainly implies that National Socialism was responsible for the instability of the European order. For example:

> The fact that the Sudetenland and Danzig arose at all as *acute, international* problems was due almost entirely to the hegemony of the National Socialist party within Germany.
> The persistent and violent disruption of ordered life in Austria and Czechoslovakia was a crucial contribution of National Socialism to pre-war international relations.... The National Socialist movement created conditions in which the actual course of events in central Europe was made very probable, if not fully predetermined.[2]

In one sense, this view is a tautology: since the National Socialists were ruling Germany, they were naturally responsible for the results of German actions. Mr Mason surely implies more than this. He is suggesting, if I understand him aright, that without Hitler and the National Socialist party there would have been no German problem – no unrest, no disputed frontiers, no shadow of a new German domination over Europe. I have heard something like this before. It is much what Metternich said about Mazzini or Cavour in regard to Italy: if only these men did not exist or were prevented from agitating, there would be no Italian problem. English Conservatives used to think this about Ireland and about India: the problems were all the fault of Sinn Fein or Congress; lock up de Valera or Gandhi, and all would be well. I doubt whether Mr Mason would accept this view, except apparently in regard to Germany.

There were new things in National Socialism. Antisemitism was new, at any rate in such an extreme form. The discontent against unemployment and old-style capitalism was new. The foreign policy of National Socialism merely restated the German problem. There is an almost universal misunderstanding about this problem, a misunderstanding perhaps shared even by Hitler. Most people think that the Germans wanted international equality – a state free from all restrictions on its armed forces and including all Germans. This is correct. But the inevitable consequence of fulfilling this wish was that Germany would become the dominant state in Europe. Again, many people, including many Germans, said that Germany merely wanted to reverse the verdict of the First World War. This also is correct. But they misunderstood what was implied. They thought that it meant only undoing the consequences of defeat – no more reparations, the recovery of the European territory and the colonies lost by the Treaty of Versailles. It meant much more than this: not only that things should be arranged as though Germany had not been defeated, but that they should be arranged as though she had won.

We now know, thanks to Professor Fritz Fischer,[3] what the Germans would have arranged if they had won the First World War. It was a Europe indistinguishable from Hitler's empire at its greatest extent, including even a Poland and a Ukraine cleared of their native inhabitants. Hitler was treading, rather cautiously, in Bethmann's footsteps. There was nothing new or unusual in his aims and outlook. His methods were often new. He was a gambler in foreign, as in home, affairs; a skilful tactician, waiting to exploit the opportunities which others offered to him. His easy successes made him careless, as was not surprising, and he gambled steadily higher. He found the path of violence increasingly attractive and the path of negotiation increasingly tedious. But essentially his stake, if I may for once allude to profound forces, lay in the logic of the German problem.

I fear I may not have emphasised the profound forces. Of course there was a general climate of feeling in the Europe of the nineteen-thirties which made war likely. Everyone talked about the coming war. In particular, military men – in Great Britain and France as much as in Germany – treated war as inevitable. This was quite right from their point of view. It is the job of military men to prepare for war and indeed to assume that it is coming. But their talk washed over on to the politicians, as it still does, and they, too, began to regard war as inevitable. Anyone, including Hitler, who tried to rearrange Europe without a war, felt that he was going against the grain. Of course historians must explore the profound forces. But I am sometimes tempted to think that they talk so much about these profound forces in order to avoid doing the detailed work. I prefer detail to generalisations: a grave fault no doubt, but at least it helps to redress the balance.

We do right to ask: why did war seem likely in the nineteen-thirties? But wars, however likely, break out at a specific moment and presumably over some specific issue. On 1 September 1939 the German armies invaded Poland. On 3 September Great Britain and France declared war on Germany. These two events began a war, which subsequently – though not until 1941 – became the Second World War. Perhaps I should have called my book: The Origins of the Outbreak of War in 1939. Then my obsession with detail would have had more excuse. At any rate, I think we are entitled to ask: why did Hitler invade Poland when he did? why did Great Britain and France declare war on Germany? These questions may seem trivial, but historians spend much of their time on trivialities, and some of them believe that only by adding up trivialities can they safely arrive at generalisations. Take care of the pence, and the pounds will look after themselves. This is an old-fashioned view. But I am an old-fashioned, hack historian.

Notes

[1] G. Meinck, *Hitler und die deutsche Aufrüstung 1933–37* (Wiesbaden, 1957). It is characteristic that this excellent book, which gives full details about Hitler's statements in regard to German rearmament, provides no information whatsoever about what rearmament actually took place. Words are everything; deeds nothing.

[2] p. 110 above.

[3] Fritz Fischer, *Griff nach der Weltmacht* (Düsseldorf, 1961).

C. Robert Cole

Since its publication in 1961, *The Origins of the Second World War* has been closely read by friend and foe. Its general argument that the Second World War resulted from misunderstanding, mistakes and traditional patterns of statecraft for which no one can be blamed proved unpalatable to many English and American scholars, who raised two basic objections to Taylor's book. Firstly, he had cast doubt on the validity of moral judgements in dealing with Nazi Germany and historical events generally, and he had also repudiated the Nuremberg verdict that the war was an integral part of National Socialist policy. It was feared that the first point would obfuscate historiographical thought while the second could endanger current and future political developments.

Taylor argued that Hitler had acted the role of a traditional German statesman seeking traditional German goals; that the results of his policy were accidental since, in fact, he had no real policy other than to wait and make the most of the opportunities presented by the ineptitude of his opponents; that many provisions of the Versailles Treaty made the Second World War inevitable, and that ultimately Hitler became involved in war 'through launching on 29 August a diplomatic manoeuvre which he ought to have launched on 28 August'.[1] Taylor's critics claimed that these conclusions were based on misstatements, contradictions, omissions and misuse of evidence. They felt, more-

Reprinted from *The Wiener Library Bulletin*, xxii, iii (summer, 1968), by permission of the author and the Wiener Library. See also Introduction, pp. 15–16.

over, that he was wrong to discount significant social, economic, political and intellectual developments, thereby eliminating secondary and profound historical factors, only to leave himself with a 'non-philosophy of history', according to which history evolves accidentally. Major events, then, are not preconceived; it is therefore neither possible nor even desirable to assess history on a moral basis. The critics were equally disturbed about the book's potential impact on neo-Nazism and cold-war attitudes. Taylor's 'non-philosophy', using the metaphor of the 'road accident', argues: 'The blame for war can be put on Hitler's nihilism instead of on the faults and failures of European statesmen – faults and failures which their public shared. Human blunders, however, usually do more to shape history than human wickedness.'[2] While admitting the influence of Nazi nihilism on the causation of the war, he dismisses it from further consideration by assigning primary importance to human frailty. The Second World War was as little due to National Socialist theory as road accidents are due to the existence of cars and roads. Accidents are not the result of the driver's intent, but to poor handling and conditions outside his control. The Nazis did not intend war: it came about through mistakes and chance events. Wars, like road accidents, are the result of human mistakes and to affix guilt would be to argue that man controls history.

The critics repudiated this view of history on two counts. Firstly, Taylor had dealt mainly with diplomatic events and documents, disregarding the role of the deeper underlying factors which had made war inevitable. Secondly, by denying these factors he had implicitly rejected all assumptions of moral responsibility, which his critics regarded as fundamental when confronted with the Nazi problem. Intentionally or not, Taylor, they argued, defended Nazi achievements by dissociating them from the effects they produced. If the history of the Nazi epoch could be explored without reference to the death camps, for example, would this not invalidate all moral judgements on the period?

The licence for barbarism that this logic suggested was intolerable. Yet, however far it departed from Taylor's intentions, it was, the critics asserted, consistent with his arguments.

The most lucid attack on the accident theory came from F. H. Hinsley.[3] He could not allow Taylor's metaphors to pass unchallenged. Taylor had admitted that underlying historical causes exist, even in the history of this period. However, as Hinsley noted, 'if the war had profound causes, as he told us it did, we never learn what they were'.[4] Hinsley let Taylor off one hook by not delving into the complexities of Nazi ideology, only to impale him on another by pointing to two flaws in his diplomatic explanations. First, there was his implication that the war was caused by a combination of 'acute international anarchy', by which he meant the normal condition of independent states aggravated by the uncertainties and tensions of the thirties and the imbalance left by the removal of Germany from her traditional position at Europe's centres of power. Historical opinion, Hinsley argued, held that these factors did not cause the war, but only tended to invite it. Taylor, moreover, contradicted his own view on anarchy and imbalance by showing Hitler's excessive appetite for diplomatic success in redressing the balance, and the fatal lack of international restraint on his activities. This view, though nearer to the truth, makes nonsense of the anarchy and imbalance argument.

The second flaw was Taylor's understanding of 'general policy and precise planning' and of 'cause and occasion'. Hinsley pointed out that a long-range policy is not necessarily planned minute by minute. The apparent opportunism upon which Hitler based his daily actions did not therefore change the fact that his ends were preconceived. From Taylor's evidence, all that could be proved was that German planning did not actually occasion the crises of the period. Or as Hinsley summed it up:

Mr Taylor's version of the pre-war crises is devoid

of all regard for the policy of a man who almost wholly caused them on one level because of his confusion of plan with policy and of occasion with cause. But it also takes this course because the antithesis he has drawn between the profound causes of war and the specific events that lead to war is a false antithesis. It cannot be too much emphasised that, while the profound causes lie in the given conditions that invite war, the causes on the other level are not simply events. They are the ways in which men handle events, react to the challenge which the given conditions put to them.[5]

Hinsley concluded that the relationships between given conditions and the policies of statesmen, and those between profound causes of war and decisions that lead to war are not constant and mechanical, as Taylor's accident theory would imply. Rather, 'a war is always an alternative to some other course and is always known to be so'.[6] Taylor had provided no viable alternative to Hitler's planning in explaining the causes of the Second World War.

However, if history is not an accident, what is it? The theory opposed to Taylor's suggests that history is human action aimed at specific goals. Such actions are shaped by a variety of profound causes ranging from the pressure of economic crises to the response to evolutionary tendencies. In taking exception to Taylor, Hugh Trevor-Roper differed from Hinsley in both the direction and temper of his critique. He began by summarising his understanding of Taylor's philosophy as history determined by 'objective situations and human blunders. Objective situations consist of the realities of power; human intelligence is best employed in recognising these realities and allowing events to conform with them; but as human intelligence seldom prevails in politics, the realities generally have to assert themselves, at greater human cost, through the mess caused by human blunders.'[7] Trevor-Roper attacked Taylor's diplomatic preoccupation by reminding him that Hitler regarded himself as 'a thinker, a practical philosopher, the demiurge of a new age of history',[8] and secondly, that *Mein Kampf* was obviously a blueprint for his ultimate intentions. This blueprint was based on ideological commitments bound to lead Germany into war. Taylor had dismissed these facts as irrelevant, but they were, Trevor-Roper contended, sufficient proof that the Second World War resulted from actions specifically conceived with that end in mind.

Taylor's dismissal of *Mein Kampf* and misuse of the Hossbach Memorandum and other Hitler speeches were most vehemently attacked by critics, such as Trevor-Roper seeking proof of ideological motivations, and others pointing to the evidence that Hitler did in fact do what he said he would. P. A. Reynolds claimed to have found fifty examples of misuse, misstatement and relevant omissions in the book. He could therefore not countenance the portrayal of such an innocuous Hitler. Reynolds held that Taylor misinterpreted the events themselves:

> Here indeed is the basic weakness of the whole book. Taylor's fundamental thesis is that wars are caused more by the frailties than by the wickedness of men, that Hitler ... did not intend or plan the war of 1939 which was caused, like other wars, by the blunders of himself and others.... Taylor endeavours to show that each of the crises that marked the road to war ... developed in ways which Hitler did not intend or plan, that if he intended war at all it was against the U.S.S.R. (neutral in 1939) and not the war which occurred against Britain and France, and that the final proof that he did not intend or plan the war in which he found himself in 1939 is to be found in the state of his armaments.[9]

However, Hitler's armaments proved adequate for two years of successive victories; even if each crisis did not develop to a specific plan, this does not invalidate the fact that it represented a stage in a long-term policy which was realised only by war; and finally, if Slav extermination and eastern *Lebensraum* were his only military objectives, France and Britain had still to be neutralised first – probably by war. 'Whether Hitler was a reasonable man or not, the actions that he said he would perform, and that he did perform, were such as any sane man would expect inevitably to lead to war, protest as Taylor may (and as Hitler sometimes did) that this was not his intention.'[10] In short, Hitler was not pulled willy-nilly by events, but rather was the initiator of the crises that led to the war, crises which he had contemplated on one level far in advance of their occurrence.

These basic objections were also voiced by other critics. A. L. Rowse noted that the primary cause of the war was Hitler's drive for world power, which Britain and France had opposed with insufficient firmness.[11] G. F. Hudson thought 'the primary question is simply whether the picture of Hitler which he presents is one that should be accepted as historically true'.[12] From his reading of *Mein Kampf*, Hudson deduced that it was not. The parallels between *Mein Kampf* and the Hossbach Memorandum could not be ignored. On 23 May 1939 Hitler had said, 'There will be war.' What, asked Hudson, could be clearer than that; 'especially as these were not words spoken in casual conversation, but as an address to the heads of the armed forces charged with the military preparations for the attack which, as a matter of history, actually took place on the date assigned for it'?[13]

Accidental history simply would not do. This reaction was further illuminated by the questions raised when these same writers examined Taylor's device of using only documents dealing with diplomatic events. Robert Spencer wrote that *The Origins of the Second World War* was valuable in helping to recognise that there were some traditional aims in Hitler's policy, 'to be reminded in short that, while the 1930s can be explained in terms of twentieth century nihilism, one can explain much more about them in more familiar terms'.[14] However, according to Spencer:

One does not, in short, get the impression that

Taylor is dealing with foreign policy of a totalitarian dictatorship of the twentieth century. As one highly competent German reviewer has commented, 'the essential weakness of the book ... lies in the fact that the author has in no respect grasped the significance of the interpenetration of totalitarian seizure and consolidation of power with the formulation of ideological aims in a state sealed off ideologically from the outside; nor of the internal co-ordination (*Gleichschaltung*) and economic mobilisation with the origin of external expansion.... Without this a real understanding of National Socialist foreign policy is impossible.'[15]

T. W. Mason raised similar objections, noting Taylor's misunderstanding of German economic patterns under the Nazis – their concentration on rearmament as the prime object of the economy, and their drive towards autarky. In Mason's view, both indicated that war was uppermost in Nazi minds. As he put it, 'a war for the plunder of manpower and material lay square in the dreadful logic of German economic development under National Socialist rule'.[16] He supported this with a pin-point analysis of the totalitarian state's 'demonic' urge. To maintain the Nazi – totalitarian – hold, it was necessary to expand the economic, political and, ultimately, military horizons. In this light the interdependence of domestic and foreign affairs seemed logical and unmistakable, and it was unforgivable that Taylor should have ignored it. Spencer's and Mason's views were shared by Trevor-Roper and Rowse. Trevor-Roper saw only harm in disregarding contemporary popular opinion, and Rowse argued that ignoring the essential nature of Nazism in order to study diplomatic detail would mean that 'the heart, soul and matter are left out'.[17]

Because he denied the impact of ideology on policy, Taylor was accused of having written about a twentieth-century cataclysm in nineteenth-century terms.[18] His 'moral detachment', in Mason's eyes, 'destroys much of the point of studying history at all'.[19] The third error was perhaps the gravest as it questioned the ideological component in history. Sensing that this view might indeed reflect something of the substance of totalitarianism – its lack of creative ideas – Alfred Cobban wrote:

> It seems to me to reflect, almost in an exaggerated form, the recently dominant disposition to treat ideas as a negligible factor in history; because for all its rant, *Mein Kampf* represents this factor just as much as, say, Plato's *Republic*. Not for nothing is Mr Taylor the pupil of the late Sir Lewis Namier, in whom brilliance of style, mastery of detail (in his case perhaps more exact detail), and contempt for ideas reached their acme.[20]

The critics' objection to Taylor's apparent dismissal of the historical role of ideas implied their acceptance of a moral basis for understanding and judging history: a problem which exercised historians and philosophers for generations, particularly in England, where Macaulay and Acton are still in influence. But it had ceased to be a historiographical *cause celebre*. Suddenly, Taylor's book revived the argument.

Briefly, Taylor's critics would argue that the Germans fought the war from motives of greed and aggrandisement. A war to achieve these ends was immoral, and those responsible for it, Hitler and the Nazis, bear the moral guilt for the horrors it unleashed. As we have seen, Taylor differed considerably from this rather simple, though not entirely simplistic, conclusion. In fact Taylor held that for the following reasons Hitler was no more immoral than his opponents. Firstly, his motives were no different from – nor worse than – those of any traditional European statesman. Secondly, his actions were inspired largely by Germany's actual political weight and geographical position in Europe. Thirdly, these actions were taken in response to those of other European statesmen and were meant to answer the needs of an independent nation-state. Fourthly, the war in 1939 was caused by general misunderstandings over Poland and Danzig – areas to which Germany had some just claims, recognised even by the West. Fifthly, some resonsibility for the war lay with Joseph Beck for resisting these claims, and with England and France for supporting him. Taylor has written portentously of flicks of cigarette ash punctuating the doom of nations as Beck and the Western emissaries discussed the eventuality of war. If there was guilt to consider, it was shared.

In these writings the moral question appeared as a fundamental historical problem consistently tainted by emotional predilections. Whatever the degree of individual commitment, none of Taylor's critics excused him for ignoring moral considerations. Trevor-Roper quoted many of Hitler's utterances revealing him bent on war and conquest. There was another side to Trevor-Roper's objections which involved an interesting subtlety. By representing Hitler as a traditional statesman, Taylor was misleading the younger generation unfamiliar with the Nuremberg rallies and other displays of Nazi militancy. Trevor-Roper asserted that a proper historical appreciation stemmed in part from an awareness of the emotions and feelings of the time, 'an element of history no less important than the facts'.[21] By explaining the period from selected documents only, Taylor had reduced its impact for future generations. Ironically, Trevor-Roper was conceding Taylor's implied objection to moral judgement – that it was determined as much by the prevailing climate of opinion as by any consistent principles of right and wrong.

James Joll, less critical than Trevor-Roper, derived much interest and enlightenment from the book; even after re-examining the documents he regarded many of Taylor's conclusions as valid. Their logic appealed to him, as did the new interest they inspired in the diplomacy of the period. However, on the question of Hitler's moral responsibility he agreed explicitly with the prevailing point of view. After noting the temptation to succumb altogether to Taylor's persuasiveness, and so to forget what he omits, Joll wrote:

Whatever Mr Taylor may say, Hitler was in fact more wicked and unscrupulous than any other contemporary statesman.... It is misleading to write about Hitler as if he were just another ordinary German politician. If Hitler was a rational statesman, then Eichmann was a conscientious civil servant.[22]

F. H. Hinsley also joined the chorus of moral criticism. Taylor had rightly seen that there was much that was traditional about Hitler's aims – a Germany following the 'old free way' would 'overshadow Europe even if she did not plan to do so'.[23] However, Hitler's long-term policy, regardless of his lack of precise planning, had revealed an unpardonable craving for success. War came not because of the Polish crisis, or any of the other blunders Taylor referred to, but because Hitler was unwilling to modify his policy of exploiting Europe's imbalance for his own ends.[24]

It is worth noting a further aspect in passing moral judgement on the Second World War and Germany. Confronted with Taylor's arguments, Louis Morton wondered: 'What is the significance of this concern with responsibility for war.... Is it purely an historical question, or does it reflect deeper forces and contemporary issues?'[25] He therefore instanced political predilections and needs as factors in historical examination and judgement. Taylor's thesis on the war seemed to defend wars as instruments of national interest, a view demonstrated by his refusal to condemn Hitler's aggressions in 1939, denying indeed that they were aggressions. This was the reality of the argument: on the one hand, Taylor presented a case for justifiable use of force in support of national interest; on the other hand, his critics would justify force only when used for national defence. Morton's point was to demonstrate that, in the light of present cold-war difficulties, the necessities of survival in a hostile world, with its threats of total destruction, were forcing the historian to re-examine the principles upon which he stands regarding his material. The absolutes of right and wrong which marked the historiographical era of

Acton were giving way to the new epoch where right
and wrong are relative to existence. Comments in the
early pages of his essay on the debates over America's
war involvement served to underline the impact of
contemporary events on historical perspectives. With
regard to Taylor he notes:

> Germany is no longer the major power of Europe
> seeking to assert its natural weight in affairs. The
> Soviet Union has taken its place, and the Germans
> are now British allies. German troops assigned to
> NATO are being trained in England and the Berlin
> crisis raised the possibility of armed intervention on
> behalf of Germany. If World War II was a diplo-
> matic blunder for which the Western powers must
> bear a fair share of the blame as Taylor says, then
> perhaps Germany deserves the support of its former
> enemies. Certainly no one wishes to repeat the blun-
> der of 1939 if, indeed, the war was the result of a
> blunder.[26]

Morton's essay clarifies some of the lines leading
from Taylor's critics to the object of their debate.
Without doubt they were conscious of this political
factor in Taylor's viewpoint. In large part it was less
Taylor's treatment of the war question than his apparent pragmatism and cavalier treatment of evidence
that inspired the critics' apprehension. They feared
that his rejection of moral precepts in historical judgements would inspire a return to what a generation of
eminent historical scholars had labelled the 'Reign of
Barbarism'.

What then were the forces the critics feared? The
three they had in mind were: firstly, a tendency to
accept outrage on the grounds that no basic moral
stance can be assumed in politics; secondly, the potential usefulness of Taylor's arguments to neo- and semi-
Nazi elements, particularly in Western Germany; and
thirdly, the danger of obscuring the parallels between
the aggressive designs of Nazi Germany and those
attributed to the Soviet Union, which could be forgot-

ten if the book were taken seriously. Their apprehensions reflected a generally shared concern for the future of free men. The critics believed that the practical implications of Taylor's book were fully as important as the historiographical questions, to which they were logically connected, and provided proof of Alfred Cobban's statement that no one, least of all a historian, is without political prejudice.

The reluctance to pass judgement on evil ideologies had been criticised whenever the evidence of Hitler's duplicity had to be accounted for. Taylor's interpretation of the period was seen as a subtle and useful instrument in the hands of every peddler of anti-humanist ideas and political Machiavellism. Morton's analysis of post-war views on the use of force gave a more exact dimension to this concern. Actions involving force were to be regarded as immoral when defended in terms of national expediency or of an ideology denying human rights.[27] By ignoring the enormity of Nazi crime Taylor's book therefore produced the obvious reaction, expressed by S. William Halperin: 'This book ... is bound to give comfort to neo-Nazis in Germany and to the forces of evil everywhere.'[28]

The second problem was actually an elaboration of the first. The resurgence of Nazism in Germany was of more immediate concern to the critics than moral abstractions because the memory of Nazi savagery was ineradicable. The war had forced these men to join a desperate – and at times almost hopeless – battle. This theme is apparent in the terse comments on the neo- and semi-Nazi elements in Taylor's reading audience. Ernest Pisko quoted a reviewer in the *Frankfurter Allgemeine Zeitung* who feared that Taylor's volume might become a primer for unrepentant Nazis. Pisko repeated Gerhard Ritter's warnings against 'those all too numerous who have neither learned nor forgotten anything'.[29] Trevor-Roper concurred and suggested that Taylor's defence of Nazi foreign policy would 'do harm by supporting neo-Nazi mythology'.[30] He was not surprised to find that the book was well received in radical right-wing circles.

In a letter to *The Times Literary Supplement*,[31] Elizabeth Wiskemann drew attention to the welcome the book had received in the neo-Nazi organ *Reichsruf*, and the *Deutsche Soldaten-Zeitung*, which asserted that it had made nonsense of the Nuremberg trials. Similarly the *Nation-Europa* (published in Coburg by the ex-S.S. major Arthur Ehrhardt) was gratified to observe that Mr Taylor had denied Nazi Germany's responsibility for the Second World War. In England, Sir Oswald Mosley's Fascist *Action* had shared these views.

The anxiety about Taylor's impact on neo-Nazism was based on his treatment of the 'German Question', made doubly strange since it seemed to contradict his past writings on the problem.[32] For Germany's steadily growing economic potential – she is now the world's third largest industrial producer – is viewed with apprehension by those who on the evidence of the past fear the temptations of such power. Joll and many of the other critics doubted whether Germany had really outgrown a traditional *Weltanschauung* that has been so much a part of her past experience,[33] and they discovered no proof yet that Germany, surrounded by so many reminders of the nightmare past, had fundamentally changed.

The cold war had its effect upon these writers too, and their personal politics were bound to colour their views of Taylor. In effect, the writers were caught in a tension not unlike that of the 1930s. Isaac Deutscher wrote that Taylor's examination of Nazi Germany was directly in line with cold-war policies and international alignments. '*The Course of German History* justified the policies of Yalta and Potsdam ... and the plans which were then in vogue for the dismemberment and de-industrialisation of Germany; and *The Origins of the Second World War* is in striking harmony with the mood which is now dominant and favours the Western alliance with Germany.'[34]

Deutscher's pointed attack was too strong for most of the later reviewers. But it was fear of Eastern pressures on the Western world that produced the various anal-

ogies. Some regarded the book as an argument for repeating the mistakes of Munich in a wrongheaded
attempt to preserve peace. Trevor-Roper parodied
Taylor's Hitler in describing Khrushchev: 'He is a
traditional Russian statesman of limited aims, and
"the moral line" consists of letting him have his way
more completely than we let Hitler have his: in other
words, unilateral disarmament.'[35] *The Economist*,
while not agreeing, noted the prevalence of this attitude among Taylor's critics. According to this argument, any disregard of the lessons of Munich would be
fraught with danger.[36] This position was presented
often enough to indicate the deep cold-war commitments among a significantly large group of English and
American writers. Louis Morton's analogy, like Trevor-
Roper's, was an excellent example:

> If Hitler had no blue print for conquest ... then
> to follow Taylor's reasoning, how much weight
> should we attach to Khrushchev's claim that he will
> bury capitalism? If Hitler was only acting under the
> pressure of events to secure for Germany only what
> was right and just, may not Khrushchev be taken as
> merely a Russian version of the German model?[37]

The common denominator of all these comparisons is
their attempt to apply the underlying philosophy of
The Origins of the Second World War to familiar
contemporary situations, leaving the reader to decide
whether history-writing in these terms makes sense.

Notes

[1] A. J. P. Taylor, *The Origins of the Second World
War* (American ed., Greenwich: Fawcett Publications,
1963) p. 267.

[2] Ibid., p. 209.

[3] F. H. Hinsley, *Historical Review*, no. 1, IV (1961)
222–9.

[4] Ibid., p. 223.

[5] Ibid.

[6] Ibid.

[7] Hugh Trevor-Roper, Paper 3.

[8] Ibid.

[9] P. A. Reynolds, *History*, XLVI (Oct 1961) 217.

[10] Ibid.

[11] A. L. Rowse, *New York Review of Books* (7 Jan 1962) 7.

[12] G. F. Hudson, *Commentary*, XXXIII (June 1962) 179.

[13] Ibid., pp. 182–3.

[14] Robert Spencer, *Canadian Historical Review*, XLIII (June 1962) 139–40.

[15] Ibid., pp. 142–3.

[16] T. W. Mason, Paper 5.

[17] Rowse, in *New York Review of Books* (7 Jan 1962) 6.

[18] Frank Freidel, *Reporter*, XXVI (18 Jan 1962) 52.

[19] Mason, in *Past and Present*, no. 29, p. 87.

[20] *History*, XLVI (Oct 1961) 227.

[21] Trevor-Roper, Paper 3.

[22] James Joll, *Spectator* (21 April 1961) 561.

[23] Hinsley, in *Historical Review*, no. 1, IV 224.

[24] Ibid., p. 228.

[25] Louis Morton, *World Politics*, XIV (Jan 1962) 387.

[26] Ibid., p. 292.

[27] Ibid., p. 288.

[28] S. William Halperin, *Chicago Sunday Times* (12 Jan 1962) 8.

[29] Ernest Pisko, *Christian Science Monitor* (11 Jan 1962) 7.

[30] Trevor-Roper, Paper 3.

[31] *The Times Literary Supplement* (2 June 1961) 361.

[32] Cf. A. J. P. Taylor, *The Course of German History*. A fundamentally unsympathetic treatment, particularly of the Nazi period.

[33] Joll, in *Spectator* (21 April 1961) 561.

[34] Letter in *The Times Literary Supplement* (2 June 1961) 361.

[35] Trevor-Roper, Paper 3.

[36] 'Foresight and Hindsight', *The Economist*, CLXCIX (13 May 1961) 655.
[37] Morton, in *World Politics*, XIV 392.

8 Hitler and the Origins of the Second World War:
   Second Thoughts on the Status of Some of the
   Documents[1]

H. W. Koch

Ernst Nolte in his *Die Epoche des Faschismus* writes
that Hitler undoubtedly in principle had wanted war
'but hardly *that* war at *that* time',[2] meaning the war of
1939. This somewhat muddled thesis conceals two distinct issues, namely the argument that in 1939 contingencies were not entirely to Hitler's liking and the
argument that in 1939 contingencies were so little to
his liking that we must conclude that Hitler took no
conscious steps to risk a *general* war. Few would question the first argument, it is the second which is in need
of further examination. Did Hitler in 1939 set out on a
premeditated course towards war with Poland and
with France and Britain as Walter Hofer implies;[3] or
was his aim confined to war with Poland exclusively?
Or, last but not least, while accepting the risk of war
with Poland, were his diplomatic manoeuvres calculated to repeat Munich all over again?
    Walter Hofer implicitly denies the validity of the
third of these alternatives and so does most of the historiography concerning the outbreak of the Second
World War. The exception, of course, is A. J. P. Taylor's *Origins of the Second World War*, which seems to
have withstood the mauling of its critics, a test of its
quality perhaps.[4] However, it does bear the hallmarks
of a rapidly executed intellectual exercise and lacks a
close examination of some of the key documents which

Reprinted from *The Historical Journal*, XI i
(1968), by permission of the author and *The Historical
Journal*. See also Introduction, pp. 16–18.

form its basis. In addition, Taylor's thesis that Hitler behaved no differently from how any other statesman would have behaved in similar circumstances, that there is little to distinguish him from his Weimar predecessors, seems on balance untenable. But the emotionally charged response to Taylor's book saw in this thesis a means which could primarily be used to whitewash Hitler. It failed to see that Taylor does not so much attempt to exonerate Hitler as endeavour to illustrate that Hitler was as normal a German as Germans normally are: therefore beware of them.

The purpose of this article is not to supply a conclusive answer to the above questions, but to review some of the key documents and examine how far they support the present-day historical consensus on the origins of the Second World War. If a reasonably valid alternative interpretation of these documents can be put forward it might bring about a change in that consensus.

Of course, any discussion of documents, their relevance and authenticity, concerning Nazi Germany could be met by the understandable objection that nothing but a purely destructive purpose is served if all one does is to show that some evidence is suspect without indicating what the upshot is when the evidence is sanely considered. Documentary evidence is hardly needed where visible evidence – mass graves, remnants of places of extermination, a divided Europe – is around us in pitiful abundance. This would take us to the position of the late Sir Lewis Namier, who wrote: 'For who wants to read documents? And what are they to prove? Is evidence needed to show that Hitler was a gangster who broke his word whenever it suited him?' This objection, this attitude is understandable but not necessarily valid, certainly not for the historian. Any discovery which may change certain nuances of interpretation will not undo Auschwitz. The possibility that Hitler in 1939 miscalculated, rather than premeditated general war, will not undo genocide. Nor does it undo his responsibility for general war – which lies in the fact that by accepting the uncertainty of being able to isolate Poland he was prepared to accept the risk that the Western Powers would refuse to stand aside, and that the outcome might thus be a general war. The area of manœuvre in 1939 was incomparably more restricted than it had been in 1938, and Hitler was aware of this.

The documents to be examined are the fourteenth chapter of Hitler's *Mein Kampf* – the famous 'foreign policy chapter'; the Hossbach Memorandum; Hitler's speech to the press of 10 November 1938; his speech to senior *Wehrmacht* officers on 23 May 1939; and finally Hitler's speech to his *Wehrmacht* commanders on 22 August 1939.

Underlying this examination and especially that of *Mein Kampf* are two basic questions:

(*a*) Did Hitler deliberately plan and unleash a world war aimed at world conquest?

(*b*) If such a plan did exist was it Hitler's intention to initiate it in 1939?

Professor Trevor-Roper in his review of Taylor's book[5] writes that between 1936 and 1939 the British people came to accept that Hitler meant what he said, 'that he was aiming – *so oder so* as he used to say – at world conquest'. While the present writer finds it extremely difficult to define what Hitler meant as no evidence exists setting forth Hitler's declared intention to conquer the world, in Professor Trevor-Roper's view Hitler had published a blueprint of policy which he intended to carry out. This blueprint, according to Trevor-Roper, is Hitler's *Mein Kampf*, written in 1924.

Hitler's views on foreign policy in 1924 are spread erratically over the whole of his book. Finally, however, they are concentrated in chapter XIV, which in spite of its title 'East Orientation or Eastern Policy?' summarises what in Hitler's view foreign policy ought to be like, rather than, as is the case with most of the book, telling the reader what course German history ought to have taken.[6]

Two reasons, Hitler writes in this chapter, warrant a

particular examination of Germany's relations with Russia. First, because this relationship is probably the most important matter of concern to German foreign policy; and secondly, it provides the test for the ability of the young National Socialist movement to think clearly and act accordingly.

For a state built upon the notion of the *Volk*, foreign policy has as its major aim to secure the existence of the race by aiming at a healthy relationship between the size of population and its growth potential on the one hand and the living space available on the other. A healthy relationship can only mean conditions under which all the necessary resources in foodstuffs and raw materials can be obtained for a growing population. Only in that way can a nation remain free from outside pressures.

Hitler then goes on to discuss German foreign policy before 1914 in the light of this dictum, and judges it as totally misguided because it did not correspond with his own definition of Germany's national interest. From the point of view of their respective national interests, the policies of Britain and France, on the whole, gain his approval. What course, Hitler asks, are the National Socialists to pursue? Mainly, he replies, to bring into harmony the national territory with the size of the population, the corollary being that territorial expansion must be the aim of Germany's foreign policy.

Having stated this, Hitler draws the following consequences. Any endeavour to return to the territorial *status quo ante bellum* would be absurd. Indeed it would amount to a crime, for Germany's borders of 1914 were anything but logical, ethnologically or militarily. Any foreign policy aiming at the revision of the Versailles Treaty, in order to return to the pre-1914 boundaries, would make it impossible for potential allies of Germany to leave the company of her present antagonists. Hitler refers here to Britain and Italy, which are to be the pillars of Germany's future system of alliances. German demands for the return of her colonies or for the Southern Tyrol would inevitably alienate Germany's potential allies. Moreover, a policy aiming at the return of pre-Versailles conditions is made nonsensical by Germany's lack of power and because the actual result would hardly be worth the sacrifice of blood involved. No one, Hitler insists, should have any illusions that such revision could be carried out without bloodshed. If, contrary to expectation, the application of force to correct Versailles should be successful, the cost in blood would be so expensive as to deprive the race of such reserves as are inevitably needed for future endeavours.

In the context of a foreign policy designed to increase Germany's living space France appears a problem only in so far as she threatens Germany's rear, a threat that must be eliminated. But above all stands the quest for *Lebensraum*. With that Hitler turns his gaze upon the future of Germany which, unlike Kaiser Wilhelm II, he did not seek upon the water but beyond Germany's eastern frontier, in Russia. In Hitler's view Russia was a country in which Jewish Bolshevism had eliminated the intelligentsia and ruling class of Germanic stock, which so far had guaranteed the continuance of the Russian state. 'Fate has chosen us to become witnesses of a catastrophe which will supply the most powerful confirmation of our racial theory.'[7] (One ought to note here that Hitler speaks of 'witnesses' and not of 'initiators'.) And then follows the fateful statement: 'Our task, the mission of the National Socialist movement, however, is to lead our people to a degree of political insight in which it does not see the fulfilment of its future aims in an intoxicating Alexandrian campaign of conquest but rather in the diligent and persistent work of the German plough, to which the sword has only to give the soil.'[8]

After dealing cursorily with objections to this policy, Hitler continues by emphasising that any positive German foreign policy also requires assistance by powerful allies, and that those who support a Russo-German alliance against the West ignore the realities of power. Russia was in decay and any possible war was bound to take place not on Russian but on German soil. Russia's lack of industry eliminates her altogether as a source of supply, on the contrary Germany would have to play the role of a supplier nation. Germany's state of weakness did not allow any kind of offensive action against the West. Hence, of what value is an alliance, if one cannot face a potential conflagration with a relative sense of security? 'Either a Russo-German coalition would be of paper value only, in which case it is valueless, or the letter of the treaty would be turned into reality – and thereby the entire world warned.... Inherent in an alliance is the next war. Its results would be the end of Germany.'[9] Quite apart from that, he asks with what right one could condemn the large numbers of Germans sympathising with Communism, if the leaders of the state made the representatives of that *Weltanschauung* their allies.

A future National Socialist government had only one acceptable alternative, to turn to Britain and Italy. This carried no inherent risk of war. France would be isolated and the law of action would reside within the new coalition; Germany's unfavourable strategic position would be eliminated. Only under such conditions could Germany pursue a positive and active eastern policy.[10]

If *Mein Kampf* is, as is usually maintained, a blueprint, and if by a blueprint we mean a detailed plan guiding Hitler's actions, then we have to ask how far Hitler's actions between 1933 and 1939 correspond with it. The purpose of this exercise is not to prove the obvious – that Hitler was an opportunist – nor is it intended to go to extremes in trying to prove that, since he was merely an opportunist in circumstances which had rendered *Mein Kampf* out of date, he had no aggressive intentions of the kind that might cause war. The purpose of comparing Hitler's actions with *Mein Kampf* is to show that *Mein Kampf* does not amount to a blueprint of Hitler's foreign policy, nor to a scheme of strategy. This does not mean that because of changed circumstances between 1924 and 1939 Hitler abandoned his social Darwinian premises and renounced (what appears to be) his primary objective, the increase of Germany's *Lebensraum*. Nor does the lack of correspondence between *Mein Kampf* and Hitler's policy mean that he had at any time abandoned his belief in the primacy of force. On the contrary, Hitler's belief in the need for territorial expansion at Russia's expense, and in the need of force, represent the two elements which characterise his thinking throughout his adult life. But from this it does not follow that in 1939 he consciously and deliberately engineered the Polish crisis with the intention of beginning his eastward expansion.

On the contrary, Hitler's foreign policy between 1933 and 1939 represents a strong contradiction to that outlined in *Mein Kampf*; that is to say, to what Hitler had written in 1924 that it ought to be like. Of course, it can be argued that steps like the renunciation of the military clauses of the Versailles Treaty in 1935 and the remilitarisation of the Rhineland in 1936 were necessary in order to prepare a basis for future action. If so, one is nevertheless surprised by the methods Hitler employed to gain his objectives for, to say the least, these methods implicitly contradicted his policy as outlined in 1924. A substantial and vocal part of British public opinion acknowledged the apparent need for a revision of the Versailles Treaty. And Hitler's public claims, such as parity of armaments and even the demand for a revision of the territorial status quo in Eastern Europe, received a fundamentally sympathetic hearing. Neither is there any doubt that however much Hitler's apparent objectives may have been justifiable within the context of national values and status then existing in Europe, his coarse methods on the international scene (quite apart from those employed domestically) certainly hardened those who were suspicious and turned tentative sympathies into suspicion. The Anglo-German naval agreement is indicative of what might have been obtained by way of slow negotiation.

His revisionist policy did not usually proceed by slow negotiation and its aims were extended as far as the demand for the return of Germany's colonies.

While he was pursuing it, moreover, his eastern project receded. Even the *Anschluss,* Hitler's declared aim in the first paragraph of *Mein Kampf,* upon close analysis has been shown to be a response to a situation only partly of his own making and 'achieved almost against his own will'.[11]

The Sudetenland and the question of Czechoslovakia appear at first glance as a departure from his revisionist policy but if one takes into account Hitler's Austrian background and heritage they become its corollary. Moreover, like Danzig, they were not problems created by Hitler. But be that as it may, it is difficult to see the relevance of *Mein Kampf* as a blueprint for the particular actions in these questions.

Hitler's foreign policy between 1933 and 1939 amounts to the pursuit of that which he had disavowed in 1924, namely the restoration of Germany's pre-1914 frontiers, while the means he used were the direct antithesis of those laid down in *Mein Kampf,* particularly so in respect to Britain, in return for whose support he had once stipulated that nothing must be considered too difficult and no self-denial too great. Naturally, it may be said that what Hitler had written in 1924 could hardly be applicable in the changed environment of the mid- and late 1930s when Hitler apparently could get all he wanted without bloodshed. But this precisely confirms the argument put forward here, that *Mein Kampf* as a supposed blueprint of Hitler's plans is at most remotely relevant to the actual policy pursued.

Living space in Russia had always been Hitler's aim and yet, although the war of 1939 was supposedly 'premeditated' and to be the initiation of the quest for *Lebensraum,* there existed no plan for a military campaign in Russia. When such planning began in 1940, even then it was under the reservation 'that clarification with Russia by diplomatic ways and means' would not succeed.[12] The Hitler–Molotov conversations of November 1940 crystallised the issues, and as far as Hitler was concerned, caused political expediency to coincide with his anti-Marxist bias and with the direction in which living space could be acquired.

But irrespective of whether the campaign against Russia was irrevocably decided upon in July or in November 1940 or not, Hitler had failed in what he had set out to be the National Socialist movement's primary task, 'to lead our people to a degree of political insight in which it does not see the fulfilment of its future aims in an intoxicating Alexandrian campaign...'[13]

Finally, the manner of planning 'Barbarossa' shows again the absence of a relationship between blueprint and execution. Between July 1940 and March 1941 planning was entirely military. Economic planning did not really begin until 1941, civilian administration not before April, while it was only towards the end of August 1941 that the form and character of the civil government was decided. 'Far from acting on the basis of a long-term plan for colonisation, Hitler approached the subject empirically, seeing present alternatives clearly but rarely perceiving anything beyond the successful achievement of the immediate objective.'[14]

Relating the content of *Mein Kampf* to the events of 1939, it is virtually impossible to conclude that Hitler in 1939 set out deliberately to conquer Europe or the world in accordance with his postulates of 1924. His aim as set out in *Mein Kampf* was with Britain's aid to make Germany a World Power by expansion into Russia.

The Polish problem had little relation to Hitler's fudamental aim, yet out of it came the Second World War. Of course he could not expand into Russia without dealing with Poland but again this could be accomplished in ways other than war, as the example of Slovakia shows. A satellite relationship with Germany, such as Poland has had since 1945 with Russia could have solved Hitler's problem – if that was the problem – of finding a broad base for attack on Russia. The British guarantee hardly meant that the alternatives confronting Hitler were either to give up his claim to Danzig or face general war. There was still, on the surface at least, room for diplomatic manoeuvre and for the exercise of all pressure short of war, as the

Russo-German Pact demonstrates.

Hitler's initial stupendous military successes increased his appetite, and the ramblings of his 'secret conversations' are much more a reflection of that than a continuation and elaboration of what he had written in 1924: except, of course, that they continued to illustrate Hitler's basic premise of political action, the primacy of force.

The policy in *Mein Kampf* therefore has little connection with the actual policy followed by Hitler in the 1930s. It is a character statement, indicative of the primitive passions of its author, a creed of violence; it is public oratory become 'literature'. It reflects the essential coarseness and crudity of Hitler's mind, but it is only a guide-book to Hitler's diplomacy in 1933 to 1939 by way of a very long stretch of imagination and then only in the widest sense and not in the detail associated with a blueprint.

Konrad Heiden's verdict of some twenty years ago seems to hold true still: 'Far too much has been read into the so-called foreign policy chapters. No statesman is in a position to indicate ten years in advance what he is going to do twenty years later.'[15] Is there, then, anything in *Mein Kampf* which could give us a clue to Hitler's actions? Perhaps. 'Considerations of foreign policy,' Hitler wrote, 'can only be made from one point of view: is it of benefit to our people now and in the future, or will it be harmful?'[16]

From that perspective, in the way in which he from time to time interpreted the 'benefit' of his people, Hitler's actions in the realm of foreign policy can be rationally assessed, rather than when they are forced with great industry and artifice into a scheme of strategy planned ten to fifteen years ahead. In place of following a long-term scheme, Hitler up to 1939 pursued a policy of national restitution on Greater German lines which seemed to contain little coherent planning but evolved from case to case. But this raises a genuine problem which it will be difficult to solve. This is the discrepancy between Hitler's beliefs, his principles, such as the need for *Lebensraum*, and the extremely haphazard nature of his planning and preparations, military, economic and political, to turn these principles into reality. This is not the place to solve this problem, but, perhaps, one may suggest tentatively that in spite of his prominence on the political stage, Hitler himself was as much surprised by the speed with which events unfolded, by the quickness of his success, as was the rest of the world. Hence it is only with the beginning of the war and particularly with its extension into Russia that we notice the gradual establishment of a direct relationship between theory and practice.

One of the major documents used hitherto as providing – in the words of the editors of the *Documents on German Foreign Policy* – 'a convenient summary of German Foreign Policy in 1937–8',[17] has been the Hossbach Memorandum of 10 November 1937. It is not the purpose of this article to give a detailed analysis of its contents or to relate it to the actual course of events. This has already been done elsewhere.[18] All that is intended is to ask some salient questions on the nature of the document and to throw light on what is generally still its very obscure history.

The first striking feature of the Hossbach Memorandum when compared with *Mein Kampf* is the almost complete lack of connection between the two documents, save the insistence on the primacy of force and the desire to annex Austria. This lack, however, should not be interpreted as meaning that, as there is little practical connection in detail between the postulates of *Mein Kampf* and Hitler's actual foreign policy, his words on 5 November 1938 in the Reichskanzlei represent, for once, the true policy he intended to follow. Perhaps, perhaps not. But what is significant is that the main theme of foreign policy in *Mein Kampf*, the obtaining of living space in Russia, is not mentioned at all in the memorandum. And yet Hitler in his introductory remarks asked for his views expressed at the meeting to be considered as his testament in case of death. This, in Professor Trevor-Roper's opinion, 'suggests that he was not talking irresponsibly'.[19] It is doubtful whether Hitler on an occasion like this would talk 'irresponsibly' but a motive can equally well be found in the realm of German domestic politics. Jurgen Gehl, for instance, maintains that Hitler wanted to convince his generals that the armaments programme had to be expanded and therefore exaggerated the possibilities of an armed conflict.[20] But, be that as it may, if Hitler meant what he said, if his discourse at the Reichskanzlei was a full exposition of his policy intentions, if he meant it to be his testament, Hitler's refusal on two separate occasions to read the memorandum and approve it when asked to do so by his adjutant requires an adequate explanation.[21] Whatever the explanation, it is bound to be so highly speculative as to make the document inadmissible in any other court except the Nuremberg tribunal.

This impression is reinforced when we bear in mind the actual history of the document. On 18 June 1946 Hossbach, upon the request of Dr Laternser, the defence counsel of the General Staff and the O.K.W., submitted an affidavit in connection with his testimony concerning the meeting at the Reich Chancellery on 5 November 1937. On oath Hossbach declared that he had made no protocol of the conference, instead a few days later (five to be exact) he wrote minutes based on his memory and written according to the best of his knowledge and conscience.[22] In 1948 Hossbach published a book in which, in contradiction to his affidavit of 1946, he writes that the memorandum was based on notes made at the conference as well as on his own memory.[23]

The problem is further complicated by the subsequent history of the document.[24] Hossbach had made no copy besides the original which he handed over to Blomberg.[25] From Blomberg the original apparently went to the O.K.H. files at Liegnitz in Silesia where, towards the end of 1943, it was discovered by a general staff officer, Colonel Count von Kirchbach. Kirchbach, while leaving the original in its place of deposition, did make a copy which he handed to one of his relations, by whom the document was forwarded to the prosecution team of the first Nuremberg trials. It finally reached the floor at Nuremberg as Document PS-386. The considerable objections to Hitler's plans which Neurath, Blomberg and Fritsche put up are not recorded in it, and in consequence the document does not agree with Kirchbach's own copy.[26] Hence, the original plus Kirchbach's own copy are missing.

It is therefore surprising that the relevant volume of the *Documents on German Foreign Policy* contains no reference to the somewhat chequered career of the 'memorandum' and to the fact that it is a copy of a copy, the original as well as the first copy of which are missing.[27] While there is little doubt that the document such as it is does reflect Hitler's mentality and attitude in a general sense, its value as Hitler's 'testament' and as an indicator of his future policy can be seriously disputed.[28]

Another argument which has been raised is that once it had overcome all resistance to the assumption of full power inside Germany, the inherent dynamic of National Socialist policy would end inevitably in an aggressive foreign policy. This may be so, but it appears doubtful whether an aggressive foreign policy is a specifically National Socialist characteristic. After all, revisionism, meaning the revision of the Versailles Treaty, was accepted and endorsed by the majority of Germans and was thus bound to be aggressive in terms of policy, which does not necessarily mean aggressive to the point of war. This determinist thesis has now been extended to mean that by 1936 the German economy had arrived at the crossroads at which Schacht's policy of expedients had to be abandoned, the alternative facing Hitler being a return to the ordered channels of the international economy. Since the basic premise of Hitler's policy was the extension of *Lebensraum*, such a return would tend to frustrate any rapid mobilisation of Germany's economic and military resources necessary for such a course. Consequently, Hitler had not only to continue the course of expedients but indeed to endeavour to extend it on a scale far wider

than practised hitherto, with the result that, meta-
phorically speaking, cheques were drawn on non-
existent capital, or more correctly the proceeds of living
space were used before this space had actually been
obtained.[29]

This seems plausible enough, but the theory is as
good or as bad as any other. Its inherent major problem is the unsatisfactory state of the evidence cited,
mostly polemical in nature, and the almost complete
lack of figures. The one (but certainly not definitive)
survey whose conclusions are backed up by relatively
reliable figures, shows no evidence of an economic crisis
between 1936 and 1939; moreover it reduces to its true
proportions the myth, purposefully and apparently
very successfully put about by Hitler, of the extent of
German rearmament.[30]

The propounders of the thesis of inevitability of war
for economic reasons interpret the Hossbach notes as
being the military and political equivalent of Hitler's
Four-Year Plan of 1936 in the economic field. This
equation is juxtaposed with excerpts from Hitler's
Table Talk of 1942–3. Apart from demonstrating that
the method of juxtaposition is no satisfactory substi-
tute for reliable and unequivocal evidence, since the
Hossbach notes deal only with Austria and Czechoslovakia, they are irrelevant to Hitler's concept of
Lebensraum as such. Secondly, these territories hardly
add – and this was clear to see in 1937–8 – sufficient
resources to cope with a long-term economic crisis.
This, of course, is provided such a serious crisis did
exist, which is itself more than doubtful.

Hitler's address to representatives of the German press
on 10 November 1938 has only come to light in recent
years.[31] It has been interpreted as Hitler's order for
the psychological preparation for war,[32] as well as an
expression of his bitterness at the silent opposition of
the German population against his warlike policy,[33] of
his disappointment at Germany's defeatist mood, for
which Hitler saw himself as partly responsible.

In actual fact, far from expressing despondency over

the reaction of public opinion, his attitude from the
outset of his address is congratulatory at the achievement of the German press. It had influenced the public
to the extent of helping to maintain its nerve, while
the nerve of Czechoslovakia in particular had failed.
The frequently quoted passage in which Hitler says
that only circumstances forced him to speak of peace
for decades, and that this contained the inherent danger of giving the impression that he wished to maintain
peace at all costs – this passage is meant retrospectively.
Underlying it are Hitler's social Darwinian premises,
according to which excessive love of peace will make a
nation unfit for the 'struggle for survival'. But, Hitler
says, with the help of the press he had succeeded in
avoiding this dangerous pitfall. It would now be their
task to continue along that line 'and to reinforce step
by step the self-confidence of the German people...', a
task which could not be carried out in a year or two,
and whose objective was not immediate, not 'for the
spring or summer of 1939, but ... for the coming
decades' and years.[34]

The last third of Hitler's address contains his cus-
tomary diatribe against intellectuals and then finally
an admonition to the press, amounting to a demand
that Germany's leadership be treated by the press as
infallible.

In essence Hitler demanded psychological war preparation, though the view of the speech as an emphatic
and expressive directive to prepare public opinion for
an imminent war cannot be substantiated. To support
this point by quoting Hitler as saying that the press
ought to throw certain events into a perspective as a
result of which the inner voice of the people would
slowly *'begin'* to scream for the use of force,[35] is a
subtle distortion. The quotation taken in its actual
context shows Hitler reviewing the events leading up
to Munich. He is speaking in the past tense; he says
that there are matters which, if they could not be
solved peacefully, 'had to be solved by way of force. For
that purpose it has been necessary not to propagate the
use of force as such but to represent to the German

people certain foreign events in such a manner that the inner voice of the people slowly *began* to scream for the use of force.'[36] Hitler expressed his great appreciation of the efforts of the German press and asked for its continuation. There is nothing to suggest, as does Erich Kordt, that Hitler ordered the press within two years to arouse in the people the will to war.[37] The great significance with which the speech has been invested since its discovery was apparently lost to some of the major personalities present, particularly to Dr Otto Dietrich, the government press chief.[38] A more recent study by Ernest K. Bramsted interprets Hitler's speech as giving praise 'for the performance of the press',[39] an interpretation shared by Oron J. Hale.[40]

On 22 August 1939 Hitler entertained his senior commanders to one of his most ferocious displays yet. The accounts of that display vary, and for the historian three separate records exist.[41] The first version comprises two documents of a total of $6\frac{3}{4}$ pages in the *Documents of German Foreign Policy*.[42] It purports to record two speeches Hitler made on that day, but according to Halder's diary there seems to have been only one speech.[43] The second version, reproduced in the *British Documents*,[44] is of a highly sensational nature and was rejected by the Nuremberg tribunal – a fact which did not prevent it from becoming a standard document in many publications on the period. The third version is the record made by one of the attendants at the conference, Admiral Boehm, and is considerably more substantial than the first version and much less sensational than the second.

The principal difference between the first and second version on the one hand and the third on the other is that the authorship of the latter is clear. Admiral Boehm recorded Hitler's speech on the evening of 22 August 1939, at the hotel 'Vier Jahreszeiten' in Munich.[45] The authorship of the other two versions of Hitler's speech cannot be clearly ascertained.

There is no need here to recapitulate the text of Hitler's speech. Those who attended had the impression that Hitler was trying to impress his commanders with the necessity of the course which he was taking,[46] an attempt for which there appeared to have been great need, for, as Hitler said, 'A great deal of harm was done by many Germans, who were not in agreement with me, saying and writing to English people after the solution of the Czech question: The Führer succeeded because you lost your nerve, because you capitulated too soon.'[47] But of greater immediate importance was Hitler's emphatic expression of his opinion to his generals that, in view of the Russo-German Pact about to be concluded, there was no fear of British intervention, and that for this reason Poland might not drive the situation to the extreme.[48] In other words, Hitler was aware of the strong opposition to his course and that this opposition was in contact with Britain.[49]

Does this suggest that Hitler hoped in that way to deter some generals from encouraging the British to intervene and oppose him? Clearly no, otherwise Hitler would hardly have chosen a full assembly of *Wehrmacht* commanders and instead would have followed his usual method of informing only a highly select group of which each individual would know no more and no less than was absolutely necessary for the accomplishment of a specific task. What is meant is precisely the opposite. Assuring the generals that he had little fear of British intervention, he displayed on the other hand a firmness of intent and purpose and he may have hoped that if relayed by the elements of opposition with the intent of strengthening Britain's resolve, this would in effect have the opposite result upon the frayed nerves of Chamberlain's government. Taylor's suggestion, therefore, that Hitler was talking for effect seems extremely plausible.[50] Within 48 hours the British Embassy in Berlin had in its hands the second version of the address, later to become known as document L-3. It was communicated to the British Embassy by the American A.P. correspondent in Berlin, Louis P. Lochner.[51] This most sensational of all versions has Hitler express himself with a degree of callousness, vulgarity and brutality which even for Hitler is rare.[52] Referring to Chamberlain he expresses fear that some '*Saukerl*' would intervene and mediate. According to this version the meeting closed with Goering jumping on the table, thanking Hitler bloodthirstily and dancing like a wild man. The first version does not mention this incident at all and according to it 'Goering thanked the Führer and assured him that the *Wehrmacht* would do their duty'. The reference to fear of mediation is also there,[53] only it appears that the expression Hitler used has changed to *Schweinehund*.[54]

Admiral Boehm's account, which it ought to be emphasised again is the most substantial and detailed of the three, confirms the tenor of the first version but does not contain Hitler's expression of such fears of his use of either *Saukerl* or *Schweinehund*; nor does it contain a record of Goering's war dance or Hitler's call to deal mercilessly with the Poles. Boehm is supported by three other persons attendant at the meeting who otherwise had little reason to rally to Hitler's defence, the late Grand Admiral Raeder, Field-Marshal von Manstein and Hitler's own chief of staff, General Halder.[55] Against this we have firstly Lochner's document and secondly a document consisting of two pages of typescript without heading, filing indication or any of the other bureaugraphic paraphernalia which would allow us to ascertain its precise origin.[56]

Hoggan all too readily views document L-3 as Lochner's own fabrication.[57] The fact that similarities exist between all three documents would suggest that this is not so, moreover it has since become clear that the material if not the documents were supplied to Lochner via Beck.[58] Hoggan's own kind of history tends to yield too quickly to conspiratorial notions – though as an afterthought Goering's war dance sounds very much like a journalistic embellishment.

One may therefore ask why in one particular detail which is directly relevant to any assessment of Hitler's attitude prior to the immediate outbreak of war, the two records of the meeting which are of uncertain origin should so strongly diverge from that of an actual

participant and from the testimony of other participants.

Perhaps the Lochner version provides the clue, in
that it turned up shortly afterwards at the British Embassy. If Hitler had spoken for effect, his estimate of
what would occur was certainly right. The amount of
'resistance' literature is too prolific, at least in quantity,
to be examined here, but it emerges fairly clearly that
the opposition to Hitler did as much as it could to
reinvigorate the moral fibre of Chamberlain's government against Hitler. The fear which dominated the
opposition's activities in the last month or so before the
war was that of a repetition of Munich. Not that they
resented Munich or its repetition in principle, but that
it should have been concluded with Hitler! [59]

The document makes it clear that it originated from
one of the generals present opposed to Hitler. Facing
the possibility of another British and French acquiescence in another bloodless victory for Hitler, a reference such as the first two versions contain was just the
kind of phrase with which the originators of the document would hope to prevent this. True, this interpretation still leaves open the question of how a similar phrase came to be recorded in the first version, but
in the last analysis the historian is faced with the choice
between two documents of extremely uncertain and
even doubtful origin and a third document which in
contrast to the other two is the most substantial and
detailed; its origins are clear and its testimony supported by verifiable witnesses. [60]

But one ought to emphasise again that Hitler's
actions in the summer of 1939 were part and parcel of a
complex war of nerves. Hitler was decided upon a
fairly early solution of the Polish question, a solution
which was to his liking. One of the effects of the Russo-
German Pact could well have been Polish acquiescence
over Danzig, another Britain's realisation of the practical impossibility of assisting the Poles. To gain his
objective Hitler was prepared to risk war with Poland
– but this diplomacy appears to have been aimed at a
repetition of Munich.

A short resume of the Polish crisis may perhaps serve as a test of some of the key documents, in particular of *Mein Kampf*, as well as throwing light on the last document in question, the minutes of a conference on 23 May 1939, with senior officers of the *Wehrmacht*.[61]

Shortly after the Munich Agreement Hitler initiated his attempts to come to an arrangement with Poland over Danzig and the Polish corridor. All of these attempts proved to be abortive and, in conjunction with the German occupation of the Czech rump state, they precipitated the British guarantee to Poland. If Hitler now pursued the return of Danzig to the Reich, he risked the greater probability, though not the certainty, of Western intervention.

The first German move therefore was to endeavour to extend the existing treaties with Japan into a full military alliance directed against the British position in the Far East, thus diverting British military resources away from Europe, an endeavour which really goes back into the autumn of 1938. Ribbentrop pressed the matter early in 1939 but without much success.[62] Japan was interested in a military alliance directed against Russia,[63] a measure hardly conducive to relieving pressure on Germany, let alone allowing her to exert it on Poland.

Obviously this reduced the number of alternatives available to Hitler. After 31 March 1939, he could drop his claims to Danzig and, in view of the significance of the British guarantee, suffer a major diplomatic defeat, a course which, as the May crisis of 1938 had clearly shown, was simply unacceptable to a man of Hitler's character. A different alternative was to continue wooing Poland and try to get his friendship pact, with Danzig thrown in into the bargain. But the British guarantee had reduced the chances of success of this policy to zero. Consequently, the last alternative short of using direct force was the coercion of Poland by means of a Russo-German rapprochement. At the end of March Hitler had already asked Brauchitsch what he thought of the Reichskanzler visiting Moscow.[64] The upshot was the Russo-German Pact of August 1939.

In the light of Hitler's intention of coming to terms with Russia, his speech made on 23 May 1939 to senior *Wehrmacht* officers is of particular significance. In it Hitler said 'Danzig is not the objective, it is a question of expanding our living space in the east ... of securing our food supplies as well as solving the problem of the Baltic states.'[65] At first sight the meaning seems clear enough: war *so oder so*, as Hitler used to express himself. The quest for *Lebensraum* seems confirmed. But is it? To begin with, Hitler's living space, the area where it could be obtained, had always been the Ukraine: Russia, not Poland. But with Russia negotiations were already in progress, with the ultimate end of making her his partner in the coercion of Poland. In other words, far from solving the problem of *Lebensraum* or that of the Baltic states, by his very action Hitler was in the process of shutting off – possibly only for the short term – the source of his potential living space.

On the basis of the available evidence it seems reasonable to assume that Hitler viewed the pact as a mere expedient, in the long run to be jettisoned whenever convenient. Nevertheless, within the immediate context of the diplomatic prelude to the Second World War, Hitler's invocation of the need to secure food supplies by territorial expansion and the settling of the problem of the Baltic states was a reference to aims which could hardly be secured in the desired form if a Russo-German Pact were concluded.

What then remains of Hitler's actual objectives are Danzig and the Corridor, in fact nothing but Germany's pre-1914 frontiers which, even if one includes the western hulk of Poland, in the terms in which Hitler saw the problem of living space were neither here nor there. Seen in this perspective, the intention underlying Hitler's speech may well have been different from that which has been accepted hitherto.

Seeckt had succeeded in making the *Reichswehr* a state within a state, a circumstance which still existed in 1939. Admittedly, through conscription, nazification of the army had set in in its lower levels, but though many supported Hitler as head of state, the majority of commanders and staff officers kept their distance and resented the permeation of their profession by National Socialist party doctrine. This, it appears, Hitler intuitively felt; as yet it was doubtful whether the army was an instrument instantly ready to follow the dictator's every whim. It might; but there was not yet that absolute certainty which existed after the successful campaigns in Poland, Scandinavia and the West. Hitler, as we have seen, was not unaware of the existence of a body of opposition to him.

Having laid down in *Mein Kampf* the principle that Germany's pre-1914 frontiers were not worth the sacrifice of German blood, Hitler stuck to it in the face of contrary evidence before his generals, simply by denying that Danzig was his objective. Instead he invoked what he had described as being Germany's fundamental problem. But at the back of his mind he must have had the thought that in 1939, as in 1938, war might yet be avoided, Poland might give in, and Hitler would have another bloodless conquest over which his generals would forget the original objectives he had said were at stake. Hitler's choice of words in this speech, it is suggested, was a product of expediency as much as the Russo-German Pact was to be a few months later.

As the crisis wore on, particularly in August 1939, this was no idle speculation. Especially after the conclusion of the Russo-German Pact Hitler could legitimately hope that it nullified any hopes the Poles might entertain of Anglo-French military intervention on their behalf. And even if the Poles persisted in not giving way to Hitler's claims without the use of force, Hitler, who could not know the secret stipulation of the Anglo-Polish treaty, according to which the British guarantee was limited to the sole contingency of German aggression, had to assume that it applied also to Russian intervention in Poland. Since this meant war between the Russo-German alliance and the Anglo-French-Polish combination, a war in which neither French nor British could do anything effective to aid their Polish ally, there was good reason to suppose that Britain and France would not aid their ally. In Hitler's view if the Poles had any sense of realities they would see it the same way. The extent to which Hitler discounted Anglo-French intervention is best seen when one looks at the troop dispositions on Germany's western frontier between September and October 1939. Moreover Hitler and Ribbentrop tried very hard to get Russian military demonstrations on Poland's eastern frontier prior to 1 September 1939 (which Stalin and Molotov judicially avoided).[66] This is surely inconsistent with the thesis underlying Walter Hofer's book *War Premeditated*: the thesis that in 1939, Hitler's objective was war (a war of which Chamberlain in 1938 had deprived him), for this kind of demonstration would have been the likeliest thing to make Poland more amenable to German demands, and thus kill Hitler's chance of having his own little war. One can hardly exclude the possibility that in spite of all Hitler was aware that another diplomatic victory might not be granted to him. But weighing the possibilities it seems likely that Hitler gambled in the conviction that the odds, or providence, as he would have put it, favoured this.

This examination of evidence already known puts forward no dogmatic claims; the intention simply is to supply and substantiate an approach to a reasonable alternative interpretation, consistent with the evidence and one that is in keeping with Hitler's character.

Far from having been a far-sighted planner of genius, Hitler was more of a superb tactician, a Rommel in politics, who very often because of his lack of a detailed strategic long-term conception defeated his own ends (e.g. his declaration of war on the United States of America in 1941!). One of Hitler's major character traits, as Nolte rightly points out, was his monomania, his concentration upon one objective to the exclusion of anything else. In foreign policy, as for instance in the Czech and Polish crises, this meant following courses of action which surprised people through the impatience and violence with which the case was put and later the action pursued, once obstacles or provocations were put in the way. Once Czech mobilisation had taken place or Poland had become demonstrably active in the Danzig question, there was no holding Hitler back from solving the particular problem in hand.

Policy in that way dependent on the play of individual temper played havoc with military planning, as E. M. Robertson's study has shown.[67] Although Hitler's long-term political objective as set out in *Mein Kampf* seems to have been *Lebensraum* in Russia, his streak of monomania when provoked led him into a pact with his potential victim. But even if we accept that this pact was a temporary expedient as far as Hitler was concerned, until September 1940 there had never been a military plan to this effect and even then Hitler, until Molotov's visit to Berlin, envisaged the possibility of an amicable settlement with Russia. The discrepancy between Hitler's principles as expounded in *Mein Kampf* and the policy actually pursued is still apparent. Up to 1939 Hitler had waited and taken those pickings which conveniently offered themselves. If there was a plan, it was not in *Mein Kampf* nor in the Hossbach Memorandum: it evolved from picking to picking as it were.

That Poland was one picking too many became evident on 3 September 1939. To Hitler at the time it was not. His belief in the spinelessness of Britain and France apart – and this in itself came very near to being justified – Hitler always prided himself on being an ice-cold *Verstandsmensch* and a realist, which was the quality he believed British politicians were supremely endowed with, and which he so much admired. To him the Polish guarantee was no more than an unfulfillable gesture, even more so after the conclusion of the Russo-German Pact. Britain, after all, could provide no effective help for her ally while taking the risk of becoming involved in war not only with Germany but also with Russia. His mistake was not to believe that Britain could take a seemingly unrealistic attitude. This lesson was lost on Hitler, in whom the *Verstandsmensch* was unable to see why on earth Britain should continue the war after the defeat of Poland, or again after the fall of France.

Finally, this persistent belief in the rationality of the Anglo-Saxons may have been responsible for Hitler's faith that ultimately they would not allow the domination of Europe by Russia, and that consequently every step which in early 1945 brought Russians and Western allies closer together would bring nearer the moment of rupture. All that was wrong with this calculation was that Hitler was three years ahead of his time.[68]

Notes

[1] I wish to express here my gratitude to my colleagues Professor G. E. Aylmer and Dr K. G. Robbins and especially to Mr F. H. Hinsley, all of whom by their suggestions have helped to improve the presentation of this article.

[2] Ernst Nolte, *Die Epoche des Faschismus* (Munich, 1963) p. 432 (now also available in English as *The Three Faces of Fascism*, London, 1965). See also footnote no. 189, p. 604, of the German original.

[3] Walter Hofer, *Die Entfesselung des Zweiten Weltkrieges* (Frankfurt: Fischer Bucherei, 1960).

[4] D. L. Hoggan's *Der erzwungene Krieg* does not warrant inclusion here as it is more of a historical curiosity than a work of scholarship.

[5] H. R. Trevor-Roper, 'A. J. P. Taylor, Hitler and the War', *Encounter*, xvii (July 1961) 88–96 (Paper 3).

[6] Adolf Hitler, *Mein Kampf* (227–31 Auflage, Dunndruckausgabe, Munich, 1937) pp. 726–58; see also pp. 687–712.

[7] Ibid., p. 743.

[8] Ibid.

[9] Ibid., p. 749.

[10] See also Werner Maser: *Hitler's Mein Kampf, Entstehung, Aufbau-Stil, Anderungen, Kommentierte*

Auszüge (Munich, 1966), an example of systematic omission of all those passages of chapter xiv which contradict Maser's attempt at demonstrating a clear detailed continuity between the arguments set out in *Mein Kampf*, and the policy Hitler pursued.

[11] See Jurgen Gehl, *Austria, Germany and the Anschluss 1931–1938* (Oxford, 1964).

[12] General Warlimont's evidence, *International Military Tribunal*, xv 562 ff. See also *Hitlers Weisungen für die Kriegsführung*, ed. Walter Hubatch (dtv-Taschenbuchausgabe) Weisung no. 18, 12 Nov 1940, p. 77, which makes reference to Russo-German talks the aim of which was to clarify Russia's attitude 'for the immediate future'.

[13] Hitler, *Mein Kampf*, p. 743.

[14] Gerald Reitlinger, *The House Built on Sand* (London, 1960) p. 10.

[15] Konrad Heiden, *Der Führer* (London, 1944) p. 226.

[16] Hitler, *Mein Kampf*, p. 687.

[17] *DGFP*, series D, 1, no. 29, n. 25a.

[18] A. J. P. Taylor, *The Origins of the Second World War* (London, 1961); Gehl, *Austria, Germany and the Anschluss*, also B.B.C. transcript of the Taylor–Trevor-Roper debate, 9 July 1961; T. W. Mason in *Past and Present*, no. 29 (Dec 1964) (Paper 5).

[19] Trevor-Roper, in *Encounter*, xvii (Paper 3), also see letter by Margaret Lambert to *The Times Literary Supplement* (2 June 1961).

[20] Gehl, *Austria, Germany and the Anschluss*, p. 162, see also Taylor, *Origins of the Second World War*, pp. 131–4 and Gerhard Meinck, *Hitler und die deutsche Aufrüstung 1933–37* (Weisbaden, 1957).

[21] Friedrich Hossbach, *Zwischen Wehrmacht und Hitler* (Hanover, 1949) p. 219.

[22] *IMT* xlii 228 ff.

[23] Friedrich Hossbach, *Von der militärischen Verantwortlichkeit in der Zeit vor dem Zweiten Weltkrieg* (Göttingen, 1948) p. 28.

[24] Meinck, *Hitler und die deutsche Aufrüstung*, pp. 236–7.

[25] *IMT* XLII 218.

[26] Ibid., 236.

[27] Mason in Paper 5, contends that the Hossbach Memorandum, i.e. the Nuremberg version, corresponds with the notes taken at the time by General Beck. This is substantially true but for one significant omission. Beck in his notes makes no reference whatsoever to Hitler's plan to drive out large parts of the populations of Austria and Czechoslovakia, the kind of plan which because of its inherent inhumanity one would have expected a man of Beck's character to take exception to and to comment upon. See also Wolfgang Forster, *Ein General kämpft gegen den Krieg* (Munich, 1949).

[28] See Nolte, *Epoche des Faschismus*, pp. 602–3, n. 177, for a pertinent assessment of the value of the Hossbach Memorandum in a general sense.

[29] K. D. Bracher, W. Sauer, G. Schulz, *Die nationalsozialistische Machtergreifung* (Cologne, 1962) pp. 745 ff.; Meinck, *Hitler und die deutsche Aufrüstung*; H. Buchheim, *Das Dritte Reich* (Munich, 1958) pp. 27 ff.; Rene Erbe, *Die nationalsozialistische Wirtschaftspolitik im Lichte moderner Theorie* (Zürich, 1958).

[30] Burton H. Klein, *Germany's Economic Preparations for War* ('Harvard Economic Studies', Harvard, 1959). See n. 68, below.

[31] Wilhelm Treue, 'Hitlers Rede vor der deutschen Presse, 10. November 1938', *Vierteljahrshefte für Zeitgeschichte*, VI (1958) 175–91.

[32] Bracher, Sauer, Schulz, *Die nationalsozialistische Machtergreifung*, p. 758.

[34] See also *DGFP*, series D, IV, no. 400, recording a conversation between Ribbentrop and Ciano, 28 Oct 1938, in which a conflict with the Western democracies is regarded 'within the bounds of possibility in 4 to 5 years time'.

[35] Bracher, Sauer, Schulz, *Die nationalsozialistische Machtergreifung*, p. 759.

[36] Treue, in *Vierteljahrshefte für Zeitgeschichte*, VI 182. The mutation of a distortion of this nature is amply demonstrated in *Hitler and Nazi Germany* (ed.

R. G. L. Waite, 'European Problem Studies', New York, 1966) p. 91. The editor, who has translated the work of Bracher, Sauer and Schulz, quotes Hitler in direct speech that it was necessary 'to explain certain events to the German people in such a way that the inner voice of the people will itself cry out for force'. R. G. L. Waite is not only taking great liberty with the original of Hitler's speech but also with the text of the work he has translated. At least Wolfgang Sauer does not put the present tense *begin* under quotation marks, but the immediate part which follows. Waite, who has obviously never looked at the original, not only mistranslates that but his secondary source as well.

[37] Erich Kordt, *Wahn und Wirklichkeit* (Stuttgart, 1948) p. 135.

[38] Otto Dietrich, *12 Jahre mit Hitler* (Cologne, 1955) pp. 250 ff.: O. Meissner, *Staatssekretär unter Ebert, Hindenburg, Hitler* (Hamburg, 1950) p. 470.

[39] Ernest K. Bramsted, *Goebbels and National Socialist Propaganda 1925–1945* (London, 1965) pp. 101–2, 176–7.

[40] Oron J. Hale, *The Captive Press in the Third Reich* (New Jersey, 1964) pp. 319–20.

[41] (a) Nuremberg Documents 798-PS and 1014-PS.

(b) N.D. L-3.

(c) Admiral Boehm's version, Raeder Defence Document Book no. 2, doc. 27.

[42] *DGFP*, series D, VII, nos. 192, 193.

[43] Ibid., pp. 557 ff. Generaloberst Halder, *Kriegstagebuch* (Stuttgart, 1964) 1, entry for 22 Aug 1939; Gerhard Ritter, *Goerdeler und die deutsche Widerstandsbewegung* (dtv-Taschenbuchausgabe, Munich, 1964) p. 498, n. 54.

[44] *Documents on British Foreign Policy, 1919–1939*, 3rd series, VII, no. 314 (enc.).

[45] Alan Bullock, *Hitler: A Study in Tyranny* (Odhams, 1954) p. 482; *IMT* XLI 16 ff.; Wheeler Bennett, *The Nemesis of Power* (London, 1954) p. 447 n.

[46] Warlimont, *Im Hauptquartier der Wehrmacht 1939–1945* (Frankfurt, 1964) p. 40.

[47] *DGFP*, series D, VII, no. 192. This passage also corresponds with Boehm's account. See also Fabian von Schlabrendorff, *Offiziere gegen Hitler* (Frankfurt, 1959) pp. 49 ff.

[48] Ibid.; also Warlimont, *Im Hauptquartier der Wehrmacht*, p. 40, and Manstein, *Verlorene Siege* (Bonn, 1958) p. 19. For the view that as late as 29 Aug 1939 Hitler still considered a negotiated settlement possible, see *DGFP*, series D, VII, app. i, p. 567.

[49] See for instance Winston Churchill's B.B.C. broadcast on 17 Oct 1938, in which he, in the words of Hans Rothfels, 'divulged in a manner hardly justifiable confidential information which in this case was primarily based on that provided by Ewald von Kleist' (Hans Rothfels, *Die deutsche Opposition gegen Hitler* (Frankfurt, 1958) pp. 137–8).

[50] Taylor, *Origins of the Second World War*, p. 264.

[51] *DBFP*, 3rd series, VII, no. 314 (enc.).

[52] Also Halder, who was present, denies emphatically Hitler's display of brutality: Ritter, *Goerdeler und die deutsche Widerstandsbewegung*, p. 498, n. 54.

[53] *DBFP*, 3rd series, VII, no. 314 (enc.).

[54] Ibid.

[55] Erich Raeder, *Mein Leben* (Tübingen, 1957) pp. 165 ff.; Manstein, *Verlorene Siege*, p. 19; Ritter, *Goerdeler und die deutsche Widerstandsbewegung*, p. 498.

[56] Gerald Reitlinger, *The S.S.—Alibi of a Nation* (London, 1956), and Bullock, *Hitler*, p. 482, state in accordance with statements of the Nuremberg prosecutors that these sheets of typescript (N.D. 798-PS and 1014-PS) were aken from O.K.W. files captured in the Tyrol. Reitlinger goes on to say that these were based on shorthand notes taken surreptitiously by Admiral Canaris. As his source he quotes H. Greiner, *Die Oberste Wehrmachtsführung 1939–1943* (Wiesbaden, 1951) p. 38. What Greiner states, however, is that he himself made these notes on the evening of 22 August 1939 and based them on the account which General Warlimont supplied, who had just returned from Berchtesgaden. These notes, so Greiner goes on, were supplemented the next day by those which Canaris had

made 'surreptitiously'. Incidentally, Greiner's own account does not mention the words *Saukerl* or *Schweinehund*.

⁵⁷ Hoggan, *Der erzwungene Krieg*, p. 624.

⁵⁸ According to Lochner the document originated from an unnamed officer who handed it to Beck, who in turn through Hermann Maass, a former youth movement official, forwarded it to Lochner. Ritter, *Goerdeler und die deutsche Widerstandsbewegung*, p. 498.

⁵⁹ Schlabrendorff, *Offiziere gegen Hitler*, pp. 49 ff.

⁶⁰ A good example of the manipulation of sources examined here is provided by Alan Clark's recent book, *Barbarossa* (London, 1965). On p. 20 Hitler's conference of 22 Aug 1939 is reported in the light of document L-3, i.e. *DBFP*, 3rd series, VII, no. 314, without reference being made to differing and less sensational versions. Goering's alleged war dance is mentioned, and supplemented by a footnote which reproduces Manstein's acid remark on Goering's extravagant attire. To the unsuspecting reader this juxtaposition appears very much as confirmation by Manstein of Goering's extraordinary behaviour. What he does not know, without actually referring to Manstein, is that the latter categorically denies this performance having taken place.

⁶¹ *DGFP*, series D, VI, no. 433.

⁶² *DGFP*, series D, IV, nos 400, 421, 426, 542, 543, 547, 549.

⁶³ *DGFP*, series D, VI, no. 70.

⁶⁴ Professor Harold C. Deutsch, 'Strange Interlude: The Soviet–Nazi liaison of 1939–41', in *Historian*, IX (1946–7) (Brauchitsch's testimony to Professor Deutsch in his capacity as chief of the State Department Special Interrogation Mission).

⁶⁵ *DGFP*, series D, VI, no. 433.

⁶⁶ *DGFP*, series D, VII, nos 360, 383, 387, 388, 413, 414, 424, 446.

⁶⁷ E. M. Robertson, *Hitler's Pre-War Policy and Military Plans 1933–1939* (London, 1963).

⁶⁸ Since completing this article my attention has

been drawn to a document recently discovered in the Hungarian National Archives which bears on p. 170. If this document is genuine in all respects it seems that the 'appeasers' were more realistic and accurate about the pace of German rearmament than Churchill before 1939 or others since 1945. See Eva Haraszti, 'Two Secret Reports from the Hungarian Archives', *New Hungarian Quarterly*, VIII xxvii 107–34.

9 Hitler and the Origins of the Second World War

Alan Bullock

I

In the twenty years since the end of the war and the Nuremberg trials, historical controversy has been largely concerned with the share of the other Powers in the responsibility for allowing war to break out in 1939. Thus, the British and French governments of the 1930s have been blamed for their policy of appeasement and for failing to secure an agreement with Russia; Mussolini for his alliance with Hitler; Stalin for the Nazi–Soviet Pact; the Poles for the illusions which encouraged them to believe that they could hold Russia as well as Germany at arm's length. Taking a wider sweep, historians have turned for an explanation of the origins of the Second World War to the mistakes made in the peace settlement that followed the First; to the inadequacies of British and French policy between the wars; the retreat of the United States into isolation; the exclusion of the Soviet Union; the social effects of the Great Depression, and so on.

All this is necessary work, in order to establish the historical situation in which the war began, but as the catalogue grows, I find myself asking what is left of the belief universally held outside Germany twenty years ago that the primary responsibility for the war rested on Hitler and the Nazis?

No one suggests that theirs was the sole responsibility. Hitler would never have got as near to success as he did if it had not been for the weakness, the divi-

Reprinted from *Proceedings of the British Academy*, LIII (1967), by permission of the author and Oxford University Press. See also Introduction, pp. 16 and 19.

sions, the opportunism of the other governments, which allowed him to build up such power that he could not be prevented from conquering Europe without a major war. Still, there is a lot of difference between failing to stop aggression, even hoping to derive side profits from it – and aggression itself. Indeed, much of the criticism directed at the other Powers for their failure to stop Hitler in time would fall to the ground if there proved to have been nothing to stop.

Is the effect of filling in the historical picture to reduce this difference to the point where it no longer appears so important, where the responsibility for the war becomes dispersed, or is shifted on to the shortcomings of an anarchical system of international relations, or of militarism or of capitalism, as happened after the First World War? Is Mr A. J. P. Taylor[1] the harbinger of a new generation of revisionist historians who will find it as anachronistic to hold Hitler – or anyone else – responsible for the outbreak of the Second World War as to hold the Kaiser responsible for the outbreak of the First?

The question is an important one, for to an extent which we only begin to realise when it is questioned, the accepted version of European history in the years between 1933 and 1945 has been built round a particular view of Hitler and of the character of German foreign policy, and if the centrepiece were removed, far more than our view of Hitler and German foreign policy would have to be revised – our view of the foreign policies of all the Powers and of the substantiality of the dangers which the other governments, and their critics, believed they confronted.

It occurred to me, therefore, when I was invited to deliver this lecture, that it would be interesting to take a fresh look at Hitler's foreign policy in the light of the new evidence that has become available in the twenty years since the Nuremberg trials (and, no less important, of new ways of looking at familiar evidence) and then to go on and ask, in what sense, if at all, it is still possible to speak of Hitler's and the Nazis' responsibility for what became a Second World War.

II

There are two contrasted versions of Hitler's foreign policy which for convenience' sake I will call the fanatic and the opportunist.

The first[2] fastens upon Hitler's racist views and his insistence that the future of the German people could be secured neither by economic development nor by overseas colonisation, nor even by the restoration of Germany's 1914 frontiers, but only by the conquest of living space (*Lebensraum*) in Eastern Europe. Here the scattered populations of Germans living outside the Reich could be concentrated, together with the surplus population of the homeland, and a Germanic empire established, racially homogeneous, economically self-sufficient and militarily impregnable. Such *Lebensraum* could only be obtained at the expense of Russia and the states bordering on her and could only be won and cleared of its existing population by force, a view which coincided with Hitler's belief in struggle as the law of life, and war as the test of a people's racial superiority.

Hitler first set these views down in *Mein Kampf*, elaborated them in his so-called *Zweites Buch*[3] and repeated them on almost every occasion when we have a record of him talking privately and not in public, down to the Table Talk of the 1940s[4] and his final conversations with Bormann in the early months of 1945[5] when his defeat could no longer be disguised. Not only did he consistently hold and express these views over twenty years, but in 1941 he set to work to put them into practice in the most literal way, by attacking Russia and by giving full rein to his plans, which the S.S. had already begun to carry out in Poland, for the resettlement of huge areas of Eastern Europe.

The alternative version[6] treats Hitler's talk of *Lebensraum* and racist empire in the East as an expression of the fantasy side of his personality and fastens on the opportunism of Hitler's actual conduct of foreign policy. In practice – so this version runs – Hitler was an astute and cynical politician who took advantage of the mistakes and illusions of others to extend German power along lines entirely familiar from the previous century of German history. So little did he take his own professions seriously that he actually concluded a pact with the Bolsheviks whom he had denounced, and when Hitler belatedly began to put his so-called programme into practice, it marked the point at which he lost the capacity to distinguish between fantasy and reality and, with it, the opportunist's touch which had been responsible for his long run of successes. Thereafter he suffered nothing but one disaster after another.

These two versions of Hitler's foreign policy correspond to alternative versions of his personality. The first stresses his insistence on a fanatical will, force and brutality of purpose, his conviction that he was a man of destiny, his reliance on intuition, his scorn for compromise, his declaration after the occupation of the Rhineland: 'I go the way that Providence dictates with the assurance of a sleepwalker.'[7]

The second takes this no more seriously than the rest of Nazi and Fascist rhetoric and insists that in practice Hitler relied for his success upon calculation, total lack of scruple and remarkable gifts as an actor. The suggestion that his opponents had to deal with a man who was fanatical in his purposes and would stop at nothing to accomplish them was part of the act, and a very successful part. His threats were carefully timed as part of a war of nerves, his ungovernable rages turned on or off as the occasion demanded, his hypnotic stare and loss of control part of a public *persona* skilfully and cynically manipulated. And when Hitler, carried away by his triumphs, himself began to believe in his own myth, and no longer to manipulate it, success deserted him.

It is a mistake, however, I believe, to treat these two contrasting views as alternatives, for if that is done, then, whichever alternative is adopted, a great deal of evidence has to be ignored. The truth is, I submit, that they have to be combined and that Hitler can only be understood if it is realised that he was at once both fanatical *and* cynical; unyielding in his assertion of will-power *and* cunning in calculation; convinced of his role as a man of destiny *and* prepared to use all the actor's arts in playing it. To leave out either side, the irrational or the calculating, is to fail to grasp the combination which marks Hitler out from all his imitators.

The same argument, I believe, applies to Hitler's foreign policy, which combined consistency of aim with complete opportunism in method and tactics. This is, after all, a classical receipt for success in foreign affairs. It was precisely because he knew where he wanted to go that Hitler could afford to be opportunistic and saw how to take advantage of the mistakes and fears of others. Consistency of aim on Hitler's part has been confused with a time-table, blueprint or plan of action fixed in advance, as if it were pinned up on the wall of the general staff offices and ticked off as one item succeeded another. Nothing of the sort. Hitler frequently improvised, kept his options open to the last possible moment and was never sure until he got there which of several courses of action he would choose. But this does not alter the fact that his moves followed a logical (though not a predetermined) course – in contrast to Mussolini, an opportunist who snatched eagerly at any chance that was going but never succeeded in combining even his successes into a coherent policy.

III

Hitler had established his power inside Germany by the late summer of 1934. By securing the succession to President Hindenburg, he became head of state and commander-in-chief of the armed forces as well as leader of the only party in the country and head of a government in which no one dared to oppose him. From now on, apart from the one thing which he put before everything else, his own supremacy, Hitler took no great interest in internal affairs or administration. He turned his attention almost wholly to foreign policy and rearmament.

Shortly after he became chancellor, on 3 February 1933, Hitler had met the leaders of the armed forces privately and told them that once his political power was secure, his most important task would be to rearm Germany and then move from the revision of the Versailles Treaty to the conquest of *Lebensraum* in the East.[8]

Just over a year later, on 28 February 1934, Hitler repeated this at a conference of army and S.A. leaders, declaring that here was a decisive reason for rejecting Roehm's plan for a national militia and for rebuilding the German army. The Western Powers would never allow Germany to conquer *Lebensraum* in the East. 'Therefore, short decisive blows to the West and then to the East could be necessary', tasks which could only be carried out by an army rigorously trained and equipped with the most modern weapons.[9]

None the less, in the first two years, 1933 and 1934, Hitler's foreign policy was cautious. Politically, he had still to establish his own supremacy at home. Diplomatically, Germany was isolated and watched with suspicion by all her neighbours. Militarily, she was weak and unable to offer much resistance if the French or the Poles should take preventive action against the new regime.

These were all excellent reasons for Hitler to protest his love of peace and innocence of aggressive intentions. As he told Rauschning, now that Germany had left Geneva, he would more than ever speak 'the language of the League'.[10] There is, in fact, a striking parallel between his conduct of foreign policy in this early period and the tactics of 'legality' which he had pursued in his struggle for power inside Germany. By observing the forms of legality, staying within the framework of the constitution and refusing to make a *Putsch* – which would have brought the Nazis into open conflict with the army – Hitler was able to turn the weapons of democracy against democracy itself.

His appeal to Wilsonian principles of national self-determination and equality of rights had precisely the same effect – and those who believed him were to be as sharply disillusioned as those who supposed Hitler would continue to observe the limits of legality in Germany once he had acquired the power to ignore them.

Although Nazi propaganda made the most of them, none of Hitler's foreign policy moves in his first two years did much to improve Germany's position. Leaving the Disarmament Conference and the League was a gesture; the pact with Poland clever but unconvincing, and more than counterbalanced by Russia's agreement to join the League and start negotiations for an alliance with France. The hurried repudiation of the Austrian Nazis in 1934 was humiliating, and the Saar plebiscite in January 1935 was largely a foregone conclusion. When Hitler announced the reintroduction of conscription in March 1935, Germany's action was condemned by the British, French and Italian governments meeting at Stresa, as well as by the League Council, and was answered by the conclusion of pacts between Russia and France, and Russia and France's most reliable ally, Czechoslovakia.[11]

Between 1935 and 1937, however, the situation changed to Hitler's advantage, and he was able not only to remove the limitations of the Versailles Treaty on Germany's freedom of action but to break out of Germany's diplomatic isolation.

It is true that the opportunities for this were provided by the other Powers: for example by Mussolini's Abyssinian adventure and the quarrel to which this led between Italy and the Western Powers. But Hitler showed skill in using the opportunities which others provided, for example in Spain, where he reduced the policy of non-intervention to a farce and exploited the civil war for his own purposes with only a minimum commitment to France. He also provided his own opportunities: for example the offer of a naval treaty to Britain in 1935 and the military reoccupation of the Rhineland in 1936. This was a bold and risky stroke of bluff, taken against the advice of his generals, without anything like sufficient forces to resist the French if they had marched, and accompanied by a brilliantly contrived diversion in the form of the new peace pacts which he offered simultaneously to the other Locarno Powers.

Of course, there were failures – above all, Ribbentrop's failure to get an alliance with Britain. But between April 1935, when the Powers, meeting at Stresa, had unanimously condemned German rearmament, and Mussolini's state visit to Germany as a prospective ally in September 1937, Hitler could claim with some justification to have transformed Germany's diplomatic position and ended her isolation.

IV

The German Foreign Ministry and diplomatic service were well suited to the international equivalent of the policy of 'legality', but Hitler soon began to develop instruments of his own for a new style of foreign policy.[12] One was the Nazi groups among the *Volksdeutsche* living abroad. The two most obvious examples are the Nazi party in Austria and Henlein's *Sudetendeutsche Partei* in Czechoslovakia. The former had to be hastily disavowed in the summer of 1934, when the *Putsch* against Dolfuss failed, but the subsidies to the Austrian Nazis continued and so did the many links across the frontier from Munich and Berlin. Henlein's Sudeten party was also secretly in receipt of subsidies from Germany from early 1935,[13] and was to play a key role in the campaign against Czechoslovakia. These links were maintained outside the regular Foreign Ministry system and there were a number of Nazi agencies – Bohle's *Auslandsorganisation*, Rosenberg's *Aussenpolitisches Amt*, VOMI (*Volksdeutsche Mittelstelle*) – competing with each other, and with the Foreign Ministry, to organise the German-speaking groups living abroad.

At the same time Hitler began to make use of envoys

from outside the foreign service for the most important diplomatic negotiations: Goering, for instance, who frequently undertook special missions to Italy, Poland and the Balkans, and Ribbentrop whose *Buro*, originally set up to deal with disarmament questions in 1933, soon moved into direct competition with the *Auswartiges Amt*. It was Ribbentrop who negotiated the naval treaty with London; Ribbentrop who was given the key post of ambassador in London in order to secure a British alliance; Ribbentrop who represented Germany on the Non-Intervention Committee, who negotiated and signed the Anti-Comintern Pact with Japan in 1936 and a year later brought in Italy as well.

It was not until the beginning of 1938 that Hitler appointed Ribbentrop as foreign minister: until then he left the German Foreign Ministry and diplomatic service as a respectable façade but increasingly took the discussion of policy and the decisions out of their hands and used other agents to carry them out. In Hitler's eyes the diplomats – like the generals, as he came to feel during the war – were too conservative, too preoccupied with the conventional rules of the game to see the advantages of scrapping rules altogether and taking opponents by surprise. Hitler's radicalism required a new style in the conduct of foreign affairs as different from old-style diplomacy as the Nazi party was from the old-style political parties of the Weimar Republic.

This new style did not emerge clearly until 1938–9, but there were unmistakable signs of it before then in the changed tone in which Hitler and German propaganda were speaking by 1937. Hitler receiving Mussolini and showing off the strength of the new Germany,[14] Hitler beginning to talk of Germany's 'demands', was speaking a very different language from that of the man who only three or four years before had used all his gifts as an orator to convince the world of Germany's will to peace. German national pride and self-confidence had been restored, and instead of trying to conceal, Nazi propaganda now boasted of her growing military strength.

V

The Nazis' claims about German rearmament were widely believed. Phrases like 'Guns before butter' – 'total war' – 'a war economy in peace-time' made a deep impression. When Goering was appointed plenipotentiary for the Four-Year Plan in October 1936, this was taken to mean the speeding up of rearmament, and Hitler's secret memorandum to Goering found among Speer's papers after the war confirms this view.[15] Irritated by Schacht's opposition to his demands, he declared that the shortage of raw materials was 'not an economic problem, but solely a question of will'. A clash with Bolshevik Russia was unavoidable: 'No State will be able to withdraw or even remain at a distance from this historical conflict.... We cannot escape this destiny.'

Hitler concluded his memorandum to Goering with the words:

> I thus set the following task:
>
> 1. The German army must be operational (*einsatzfahig*) within 4 years.
> 2. The German economy must be fit for war (*kriegsfahig*) within 4 years.

Yet the evidence now available does not bear out the widespread belief in Germany's all-out rearmament before 1939.[16] The figures show that the rearmament programme took a long time to get under way and did not really begin to produce the results Hitler wanted until 1939. Even then Germany's military superiority was not as great as both public opinion and the Allies' intelligence services assumed.

The really surprising fact, however, is the scale of German rearmament in relation to Germany's economic resources. At no time before September 1939 was anything like the full capacity of the German economy devoted to war production. The figures are well below what German industry could have achieved if fully mobilised, below what German industry had achieved in 1914–18 and below what was achieved by the British when they set about rearmament in earnest.

The immediate conclusion which one might well draw from these facts is that they provide powerful support for the argument that Hitler was not deliberately preparing for war but was thinking in terms of an armed diplomacy in which he relied on bluff and the *threat* of war to blackmail or frighten the other Powers into giving way to his demands.

Before we accept this conclusion, however, it is worth while to carry the examination of the rearmament figures beyond the date of 1 September 1939. The attack on Poland may or may not have been due to mistaken calculation on Hitler's part (I shall come back to this later), but no one can doubt that the German attack on France and the Low Countries on 10 May 1940 was deliberate, not hastily improvised but prepared for over a six-month period. And this time it was an attack not on a second-class Power like Poland but on two major Powers, France and Britain. Yet the interesting fact is that the proportion of Germany's economic resources devoted to the war hardly went up at all. Even more striking, the same is true of the attack on Russia in 1941. In preparation for Operation Barbarossa, the army was built up to 180 divisions, but this was not accompanied by an all-out armaments drive and on the very eve of the invasion of Russia (20 June 1941) Hitler actually ordered a reduction in the level of arms production. This was put into effect and by December 1941, when the German army was halted before Moscow, the overall level of weapons production had fallen by 29 per cent from its peak in July of that year.[17]

In fact, it was not until 1942, the year in which Hitler lost the initiative and Germany was pushed on to the defensive, that Hitler was persuaded to commit the full resources of the German economy to an all-out effort.

This puts the facts I have mentioned in a different

light. For if Hitler believed that he could defeat the Western Powers, subdue the Balkans and conquer Russia without demanding more than a partial mobilisation from the German people, then the fact that German rearmament before the war had limited rather than total objectives is no proof that his plans at that time did not include war.

The truth is that both before and after September 1939, Hitler was thinking in terms of a very different sort of war from that which Germany had lost in 1914–18 or was to lose again between 1942 and 1945. With a shrewder judgement than many of his military critics, Hitler realised that Germany, with limited resources of her own and subject to a blockade, was always going to be at a disadvantage in a long-drawn-out general war. The sort of war she could win was a series of short campaigns in which surprise and the overwhelming force of the initial blow would settle the issue before the victim had time to mobilise his full resources or the other Powers to intervene. This was the sort of war the German army was trained as well as equipped to fight, and all the German campaigns between 1939 and 1941 conformed to this pattern – Poland, four weeks; Norway, two months; Holland, five days, Belgium, seventeen; France, six weeks; Yugoslavia, eleven days; Greece, three weeks. The most interesting case of all is that of Russia. The explanation of why the German army was allowed to invade Russia without winter clothing or equipment is Hitler's belief that even Russia could be knocked out by a *Blitzkrieg* in four to five months, before the winter set in. And so convinced was Hitler that he had actually achieved this that in his directive of 14 July 1941[18] he spoke confidently of reducing the size of the army, the navy and the armaments programme in the near future.

This pattern of warfare, very well adapted both to Germany's economic position and the advantages of secrecy and surprise enjoyed by a dictatorship, fits perfectly the pattern of German rearmament. What was required was not armament in depth, the long-term conversion of the whole economy to a war footing which (as in Britain) would only begin to produce results in two to three years, but a war economy of a different sort geared (like German strategy) to the concept of the *Blitzkrieg*. It was an economy which concentrated on a short-term superiority and the weapons which could give a quick victory, even when this meant neglecting the proper balance of a long-term armament programme. What mattered, as Hitler said in his 1936 memorandum, was not stocks of raw materials or building up productive capacity, but armaments ready for use, plus the will to use them. How near the gamble came to success is shown by the history of the years 1939–41 when Hitler's limited rearmament programme produced an army capable of overrunning the greater part of Europe, and very nearly defeating the Russians as well as the French,

VI

But we must not run ahead of the argument. The fact that Germany was better prepared for war, and when it began prodeeded to win a remarkable series of victories, does not prove that Hitler intended to start the war which actually broke out in September 1939. We have still to relate Hitler's long-term plans for expansion in the East and his rearmament programme to the actual course of events in 1938 and 1939.

A starting point is Colonel Hossbach's record of Hitler's conference with his three commanders-in-chief, war minister and foreign minister on 5 November 1937.[19] It was an unusual occasion, since Hitler rarely talked to more than one commander-in-chief or minister at a time, and he came nearer to laying down a programme than he ever had before. Once again he named *Lebensraum* in the East and the need to provide for Germany's future by continental expansion as the objective, but instead of leaving it at that, he went on to discuss how this was to be achieved.

The obstacles in the way were Britain and France, Germany's two 'hate-inspired antagonists'. Neither was as strong as she seemed: still, 'Germany's problems could only be solved by force and this was never without attendant risk'.

The peak of German power would be reached in 1943–5: after that, their lead in armaments would be reduced. 'It was while the rest of the world was preparing its defences that we were obliged to take the offensive.' Whatever happened, he was resolved to solve Germany's problem of space by 1943–5 at the latest. Hitler then discussed two possible cases in which action might be taken earlier – one was civil strife in France, disabling the French army: the other, war in the Mediterranean, which might allow Germany to act as early as 1938. The first objective in either case 'must be to overthrow Czechoslovakia and Austria simultaneously in order to remove the threat to our flank in any possible operation against the West'. Hitler added the comment that almost certainly Britain and probably France as well had already tacitly written off the Czechs.

To speak of this November meeting as a turning point in Hitler's foreign policy at which Hitler made an irreversible decision in favour of war seems to me as wide of the target as talking about time-tables and blueprints of aggression. Hitler was far too skilful a politician to make irreversible decisions in advance of events: no decisions were taken or called for.

But to brush the Hossbach meeting aside and say that this was just Hitler talking for effect and not to be taken seriously seems to me equally wide of the mark. The hypotheses Hitler outlined – civil strife in France, a Mediterranean war – did not materialise, but when Hitler spoke of his determination to overthrow Czechoslovakia and Austria, as early as 1938 if an opportunity offered, and when both countries *were* overthrown within less than eighteen months, it is stretching incredulity rather far to ignore the fact that he had stated this as his immediate programme in November 1937.

The next stage was left open, but Hitler foresaw quite correctly that everything would depend upon the extent to which Britain and France were prepared to intervene by force to prevent Germany's continental expansion and he clearly contemplated war if they did. Only when the obstacle which they represented had been removed would it be possible for Germany to carry out her eastward expansion.

This was a better forecast of the direction of events in 1938–41 than any other European leader including Stalin made at the end of 1937 – for the very good reason that Hitler, however opportunist in his tactics, knew where he wanted to go, was almost alone among European leaders in knowing this and so kept the initiative in his hands.

The importance of the Hossbach conference, I repeat, is not in recording a decision, but in reflecting the change in Hitler's attitude. If the interpretation offered of his policy in 1933–7 is correct, it was not a sudden but a gradual change, and a change not in the objectives of foreign policy but in Hitler's estimate of the risks he could afford to take in moving more rapidly and openly towards them. As he told the Nazi Old Guard at Augsburg a fortnight later: 'I am convinced that the most difficult part of the preparatory work has already been achieved. . . . Today we are faced with new tasks, for the *Lebensraum* of our people is too narrow.'[20]

There is another point to be made about the Hossbach conference. Of the five men present besides Hitler and his adjutant Hossbach, Goering was certainly not surprised by what he heard and Raeder said nothing. But the other three, the two generals and Neurath, the foreign minister, showed some alarm and expressed doubts. It is surely another remarkable coincidence if this had nothing to do with the fact that within three months all three men had been turned out of office – the two generals, Blomberg and Fritsch, on bare-faced pretexts. There is no need to suppose that Hitler himself took the initiative in framing Blomberg or Fritsch. The initiative seems more likely to have come from Goering and Himmler, but it was Hitler who turned both Blomberg's *mesalliance* and the allegations against Fritsch to his own political advantage. Blomberg, the minister of war, was replaced by Hitler himself, who suppressed the office altogether, took over the O.K.W., the High Command of the armed forces, as his own staff and very soon made clear that neither the O.K.W. nor the O.K.H., the High Command of the army, would be allowed the independent position of the old general staff. Fritsch, long regarded by Hitler as too stiff, conservative and out of sympathy with Nazi ideas, was replaced by the much more pliable Brauchitsch as commander-in-chief of the army, and Neurath, a survivor from the original coalition, by Ribbentrop, who made it as clear to the staff of the Foreign Ministry as Hitler did to the generals that they were there to carry out orders, not to discuss, still less question the Fuhrer's policy.

VII

I find nothing at all inconsistent with what I have just said in the fact that the timing for the first of Hitler's moves, the annexation of Austria, should have been fortuitous and the preparations for it improvised on the spur of the moment in a matter of days, almost of hours. On the contrary, the *Anschluss* seems to me to provide, almost in caricature, a striking example of that extraordinary combination of consistency in aim, calculation and patience in preparation with opportunism, impulse and improvisation in execution which I regard as characteristic of Hitler's policy.

The aim in this case was never in doubt: the demand for the incorporation of Austria in the Reich appears on the first page of *Mein Kampf*. After the Austrian Nazis' unsuccessful *Putsch* of 1934, Hitler showed both patience and skill in his relations with Austria: he gradually disengaged Mussolini from his commitment to maintain Austrian independence and at the same time steadily undermined that independence from within. By the beginning of 1938 he was ready to put on the pressure, but the invitation to

Schuschnigg to come to Berchtesgaden was made on the spur of the moment as the result of a suggestion by an anxious von Papen trying hard to find some pretext to defer his own recall from Vienna. When Schuschnigg appeared on 12 February, Hitler put on an elaborate act to frighten him into maximum concessions with the threat of invasion, but there is no reason to believe that either Hitler or the generals he summoned to act as 'stage extras' regarded these threats as anything other than bluff. Hitler was confident that he would secure Austria, without moving a man, simply by the appointment of his nominee Seyss-Inquart as minister of the interior and the legalisation of the Austrian Nazis – to both of which Schuschnigg agreed.

When the Austrian chancellor, in desperation, announced a plebiscite on 9 March, Hitler was taken completely by surprise. Furious at being crossed, he decided at once to intervene before the plebiscite could be held. But no plans for action had been prepared: they had to be improvised in the course of a single day, and everything done in such a hurry and confusion that 70 per cent of the tanks and lorries, according to General Jodl, broke down on the road to Vienna. The confusion was even greater in the Reich Chancellery: when Schuschnigg called off the plebiscite, Hitler hesitated, then was persuaded by Goering to let the march-in continue, but without any clear idea of what was to follow. Only when he reached Linz did Hitler, by then in a state of self-intoxication, suddenly decide to annex Austria instead of making it a satellite state, and his effusive messages of relief to Mussolini show how unsure he was of the consequences of his action.

No doubt the *Anschluss* is an exceptional case. On later occasions the plans were ready: dates by which both the Czech and the Polish crises must be brought to a solution were fixed well in advance, and nothing like the same degree of improvisation was necessary. But in all the major crises of Hitler's career there is the same strong impression of confusion at the top, springing directly (as his generals and aides complained) from his own hesitations and indecision. It is to be

found in his handling of domestic as well as foreign
crises – as witness his long hesitation before the Roehm
purge of 1934 – and in war as well as peace-time.

The paradox is that out of all this confusion and
hesitation there should emerge a series of remarkably
bold decisions, just as, out of Hitler's opportunism in
action, there emerges a pattern which conforms to
objectives stated years before.

VIII

The next crisis, directed against Czechoslovakia, was
more deliberately staged. This time Hitler gave preliminary instructions to his staff on 21 April 1938[21]
and issued a revised directive on 30 May.[22] Its first
sentence read: 'It is my unalterable decision to smash
Czechoslovakia by military action in the near future.'
It was essential, Hitler declared, to create a situation
within the first two or three days which would make
intervention by other Powers hopeless: the army and
the air force were to concentrate all their strength for a
knock-out blow and leave only minimum forces to hold
Germany's other frontiers.

It is perfectly true that for a long time in the summer
Hitler kept out of the way and left the other Powers to
make the running, but this was only part of the game.
Through Henlein and the Sudeten party, who played
the same role of fifth column as the Austrian Nazis,
Hitler was able to manipulate the dispute between the
Sudeten Germans and the Czech government, which
was the ostensible cause of the crisis, from within. At a
secret meeting with Hitler on 28 March, Henlein summarised his policy in the words: 'We must always demand so much that we can never be satisfied.' The
Fuhrer, says the official minute, approved this view.[23]

At the same time through a variety of devices – full-
scale press and radio campaigns, the manufacture of
incidents, troop movements, carefully circulated
rumours and diplomatic leaks – a steadily mounting
pressure was built up, timed to culminate in Hitler's

long-awaited speech at the Nuremberg Party Congress. Those who study only the diplomatic documents get a very meagre impression of the war of nerves which was maintained throughout the summer and which was skilfully directed to play on the fear of war in Britain and France and to heighten the Czechs' sense of isolation. It was under the pressure of this political warfare, something very different from diplomacy as it had been traditionally practised, that the British and French governments felt themselves impelled to act.

What was Hitler's objective? The answer has been much confused by the ambiguous use of the word 'war'.

Western opinion made a clear-cut distinction between peace and war: Hitler did not, he blurred the distinction. Reversing Clausewitz, he treated politics as a continuation of war by other means, at one stage of which (formally still called peace) he employed methods of political warfare – subversion, propaganda, diplomatic and economic pressure, the war of nerves – at the next, the threat of war, and so on to localised war and up the scale to general war – a continuum of force in which the different stages ran into each other. Familiar enough now since the time of the cold war, this strategy (which was all of a piece with Hitler's radical new style in foreign policy) was as confusing in its novelty as the tactics of the Trojan horse, the fifth column and the 'volunteers' to those who still thought in terms of a traditionally decisive break between a state of peace and a state of war.

So far as the events of 1938 go, there seem to be two possible answers to the question, What was in Hitler's mind?

The first is that his object was to destroy the Czech state by the sort of *Blitzkrieg* for which he had rearmed Germany and which he was to carry out a year later against Poland. This was to come at the end of a six-month political, diplomatic and propaganda campaign designed to isolate and undermine the Czechs, and to manoeuvre the Western Powers into abandoning them to their fate rather than risk a European war. The evidence for this view consists in the series of secret

directives and the military preparations to which they
led, plus Hitler's declaration on several occasions to
the generals and his other collaborators that he meant
to settle the matter by force, with 1 October as D-day.
On this view, he was only prevented from carrying out
his attack by the intervention of Chamberlain, which,
however great the cost to the Czechs, prevented war or
at least postponed it for a year.

The other view is that Hitler never intended to go to
war, that his objective was from the beginning a political settlement such as was offered to him at Munich,
that his military preparations were not intended seriously but were designed as threats to increase the
pressure.

The choice between these two alternatives, however
– *either* the one *or* the other – seems to me unreal. The
obvious course for Hitler to pursue was to keep both
possibilities open to the very last moment, the more so
since they did not conflict. The more seriously the military preparations were carried out, the more effective
was the pressure in favour of a political settlement if at
the last moment he decided not to take the risks involved in a military operation. If we adopt this view,
then we remove all the difficulties in interpreting the
evidence which are created either by attempting to pin
Hitler down on any particular declaration and say
now, at this point, he had decided on war – or by the
dogmatic assumption that Hitler *never* seriously contemplated the use of force, with the consequent need to
dismiss his military directives as bluff.

Neither in 1938 nor in 1939 did Hitler deliberately
plan to start a general European war. But this was a
risk which could not be ignored, and in 1938 it was
decisive. The generals were unanimous that Germany's
rearmament had not yet reached the point where she
could face a war with France and Britain. The Czech
frontier defences were formidable. Their army on
mobilisation was hardly inferior at all, either in numbers or training, to the thirty-seven divisions which the
Germans could deploy and it was backed by a first-class
armaments industry.[24] To overcome these would re-

quire a concentration of force which left the German commander in the West with totally inadequate strength to hold back the French army.

While the generals, however, added up divisions and struck an unfavourable balance in terms of material forces, Hitler was convinced that the decisive question was a matter of will, the balance between his determination to take the *risk* of a general war and the determination of the Western Powers, if pushed far enough, to take the *actual decision* of starting one. For, however much the responsibility for such a war might be Hitler's, by isolating the issue and limiting his demands to the Sudetenland, he placed the onus of actually starting a general war on the British and the French. How far was Hitler prepared to drive such an argument? The answer is, I believe, that while he had set a date by which he knew he must decide, until the very last moment he had not made up his mind and that it is this alternation between screwing up his demands, as he did at his second meeting with Chamberlain in Godesberg, and still evading an irrevocable decision, which accounts both for the zigzag course of German diplomacy and for the strain on Hitler.

In the end he decided, or was persuaded, to stop short of military operations against Czechoslovakia and 'cash' his military preparations for the maximum of political concessions.

No sooner had he agreed to this, however, than Hitler started to regret that he had not held on, marched his army in, then and there, and broken up the Czechoslovak state, not just annexed the Sudetenland. His regret sprang from the belief, confirmed by his meeting with the Western leaders at Munich, that he could have got away with a localised war carried out in a matter of days, and then confronted the British and French with a *fait accompli* while they were still hesitating whether to attack in the West – exactly as happened a year later over Poland.

Almost immediately after Munich, therefore, Hitler began to think about ways in which he could complete his original purpose. Every sort of excuse, however transparent, was found for delaying the international guarantee which had been an essential part of the Munich Agreement. At the same time, the ground was carefully prepared with the Hungarians, who were eager to recover Ruthenia and at least part of Slovakia, and with the Slovaks themselves, who were cast for the same role the Sudeten Germans had played the year before. The actual moment at which the crisis broke was not determined by Hitler and took him by surprise, but that was all. The Slovaks were at once prodded into declaring their independence and putting themselves in Hitler's hands. The Czech government, after Hitler had threatened President Hacha in Berlin, did the same. The 'legality' of German intervention was unimpeachable: Hitler had been invited to intervene by both the rebels and the government. War had been avoided, no shots exchanged, peace preserved – yet the independent state of Czechoslovakia had been wiped off the map.

IX

Within less than eighteen months, then, Hitler had successfully achieved both the immediate objectives, Austria and Czechoslovakia, which he had laid down in the Hossbach meeting. He had not foreseen the way in which this would happen, in fact he had been wrong about it, but this had not stopped him from getting both.

This had been true at every stage of Hitler's career. He had no fixed idea in 1930, even in 1932, about how he would become chancellor, only that he would; no fixed idea in 1934–5 how he would break out of Germany's diplomatic isolation, again only that he would. So the same now. Fixity of aim by itself, or opportunism by itself, would have produced nothing like the same results.

It is entirely in keeping with this view of Hitler that, after Czechoslovakia, he should not have made up his mind what to do next. Various possibilities were in the

air. Another move was likely in 1939, if only because
the rearmament programme was now beginning to
reach the period when it would give Germany a maximum advantage and Hitler had never believed that
time was on his side. This advantage, he said in November 1937, would only last, at the most until 1943–5;
then the other Powers with greater resources would
begin to catch up. He had therefore to act quickly if he
wanted to achieve his objectives.

Objectives, yes; a sense of urgency in carrying them
out, and growing means to do so in German rearmament, but no time-table or precise plan of action for
the next stage.

Ribbentrop had already raised with the Poles, immediately after Munich, the question of Danzig and
the Corridor. But there is no evidence that Hitler had
committed himself to war to obtain these, or to the
dismemberment of Poland. If the Poles had been willing to give him what he wanted, Hitler might well
have treated them, for a time at any rate, as a satellite –
in much the same way as he treated Hungary – and
there were strong hints from Ribbentrop that the Germans and the Poles could find a common objective in
action against Russia. Another possibility, if Danzig
and the Corridor could be settled by agreement, was to
turn west and remove the principal obstacle to German expansion, the British and French claim to intervene in Eastern Europe.

After Prague, the German–Polish exchanges became
a good deal sharper and, given the Poles' determination not to be put in the same position as the Czechs,
but to say 'No' and refuse to compromise, it is likely
that a breach between Warsaw and Berlin would have
come soon in any case. But what precipitated it was the
British offer, and Polish acceptance, of a guarantee of
Poland's independence. In this sense the British offer is
a turning point in the history of 1939. But here comes
the crux of the matter. If Mr Taylor is right in believ-
ing that Hitler was simply an opportunist who reacted
to the initiative of others, then he is justified in calling
the British offer to Poland a revolutionary event.[25]

But if the view I have suggested is right, namely, that Hitler, although an opportunist in his tactics, was an opportunist who had from the beginning a clear objective in view, then it is very much less than that: an event which certainly helped – if you like, forced – Hitler to make up his mind between the various possibilities he had been revolving, but which certainly did not provoke him into an expansionist programme he would not otherwise have entertained, or generate the force behind it which the Nazis had been building up ever since they came to power. On this view it was Hitler who still held the initiative, as he had since the *Anschluss*, and the British who were reacting to it, not the other way round: the most the British guarantee did was to give Hitler the answer to the question he had been asking since Munich, Where next?

The answer, then, was Poland, the most probable in any event in view of the demands the Nazis had already tabled, and now a certainty. But this did not necessarily mean war – yet.

Hitler expressed his anger by denouncing Germany's Non-Aggression Pact with Poland and the Anglo-German Naval Treaty, and went on to sign a secret directive ordering the army to be ready to attack Poland by 1 September.[26] The military preparations were not bluff: they were designed to give Hitler the option of a military solution if he finally decided this way, or to strengthen the pressures for a political solution – either direct with Warsaw, or by the intervention of the other Powers in a Polish Munich. Just as in 1938 so in 1939 Hitler kept the options open literally to the last, and until the troops actually crossed the Polish frontier on 1 September none of his generals was certain that the orders might not be changed. Both options, however: there is no more reason to say dogmatically that Hitler was aiming all the time at a political solution than there is to say that he ruled it out and had made up his mind in favour of war.

Hitler's inclination, I believe, was always towards a solution by force, the sort of localised *Blitzkrieg* with which in the end he did destroy Poland. What he had to weigh was the risk of a war which could not be localised. There were several reasons why he was more ready to take this risk than the year before.

The first was the progress of German rearmament – which was coming to a peak in the autumn of 1939. By then it represented an eighteen-fold expansion of the German armed forces since 1933.[27] In economists' terms this was not the maximum of which Germany was capable, at least in the long run, but in military terms it was more than adequate, as 1940 showed, not just to defeat the Poles but to deal with the Western Powers as well. The new German army had been designed to achieve the maximum effect at the outset of a campaign and Hitler calculated – quite rightly – that even if the British formally maintained their guarantee to Poland, the war would be over and Poland crushed before they could do anything about it.[28]

A second reason was Hitler's increased confidence, his conviction that his opponents were simply not his equal either in daring or in skill. The very fact that he had drawn back at Munich and then regretted it made it all the more likely that a man with his gambler's temperament would be powerfully drawn to stake all next time.

Finally, Hitler believed that he could remove the danger of Western intervention, or at least render the British guarantee meaningless, by outbidding the Western Powers in Moscow.

In moments of exaltation, e.g. in his talks to his generals after the signature of the pact with Italy (23 May) and at the conference of 22 August which followed the news that Stalin would sign, Hitler spoke as if the matter were settled, war with Poland inevitable and all possibility of a political settlement – on his terms – excluded. I believe that this was, as I have said, his real inclination, but I do not believe that he finally made up his mind until the last minute. Why should he? Just as in 1938, Hitler refused to make in advance the choice to which historians have tried to pin him down, the either/or of war or a settlement dictated under the threat of war. He fixed the date by which the choice would have to be made but pursued a course which would leave him with the maximum of man-oeuvre to the last possible moment. And again one may well ask, Why not – since the preparations to be made for either eventuality – war or a political settlement under the threat of war – were the same?

Much has been made of the fact that for the greater part of the summer Hitler retired to Berchtesgaden and made no public pronouncement. But this is mis-leading. The initiative remained in Hitler's hands. The propaganda campaign went ahead exactly as planned, building up to a crisis by late August and hammering on the question, Is Danzig worth a war? So did the military preparations, which were complete by the date fixed, 26 August. German diplomacy was mobilised to isolate Poland and, if the pact with Italy proved to be of very little value in the event, and the Japanese failed to come up to scratch, the pact with Stalin was a major coup. For a summer of 'inactivity' it was not a bad result.

Hitler's reaction when the Nazi–Soviet Pact was signed shows clearly enough where his first choice lay. Convinced that the Western Powers would now give up any idea of intervention in defence of Poland, he ordered the Germany army to attack at dawn on 26 August: i.e. a solution by force, but localised and without risk of a general European war, the sort of operation for which German rearmament had been de-signed from the beginning.

The unexpected British reaction, the confirmation instead of the abandonment of the guarantee to Poland – this, plus Mussolini's defection (and Mussolini at any rate had no doubt that Hitler was bent on a solution by force) upset Hitler's plans and forced him to think again. What was he to do? Keep up the pressure and hope that the Poles would crack and accept his terms? Keep up the pressure and hope that, if not the Poles, then the British would crack and either press the Poles to come to terms (another Munich) or abandon them? Or go ahead and take the risk of a general war, calcula-ting that Western intervention, if it took place, would come too late to affect the outcome?

It is conceivable that if Hitler had been offered a Polish Munich, on terms that would by now have amounted to capitulation, he would still have accepted it. But I find it hard to believe that any of the moves he made, or sanctioned, between 25 August and 1 September were seriously directed to starting negotiations. A far more obvious and simple explanation is to say that, having failed to remove the threat of British intervention by the Nazi–Soviet Pact, as he had expected, Hitler postponed the order to march and allowed a few extra days to see, not if war could be avoided, but whether under the strain a split might not develop between the Western Powers and Poland and so leave the Poles isolated after all.

Now the crisis had come, Hitler himself did little to resolve or control it. Characteristically, he left it to others to make proposals, seeing the situation, not in terms of diplomacy and negotiation but as a contest of wills. If his opponents' will cracked first, then the way was open for him to do what he wanted and march into Poland without fear that the Western Powers would intervene. To achieve this he was prepared to hold on and bluff up to the very last minute, but if the bluff did not come off within the time he had set, then this time he steeled his will to go through with the attack on Poland even if it meant running the risk of war with Britain and France as well. All the accounts agree on the strain which Hitler showed and which found expression in his haggard appearance and temperamental outbursts. But his will held. This was no stumbling into war. It was neither misunderstanding nor miscalculation which sent the German army over the frontier into Poland, but a calculated risk, the gambler's bid – the only bid, Hitler once told Goering, he ever made, *va banque*, the bid he made when he reoccupied the Rhineland in 1936 and when he marched into Austria, the bid he had failed to make when he agreed to the Munich conference, only to regret it immediately afterwards.

X

Most accounts of the origins of the war stop in September 1939. Formally, this is correct: from 3 September 1939 Germany was in a state of war with Britain and France as well as Poland, and the Second World War had begun. But this formal statement is misleading. In fact, Hitler's gamble came off. The campaign in which the German army defeated the Poles remained a localised war and no hostilities worth speaking of had taken place between Germany and the Western Powers by the time the Poles had been defeated and the state whose independence they had guaranteed had ceased to exist.

If Hitler had miscalculated at the beginning of September or stumbled into war without meaning to, here was the opportunity to avoid the worst consequences of what had happened. It is an interesting speculation what the Western Powers would have done, if he had really made an effort to secure peace once the Poles were defeated. But it is a pointless speculation. For Hitler did nothing of the sort. The so-called peace offer in his speech of 6 October was hardly meant to be taken seriously. Instead of limiting his demands, Hitler proceeded to destroy the Polish state and to set in train (in 1939, not in 1941) the ruthless resettlement programme which he had always declared he would carry out in Eastern Europe.

Even more to the point, it was Hitler who took the initiative in turning the formal state of war between Germany and the Western Powers into a real war. On 9 October he produced a memorandum in which he argued that instead of waiting to see whether the Western Powers would back their formal declaration of war with effective force, Germany should seize the initiative and make an all-out attack on the French and the British, thereby removing once and for all the limitations on Germany's freedom of action.

The German generals saw clearly what this meant: far from being content with, and trying to exploit, the good luck which had enabled him to avoid a clash with the Western Powers so far, Hitler was deliberately setting out to turn the localised campaign he had won in Poland into a general war. Their doubts did not deter him for a moment and, although they managed on one pretext or another to delay operations, in May 1940 it was the German army, without waiting for the French or the British, which launched the attack in the West and turned the *drôle de guerre* into a major war.

Even this is not the end of the story. Once again, Hitler proved to be a better judge than the experts. In the middle of events his nerve faltered, he became hysterical, blamed everyone, behaved in short in exactly the opposite way to the copy-book picture of the man of destiny: but when the battle was over he had inflicted a greater and swifter defeat upon France than any in history. And it is no good saying that it was 'the machine' that did this, not Hitler. Hitler was never the prisoner of 'the machine'. If 'the machine' had been left to decide things, it would never have taken the risk of attacking in the West, and, if it had, would never have adopted the Ardennes plan which was the key to victory. Pushing the argument farther back, one can add that if it had been left to 'the machine', German rearmament would never have been carried out at the pace on which Hitler insisted, or on the *Blitzkrieg* pattern which proved to be as applicable to war with the Western Powers as to the limited Polish campaign.

Once again, the obvious question presents itself: what would have happened if Hitler, now as much master of continental Europe as Napoleon had been, had halted at this point, turned to organising a continental New Order in Europe and left to the British the decision whether to accept the situation – if not in 1940, then perhaps in 1941 – or to continue a war in which they had as yet neither American nor Russian allies, were highly vulnerable to attack and could never hope by themselves to overcome the disparity between their own and Hitler's continental resources. Once again – this is my point – it was thanks to Hitler, and no one else, that this question was never posed. It was Hitler who decided that enough was not enough, that the war must go on – Hitler, not the German military leaders or the German people, many of whom would have been content to stop at this point, enjoy the fruits of victory and risk nothing more.

If the war had to continue, then the obvious course was to concentrate all Germany's – and Europe's – re sources on the one opponent left, Britain. If invasion was too difficult and dangerous an operation, there were other means – a Mediterranean campaign with something more than the limited forces reluctantly made available to Rommel, or intensification of the air and submarine war, as Raeder urged. The one thing no one thought of except Hitler was to attack Russia, a country whose government had shown itself painfully anxious to avoid conflict and give every economic assistance to Germany. There was nothing improvised about Hitler's attack on Russia. Of all his decisions it was the one taken farthest in advance and most carefully planned for, the one over which he hesitated least and which he approached with so much confidence that he even risked a five-week delay in starting in order to punish the Yugoslavs and settle the Balkans.[29]

Nor was it conceived of solely as a military operation. The plans were ready to extend to the newly captured territory the monstrous programme of uprooting whole populations which the S.S. – including Eichmann – had already put into effect in Poland.[30] Finally, of all Hitler's decisions it is the one which most clearly bears his own personal stamp, the culmination (as he saw it) of his whole career.

XI

It will now be evident why I have carried my account beyond the conventional date of September 1939. Between that date and June 1941 the scope of the war was steadily enlarged from the original limited Polish campaign to a conflict which, with the attack on Russia, was now on as great a scale as the war of 1914–18. The initiative at each stage – except in the Balkans, where he was reluctant to become involved – had been Hitler's. Of course he could not have done this without the military machine and skill in using it which the German armed forces put at his disposal, but the evidence leaves no doubt that the decision where and when to use that machine was in every case Hitler's, not his staff's, still less that all Hitler was doing was to react to the initiative of his opponents.

Now, it may be that the Hitler who took these increasingly bold decisions after September 1939 was a different person from the Hitler who conducted German foreign policy before that date, but this is surely implausible. It seems to me far more likely that the pattern which is unmistakable after September 1939, using each victory as the basis for raising the stakes in a still bolder gamble next time, is the correct interpretation of his conduct of foreign policy before that date. And this interpretation is reinforced by the fact that at the same time Hitler was carrying out the rearmament and expansion of the German armed forces on a pattern which exactly corresponds to the kind of war which he proceeded to wage after September 1939.

Let me repeat and underline what I said earlier in this lecture: this has nothing to do with time-tables and blueprints of aggression. Throughout his career Hitler was an opportunist, prepared to seize on and exploit any opportunity that was offered to him. There was nothing inevitable about the way or the order in which events developed, either before or after September 1939. The annexation of Austria and the attempt to eliminate Czechoslovakia, by one means or another, were predictable, but after the occupation of Prague there were other possibilities which might have produced a quite different sequence of events – as there were after the fall of France. Of what wars or other major events in history is this not true?

But Hitler's opportunism was doubly effective because it was allied with unusual consistency of purpose. This found expression in three things:

First, in his aims – to restore German military power, expand her frontiers, gather together the scattered populations of *Volksdeutsche* and found a new German empire in Eastern Europe, the inhabitants of which would either be driven out, exterminated or retained as slave-labour.

Second, in the firmness with which he grasped from the beginning what such aims entailed – the conquest of power in Germany on terms that would leave him with a free hand, the risk of pre-emptive intervention by other Powers, the need to shape German rearmament in such a way as to enable him to win a quick advantage within a limited time by surprise and concentration of force, the certainty that to carry out his programme would mean war.

Third, in the strength of will which underlay all his hesitations, opportunism and temperamental outbursts, and in his readiness to take risks and constantly to increase these by raising the stakes – from the reoccupation of the Rhineland to the invasion of Russia (with Britain still undefeated in his rear) within the space of no more than five years.

Given such an attitude on the part of a man who controlled one of the most powerful nations in the world, the majority of whose people were prepared to believe what he told them about their racial superiority and to greet his satisfaction of their nationalist ambitions with enthusiasm – given this, I cannot see how a clash between Germany and the other Powers could have been avoided. Except on the assumption that Britain and France were prepared to disinterest themselves in what happened east of the Rhine and accept the risk of seeing him create a German hegemony over the rest of Europe. There was nothing inevitable about either the date or the issue on which the clash actually came. It half came over Czechoslovakia in 1938; it might have come over another issue than Poland. But I cannot see how it could have been avoided some time, somewhere, unless the other Powers were prepared to stand by and watch Hitler pursue his tactics of one-at-a-time to the point where they would no longer have the power to stop him.

If the Western Powers had recognised the threat earlier and shown greater resolution in resisting Hitler's (and Mussolini's) demands, it is possible that the clash might not have led to war, or at any rate not to a war on the scale on which it had finally to be fought. The longer they hesitated, the higher the price of resistance. This is their share of the responsibility for the war: that they were reluctant to recognise what was happening, reluctant to give a lead in opposing it, reluctant to act in time. Hitler understood their state of mind perfectly and played on it with skill. None of the Great Powers comes well out of the history of the 1930s, but this sort of responsibility, even when it runs to appeasement, as in the case of Britain and France, or complicity as in the case of Russia, is still recognisably different from that of a government which deliberately creates the threat of war and sets out to exploit it.

In the Europe of the 1930s there were several leaders – Mussolini, for instance – who would have liked to follow such a policy, but lacked the toughness of will and the means to carry it through. Hitler alone possessed the will and had provided himself with the means. Not only did he create the threat of war and exploit it, but when it came to the point he was prepared to take the risk and go to war and, then when he had won the Polish campaign, to redouble the stakes and attack again, first in the West, then in the East. For this reason, despite all that we have learned since of the irresolution, shabbiness and chicanery of other governments' policies, Hitler and the nation which followed him still bear, not the sole, but the primary responsibility for the war which began in 1939 and which, before Hitler was prepared to admit defeat, cost the lives of more than 25 million human beings in Europe alone.

Notes

[1] In *The Origins of the Second World War* (rev. ed. 1963). See also the article by T. W. Mason, 'Some Origins of the Second World War', in *Past and Present*, no. 29 (Dec 1964) (Paper 5) and Mr Taylor's reply in the same journal, no. 30 (April 1965) (Paper 6). For a German view of Mr Taylor's book, see the review article by Gottard Jasper in *Vierteljahrshefte für Zeitgeschichte* (July 1962) 311–40.

[2] This view is well stated by Professor H. R. Trevor-Roper in an article 'Hitlers Kriegsziele', ibid. (April 1962).

[3] Written in 1928 but not published until 1961. An English translation has been published by Grove Press Inc., N.Y., *Hitler's Secret Book*. This book is almost entirely concerned with foreign policy.

[4] An English version, *Hitler's Table Talk 1941–44*, was published in 1953, with an introduction by H. R. Trevor-Roper.

[5] *The Testament of Adolf Hitler. The Hitler–Bormann Documents* (London, 1961).

[6] For this view, see Taylor, *Origins of the Second World War*.

[7] 14 Mar 1963, in a speech at Munich. For the context, cf. Max Domerus, *Hitler, Reden und Proklamationen*, 1 (Würzburg, 1962) p. 606.

[8] General Liebmann's note of Hitler's speech on this occasion is reprinted in *Vierteljahrshefte für Zeitgeschichte* (Oct 1954) 434–5. Cf. K. D. Bracher, W. Sauer and G. Schulz, *Die nationalsozialistische Machtergreifung* (Cologne, 1962) p. 748, and Robert J. O'Neill, *The German Army and the Nazi Party, 1933–1939* (London, 1966) pp. 125–6.

[9] A report of Hitler's speech on this occasion, made by Field-Marshal von Weichs, is printed by O'Neill, ibid., pp. 39–42. For further discussion of the reliability of this report see Bracher, Sauer and Schulz, *Die nationalsozialistische Machtergreifung*, p. 749, n. 14.

[10] Hermann Rauschning, *Hitler Speaks* (London, 1939) p. 116.

[11] A critical review of Hitler's foreign policy in these years is made by K. D. Bracher in *Vierteljahrshefte für Zeitgeschichte* (Jan 1957) 63–76: 'Das Anfangsstadium der Hitlerschen Aussenpolitik'.

[12] I am indebted in this section to Dr H. A. Jacobsen, who allowed me to see a forthcoming article: 'Programm und Struktur der nationalsozialistischen Aussenpolitik 1919–1939'.

[13] *Documents on German Foreign Policy*, series C, III, no. 509.

[14] Mussolini's visit to Germany took place in the last ten days of Sept 1937 and left an indelible impression on the Italian dictator. A few weeks later, in Nov 1937, Mussolini agreed to sign the Anti-Comintern Pact, a further step in committing himself to an alliance with Hitler.

[15] It is printed in *DGFP*, series C, v, no. 490. Cf. Gerhard Meinck, *Hitler und die deutsche Aufrüstung* (Wiesbaden, 1959) p. 164. Meinck's book is a valuable guide to the problems connected with German rearmament. Reference should also be made to Georg Tessin, *Formationsgeschichte der Wehrmacht 1933–39*, Schriften des Bundesarchivs, Bd 7 (Boppard am Rhein, 1959). A convenient summary is provided by O'Neill, *The German Army and the Nazi Party*, ch. 6.

[16] The evidence has been admirably summarised and reviewed by Alan S. Milward in *The German Economy at War* (London, 1965). Further details are to be found in Burton H. Klein, *Germany's Economic Preparation for War* (Cambridge, Mass., 1959).

[17] Klein, *Germany's Economic Preparations for War*, pp. 191–5; Milward, *The German Economy at War*, pp. 43–5.

[18] Reprinted in the English translation of Walter Hubatsch's *Hitlers Weisungen, Hitler's War Directives, 1939–45*, ed. H. R. Trevor-Roper (London, 1964) pp. 82–5.

[19] Text in *DGFP*, series D, I, no. 19. Cf. also Friedrich

Hossbach, *Zwischen Wehrmacht und Hitler* (Hanover, 1949) pp. 207–20.

[20] Speech at Augsburg, 21 Nov 1937: Domerus, *Hitler, Reden und Proklamationen*, I (1932–45), 759–60.

[21] *DGFP*, series D, II, oo. 133. Cf. also series D, VII, pp. 635–7.

[22] Ibid., II, no. 221.

[23] Ibid., II, no. 107.

[24] For the strength of the Czech forces, see David Vital, 'Czechoslovakia and the Powers', *Journal of Contemporary History*, I iv (Oct 1966).

[25] Taylor, *Origins of the Second World War*, ch. 10.

[26] International Military Tribunal Document C-120. Cf. also Walter Warlimont, *Inside Hitler's Headquarters* (London, 1964) p. 20.

[27] O'Neill, *The German Army and the Nazi Party*, ch. 6.

[28] It is noticeable that there were far fewer doubts in the army in 1939 than in 1938 – and the major reason for this (apart from the fact that a war with Poland fitted in far better with the generals' traditionalist ideas than one with Czechoslovakia) was their belief that a war in 1939 involved fewer risks than in 1938.

[29] See G. L. Weinberg, *Germany and the Soviet Union 1939–41* (The Hague, 1954).

[30] See Robert L. Koehl, *RKFDV, German Resettlement and Population Policy 1939–45* (Cambridge, Mass., 1957), and Alexander Dallin, *German Rule in Russia, 1941–45* (London, 1957).

The Secret Laval–Mussolini Agreement of 1935 on
Ethiopia

D. C. Watt

On 5 January 1935 the French foreign minister, Pierre
Laval, and the Italian dictator, Mussolini, met in
Rome. Two days later, on 7 January 1935, the two men
concluded eight separate agreements. Four of these
were published:[1] a general declaration; a treaty regu-
lating Franco-Italian conflicts of interest in Africa; a
special protocol on the status of the Italian minority in
French-occupied Tunisia; and a *procès-verbal* proposing a collective non-aggression pact of all the states in
Europe bordering on the Republic of Austria, then
gravely threatened by Nazi Germany. The contents of
the other four agreements, which were kept secret, purported to be covered by a communique issued the same
day.[2] On three of these four agreements, the communique was, to say the least, misleading. They com-
prised a protocol providing for joint consultation in
the event of Nazi Germany denouncing the restrictions
still imposed on her by the 1919 Treaty of Versailles; a
protocol protecting the status quo at the mouth of the
Red Sea; and two exchanges of letters, proclaiming
French disinterest in the economic sphere in Ethiopia,
and promising Italian capital participation in the
share capital of the Addis Ababa–Jibuti railroad, the
one avenue for Ethiopian trade with the outside
world.[3]

Around these last two agreements and the private

Reprinted from *The Middle East Journal*, 15 (winter, 1961), by permission of Mr Watt and *The Middle
East Journal*. See also Introduction, pp. 19–20.

conversations between the two men which accompanied them, mythology has clustered ever since their signature. They marked the first, or rather the second stage in the Italian attack on Ethiopia, and the last major part of a sinister deal between an unscrupulous and self-seeking politician, Laval, and the personification of Fascism in Mussolini. Since 1945, historians have been aware from the evidence produced at the treason trials of Laval and Marshal Pétain in France that the agreements were more complicated than that. The main intention of Laval in concluding the agreements was to bind Mussolini into an alliance in all but name against the renascent power of Nazi Germany. But somehow the stigma of underhand dealing which surrounded the agreements has never been quite cleared away, and the actual texts of the agreements remained unknown.

The Franco-Italian agreements concluded on 7 January 1935 are best understood as an illustration of the interplay, visible even in the classic period of European imperialism, between European and 'colonial' considerations. In this barter of interest for interest without even any pretence of a relation to the views of the local inhabitants, they mark perhaps the last major example of classical imperialism in action in the Middle East. While France's position was secure in Europe, between 1920 and 1933, colonial and naval rivalries had embittered Franco-Italian relations. Conversations had several times been initiated to end the actual causes of friction between the two countries in Africa, but they had always ended in renewed discord, since the real issue between the two countries was one of prestige, of Italy's claim to the status of a Great Power, sharing the primacy of Europe with France – a claim the French either dismissed contemptuously or chose to take as a personal insult. But the advent of Hitler to power in Germany and still more the Nazi threat to Austria which culminated in June 1934 with the attempt to take over Austria by *Putsch* and the murder of the Austrian chancellor, Dolfuss, threatened both countries equally. France had every incentive to reach an agreement with Italy; while as for Mussolini, it seems to have fired him with his first ideas of reaching his long-standing aims in Ethiopia.

The recently published diaries of Baron Pompeo Aloisi,[4] Mussolini's under-secretary of state for League of Nations affairs, throw a good deal of light on the origins of the agreements. From these, it appears that the idea of a French visit to Rome, and a general all-round settlement of Franco-Italian differences, was mooted before Laval's appointment as French foreign minister in October 1934, by his predecessor, Barthou, so tragically assassinated in Marseilles by a Croat terrorist. Barthou is recorded as mentioning such a plan in May and June 1934; it was at the same time that Mussolini first began his preparations for stirring up trouble in Ethiopia. On 30 June 1934 Aloisi noted:

> Conversation with the explorer Franchetti, who told of his last meeting with the Duce and how the Duce had engaged him to arrange at once the policy of acting on Abyssinia's frontiers. ... I said that ... in my opinion without a serious preparation in Europe one could not undertake anything in Abyssinia without leading to a disaster. He confided that when de Bono[5] goes with the King to Eritrea in October he will stay as Inspector-General of the Colonies.

The visit continued to be discussed throughout the summer. To judge from Aloisi's diary notes the Italians were insisting on negotiation on the various points at issue in Africa before Barthou's visit could take place. After the September meeting of the League Council, however, the Italian position weakened, largely because the Austrian question and difficulties made by Yugoslav enmity for Italy came to the forefront of Franco-Italian negotiations. On 1 October Aloisi noted:

> I informed Suvich[6] of our international position in Geneva and we recognised that it is necessary to arrive at once at an entente with France and to make

Barthou come to Rome. Then we spoke of rumours of wars in Abyssinia and said that nothing could be done without adequate international preparation. He said that the Duce had counted on this for two years, that is why it is very possible it will never take place.

From this point one can follow the negotiations from the French side in the contemporary notes[7] of Edward Herriot, the Radical Socialist leader, then in the Flandin Cabinet. On 15 November Laval read to the French Cabinet the instructions he was sending to Chambrun, the French ambassador in Rome, for the coming negotiations. The instructions covered the provision of a consultative pact in the event of a German decision to free herself from the Versailles restrictions on her rearmament, a general non-intervention agreement on Austria and the provision of an 'Economic Statute' for Central Europe. On Africa, Laval noted that the Italians were demanding the abandonment of the French Somali Coast Colony except for Jibuti. Herriot's notes continue:

In reality Italy seems likely to content herself with less; she is interested above all in the railway line, on the subject of which there exists an arrangement of 1906.[8] The danger which has appeared since then, is the question of Ethiopian independence. If these matters are settled, a declaration of Franco-Italian friendship will be drawn up and signed. The two countries will engage themselves to defend together their general interests, without concluding a treaty of alliance.

As Laval realised, the African question was to prove much less sticky than the question of Italian hostility towards Yugoslavia and vice versa, the repercussions this had on the question of a general agreement on non-intervention in Austria. Laval said as much to the French Cabinet on 20 December and again on 2

January, the day he actually left for Rome. Aloisi's
diary makes it clear that the negotiations might very
well have broken down had Mussolini not been determined on an agreement 'at all costs'. In the event, both
men were forced to abandon some of their demands,
and to postpone some questions for further negotiation, notably that of Italy's demand for all of the
French Somali Coast Colony.

What then did the two signatories obtain from the
treaty that each set such high value on it? Laval obtained in the protocol on disarmament a direct Italian
promise of Italian support and consultation should
Germany denounce the armament clauses of Versailles.
But he obtained in private more than this. He obtained Mussolini's agreement to Franco-Italian staff
talks envisaging joint military action in the event of a
German attack upon either France or Austria. And
staff agreements involving the appearance of a French
army corps in the Italian order of battle, an Italian
corps on the Franco-Swiss frontier and Italian air bases
in southern France were concluded between the
French and Italian air ministries, and between General Gamelin and Marshal Badoglio in June 1935.

In return, Mussolini obtained a clear statement of
French 'disinterest' in Ethiopia. Compared with this
all the other provisions of the agreements were of
minor importance. The questions of Tunis and of the
frontiers between Eritrea and the French Somali Coast
were, it is true, long-standing Italian grievances. But
the Italian failure in Ethiopia was felt far more deeply.
After the defeat of Adowa, itself a national humiliation, Italians believed that Britain and France alter-
nately had intrigued with the Ethiopians to defeat
Italy's ambitions and exclude her from a position of
predominance in Ethiopia. Suvich's remarks to Aloisi,
and the note in Aloisi's diary of 23 January 1935:

> The importance of the day was in the decision
> taken by the Duce on the subject of Abyssinia, which
> appears irrevocable and which we must study.
> Wherefore meetings with Suvich who reads me the

Duce's project, in my opinion it is a decision which puts at stake the future of the regime....

make it clear that the Duce can have had no motive other than Ethiopia in his mind in making the agreement. If further proof were wanted, it would lie in the Italian initiative in London on 29 January, six days later, inviting the British government to exchange ideas on 'these respective interests in Ethiopia ... with the aim of examining the possibility of the development of those interests in a manner mutually agreeable to both parties'; a mission which left the British Foreign Office in no doubt that the Italians' 'ultimate end' was not an

economic predominance pure and simple but ... the virtual absorption of whatever part of Ethiopian territory can be secured without prejudice to Italian interests and influence in other parts of the world.[9]

The question that remains unanswered in these documents is how far Laval realised and deliberately condoned Mussolini's ambitions. His enemies have advanced the theory that Laval by some wink or nod in his private conversation with Mussolini led him to understand that France would not oppose an open Italian attack on Ethiopia. Mussolini himself alleged this to Eden in June 1935, when Eden came to Rome to propose the establishment of an Italian protectorate in the non-Amharic south of Ethiopia in return for an Ethiopian opening to the sea through British Somaliland. But he did it in such terms that a misunderstanding is not altogether ruled out. Eden reported him remarking:

Since he had yielded to France 100,000 Italians in Tunis and had received in return half a dozen pine-trees in one place, and a strip of desert which did not contain a sheep in another, it must be clear that he had understood that France had disinterested herself in Abyssinia. I contested this, telling Signor Mussolini that when M. Laval had described in Geneva his interview with Signor Mussolini, he had insisted that France had only given a free hand to Italy in economic matters and that he had added to Signor Mussolini 'vous avez des mains fortes. Faites attention,' making it clear that French goodwill did not apply to other than economic enterprise. At this Signor Mussolini flung himself back with a gesture of incredulous astonishment.[10]

At Pétain's trial after the war Laval repeated this description in slightly different terms, but insisting nevertheless that he had warned Mussolini not to abuse the free hand France had given him by resorting to force, 'Imitate,' he alleged he had counselled Mussolini, 'the example of Marshal Lyautey.'[11]

The Count de Chambrun, who attended the meetings between the two men as French ambassador in Rome, throws some light on the matter in the detailed account given of Laval's visit to Rome in his memoirs.[12] According to his account, direct talks between the two men only took place on 5 and 6 January. The first day was taken up with an exchange of views in which Laval insisted right from the start on very substantial Italian concessions in Tunis. Mussolini showed himself most conciliatory on this; on Ethiopia he remarked that he sought only, 'an outlet for the economic activity of an over-populated Italy'.

The second day was devoted to discussing the draft agreements. Here the lead was taken in voicing Italian objections by the Italian under-secretary of state, Fulvio Suvich. Laval's reply was 'most direct and decisive'; he pleaded a decision by the French Cabinet which made further concession impossible. Equally bitter discussion followed on the clauses dealing with the Italian schools in Tunis. No part was taken in this by Mussolini. But, continues M. de Chambrun,

the terms in which M. Laval spoke of the cessation of French economic activity in the regions of Ethiopia

other than the Hinterland of French Somalia and
the railway zone, made a visible impression on Mussolini and effectively prepared the entente which
established itself in the evening following long discussions between MM. Léger, de Saint-Quentin and
Cherguerand on the one hand, and M. Suvich and
the Italian experts on the other.

Herriot's notes shed a little light on the discussion in
the French Cabinet. On 10 January, when Laval submitted the agreements for approval, he noted:

> we take note ... and Laval does not deny that this
> agreement on Abyssinia is alarming for the future.
> Laval qualifies the agreements reached as holding
> promise (*prometteurs*).

And again on 12 January: 'we abandon Ethiopia
whom we have introduced into the League. I am not
resigned.'

Léger himself was always inclined to believe that
Laval had given Mussolini some kind of silent assent.
Chambrun by contrast maintained that the two men
were never sufficiently alone for such a private understanding to have been possible. A little light is shed on
the question by an Italian Foreign Office report
drafted at the end of 1935, summarising the political
developments in France in that year.[13] The vital passage reads as follows:

> The fate of Ethiopia and of all the French posi-
> tion on the question of East Africa was *virtually*
> already decided at the end of the Mussolini–Laval
> talks at Rome. With the draft of the letter of
> January[14] and *Laval's verbal assurances*, the French
> government was bound to accord Italy a free hand
> for the satisfaction of her needs of expansion in East
> Africa and for the settlement once and for all of any
> questions with the Abyssinian government.

At first sight this evidence seems conclusive. But the

report needs to be interpreted with care in the light of the word 'virtually'; as the entry earlier cited from Aloisi's diary shows, the political decision to go ahead in Ethiopia was not taken until after Laval's 'assurances' had been given.[15] It was only in June, according to the same report, that Mussolini revealed to Laval his pet scheme for annexing the Galla and Danaqil-speaking areas of Ethiopia, and proclaiming a protectorate over the central Amharic-speaking plateau. Clearly Mussolini had been contemplating some action against Ethiopia for some time. Equally clearly Laval, conscious of the advantage to France of Italian support in Europe, was not the man to discourage him; but discourage him from doing what? If in June Mussolini was thinking of dismembering rather than annexing Ethiopia, his plans were probably a great deal less concrete or coherent in January. The extension of Italian influence, Italian predominance in the zones recognised as appertaining to Italy's zone of interests by the 1906 treaty, an end to Ethiopian evasions of her treaty obligations; he can hardly have· spoken to Laval in terms more concrete than these. There is room for a good deal of misunderstanding here. One is led even to wonder if the question was not tacitly left in that grey and cloudy limbo where one assumes one has been understood for fear that direct inquiry may show that one has not.

In any case the question presented itself to Laval in a very different light from that in which his detractors have always seen it. Whatever Mussolini did, so he must have thought, French interests were safeguarded. In return he was obtaining an ally against Germany in Europe, an end to Franco-Italian rivalry in the Mediterranean, possibly even in the Balkans. Like Mussolini he had not much time for the League of Nations except as a kind of twentieth-century Congress System, where the Great Powers could meet to their mutual understanding and benefit. Moreover France had never had much difficulty in managing the League in the past. He seems in fact less the sinister Machiavellian conspirator of mythology, than silly and short-sighted; a clever man overreaching himself, striving to catch a favourable constellation of forces, without realising their essential incompatibility. No one but a very self-confident and short-sighted man could have believed that British opinion could be reconciled to a major Italian economic expansion in Ethiopia, or that this was all Mussolini wanted, or that it could have been achieved without the use of force in view of Ethiopian suspicion of Italy. It would have been equally silly to imagine that British opinion could be reconciled to the use of force or pressure of any kind capable of being represented as incompatible with the Covenant of the League, or that Mussolini could be controlled once his actions had begun to attract international censure. Whether he did, or did not, tip the wink, his judgement either way appears to have been faulty to the point of ruining his own schemes and causing his exclusion from power until the hour of France's disaster. He forgot, or took a chance on, public opinion; not until the end of 1935 could he begin to hint in public at what he felt he had gained from the January agreement. His full defence only came in the hour of France's defeat, in his speech to the Senate of 10 July 1940.[16] Even then the Senate was in secret session. The agreements of January 1935 were in fact the agreements of dupes. Neither signatory could deliver on his concessions, neither could cash in his gains unopposed. At least Mussolini got Ethiopia. Laval lost all, including, ultimately, office. Mussolini's hatred for France thereafter drove him headlong into the arms of Germany.

Annex

I

Alexis Léger to Senator Henri Berenger[1]

RÉPUBLIQUE FRANÇAISE
Paris, 16 Jan 1935[2]
Ministry
of Foreign Affairs
Administration of
political and commercial affairs

EUROPE

Dear President and Colleague

I have the honour to communicate to you by the enclosure, for your personal and confidential information, a copy of the various agreements signed at Rome on the 7th of this month.

I believe that I should particularly draw your attention to the rigorously secret character of the Protocol on armaments, the Protocol annexed to the Treaty between France and Italy relating to the regulation of their interests in Africa, and of the exchange of letters relating to Abyssinia and to the Jibuti–Addis Ababa railway. /.

Please accept, dear President and Colleague, the assurances of my highest consideration,

M. Henry BERENGER
Senator
Ambassador of France
President of the Committee of Foreign Affairs
  of the Senate
Palais du Luxembourg

PARIS

> For the Minister of Foreign Affairs
> and by delegation
> AMBASSADOR OF FRANCE
> SECRETARY-GENERAL
>   Alexis Léger
>   M003178

II

Protocol on Disarmament

PROTOCOL

The Minister of Foreign Affairs of the French Republic and the Head of the Italian Government declare that they are agreed in the view that Germany cannot, any more than any other Power whose level of armament is defined by treaty, modify by unilateral action her obligations in the matter of armaments, the principle of equality of rights as defined in the Declaration of 11 December 1932[3] remaining generally intact. As a result, the two Governments agree to act as follows:

In the event of Germany wishing to free herself unilaterally from the treaty and reserving to herself complete freedom to rearm, the two Governments, animated by the desire to act by common agreement, will consult together on the attitude to be adopted.

In the event of circumstances permitting a resumption of international negotiations with a view to the conclusion of a general Disarmament agreement, the two Governments will concert their efforts so that the figures of limitation inscribed in the agreement will ensure the two countries, in relation to Germany, the advantages which will be justified for each of them.[4]

Done in duplicate,

Rome, 7 January 1935

(signed)   PIERRE LAVAL   MUSSOLINI

M003183

III

Protocol Additional to the Treaty on Africa

PROTOCOL ANNEXED TO THE TREATY BETWEEN FRANCE AND ITALY RELATING TO THE REGULATION OF THEIR INTERESTS IN AFRICA[5]

The Italian Government, anxious, as is the French Government, to ensure the free passage of the Straits of Bab el Mandeb, binds itself to maintain in their present state, in so far as fortifications and strategic works are concerned, the coastal zone of the territory mentioned in Article 4[6] of the Treaty to which the present Protocol is annexed, as also the islands and islets mentioned in Article 8[7] of the said Treaty.

Done at Rome in duplicate,

7 January 1935

(signed)   Pierre LAVAL   MUSSOLINI

M003188

IV

Mussolini to Laval

SECRET   Rome, 7 January 1935

Dear President

I have the honour to acknowledge the receipt from Your Excellency of a letter of today's date in the following terms:

'I have the honour to make to Your Excellency the following communication:

'After an examination of the situation of Italy and France in East Africa, particularly so far as the interests of Eritrea and Italian Somaliland, on the one hand, and of the French Somali Coast, on the other hand, are concerned, and in the desire to practise the policy of amicable collaboration which the two Governments pursue in the region of their African possessions, the French Government declares to the Italian Government that, on the application of the arrange-

Agreement of 13 December 1905[8] [sic], and all the agreements mentioned in Article 1 of the aforesaid Treaty, the French Government does not look in Abyssinia for satisfaction of any interests other than those economic interests relating to the traffic of the Jibuti–Addis Ababa railway in the zone defined in the annex thereto. Nevertheless, the French Government does not by this renounce the rights which its subjects and protected persons enjoy under the Franco-Abyssinian Treaty of 10 January 1908,[9] nor the concessions which it has obtained over parts of Abyssinia situated outside the zone mentioned above, nor the renewal of the aforesaid concessions.

'The French Government would esteem it highly should the Italian Government be willing to confirm its agreement on the above and bind itself to respect the rights and interests defined above, in so far as it is concerned.'

The Italian Government, confirming its own agreement on the above, takes note of the declaration made by the French Government on the application of the Agreement of 13 December 1906[8] and of all the agreements cited in Article 1 of the said Agreement; and it binds itself to respect those economic interests relating to the traffic of the Jibuti–Addis Ababa railway in the zone defined in the annex thereto, as also the rights of the French citizens, ...[10] colonists and protected persons mentioned in Your Excellency's communication.

Accept, Mr President, the expression of my highest consideration,

(S)   MUSSOLINI
M003191, 193

Mussolini to Laval

SECRET   Rome, 7 January 1935

Mr President

I have the honour to acknowledge the receipt from Your Excellency of a letter of today's date in the following terms:

'I have the honour to inform Your Excellency that
the French Government, desirous of facilitating a more
intimate collaboration of French and Italian interests
in the railway from Jibuti to Addis Ababa, is assured
that the French group of the Company holding the
concession for this line will cede two thousand five
hundred shares to an Italian group.

'In the same spirit, the French Government will
proffer its good offices with a view to enlarging the
Italian representation on the directorial boards of the
said Company."

I have the honour to take note of Your Excellency's
most courteous communication.

Accept, Mr President, the expression of my highest
consideration.

(S)   MUSSOLINI
M003192

Notes

[1] For the texts of these agreements, see *British
Foreign and State Papers*, CXXXIX 946–8, 948–50, 950–1.

[2] The communique is published in *Documents on
International Affairs, 1935*, I 18.

[3] The copies here printed in translation are taken
from photostats of the copies found by German
Foreign Office researchers in 1940, in the files of the
Committee on Foreign Affairs of the French Senate, to
whom they were sent by the French Foreign Office for
information. They were incidentally very badly copied
by the typists of the French Foreign Office, the Italian
texts being full of misspelling, grammatical errors,
typos, etc. These photostats were sent back to the German Foreign Office and placed to complete the record
in this file, closed in 1935, which dealt with the Laval–
Mussolini meeting. The originals are now again in the
custody of the German Foreign Office in Bonn, but
photostats were made by the Allied historians who
screened them for publication after their capture in
1945. They are filmed on serial M90, frames M003175–
93.

[4] Baron Pompeo Alsoisi, *Journal* (*25 Juillet 1932–14 Juin 1936*), ed. Mario Toscano (Paris, 1957).

[5] Marshal de Bono, subsequently in command of Italian forces operating in Ethiopia. See his *Anno XIII, the Conquest of an Empire* (London, 1937).

[6] Fulvio Suvich, Italian under-secretary for foreign affairs.

[7] See Edouard Herriot, *Jadis*, II (Paris, 1952).

[8] The reference is to the tripartite Anglo-French-Italian agreement of 13 Dec 1906 respecting Ethiopia. For the text, see *BFSP* XCIX 486–9. From the Italian point of view the vital provision of the agreement was article IV, which divided Ethiopia into spheres of influence, alloting to Britain the headwaters of the Nile and its tributaries, to France the hinterland of the French Somali Coast protectorate and 'the zone necessary for the construction and working of the railway from Jibuti to Addis Ababa', and to Italy the hinterland of her possessions 'in Erythrea [*sic*] and Somaliland' and 'the territorial connection between them to the west of Addis Ababa'. This arrangement was only to take place in the event of a disturbance in the status quo in Ethiopia, which the three Powers pledged themselves to uphold. The British government denounced this agreement in 1923, but it remained binding on France and Italy. There is a very considerable documentation in French and Italian on this agreement. See *Documents diplomatiques français*, 2nd series, VI, VII and VIII *passim*. For the most recent Italian discussion, see Carlo Giglio, 'La Questione del lago Tana (1902–1941)', in *Rivista di Studi Politici Internazionali*, XVIII iv (Oct–Dec 1951) 643–86; this is extensively footnoted. The only British reference is in *British Documents on the Origins of the War, 1898–1914*, VIII, no. 9.

[9] The quotations are from a Foreign Office letter of 6 March 1935, itself quoted in the report of the interdepartmental committee set up in March 1935 under the chairmanship of Sir John Maffey to report on British interests in Ethiopia. The report, dated 18 June 1935, fell into Italian hands and was published in

Italian translation in the *Giornale d'Italia*, 20 Feb 1936.

[10] Eden's report is quoted in Viscount Templewood, *Nine Troubled Years* (London, 1953) pp. 155–6.

[11] For Laval's evidence, see *Le Procès Pétain*, ed. G. London (Lyon, n.d., 1946) p. 439.

[12] Charles de Chambrun, *Traditions et Souvenirs* (Paris, 1952) pp. 192–7.

[13] The vital extracts have been published from the microfilm of the original now in the American National Archives by William C. Askew, 'The Secret Agreement between France and Italy on Ethiopia, January 1935', *Journal of Modern History*, xxv i (March 1953) 47–8.

[14] Document IV in the Annex.

[15] Marshal de Bono gives the date 20 Dec 1934 in his memoirs (*Anno XIII*, p. 116), but in the light of Aloisi's categorical statement in his diary (entry of 27 Jan 1935, *Journal*), and the instructions that de Bono himself took with him when he sailed for Eritrea on 7 Jan 1935 (*Anno XIII*, pp. 57–8), we must assume this to refer to the military rather than the political side of action against Ethiopia.

[16] The full record of the secret session of the French Senate of 10 July 1940 is printed in *Les Événements survenues en France, 1936–1940* (Paris, 1947) *Rapport*, pp. 488 ff.

Notes to the Annex

[1] The original of this document carried the following handwritten marginal notes:

(*a*) At the head of the document in the top right-hand corner, in German: Original is to be found with the files of the Archive Commission, Prince Bismarck Street 2 under the file serial, Special Section Krummer, Number 969 of 22.10.40.

(*b*) Below the date-line in two different hands, both

in French: (i) Agreements of Rome, (ii) Italy. Personal and confidential.

In the original: 'Original bei den Akten Archivkommission Furst Bismarckstr[asse] 2 unter den Aktenzeichen Sonderreferat Krummer Nr 969 v[on] 22.10.40.'

'Accords de Rome.'

'Italie.'

'Personnel et confidentiel.'

[2] The date and M. Léger's titles are rubberstamped on to the document.

[3] For the text of the declaration, see *Documents on German Foreign Policy, 1918–1945*, series C, I, editors' note pp. 18–20.

[4] The official communique on this merely said that the two governments agreed 'that no country could modify by unilateral action its obligations in the sphere of armaments, and that if such an eventuality should materialise, they would consult together'. Suvich subsequently denied to the German ambassador in Rome that this document made any specific reference to Germany: *DGFP*, series C, III, no. 417.

[5] For the French text of this treaty, see *BGFP* cxxxix 948–50.

[6] Article 4 redefined the frontier between Eritrea and the French Somali Coast established in the Franco-Italian agreements of 24 Jan 1900 and 10 July 1901 somewhat in Italy's favour.

[7] Article 8 recognised Italian sovereignty over the island of Dumeira and its adjacent and nameless islets.

[8] For the tripartite Anglo-Franco-Italian agreement of 13 Dec 1906, see *BFSP* xcix 486–9.

[9] For the Franco-Ethiopian Treaty of 10 Jan 1908, see *BFSP* ci 997–1000. The treaty bound the Ethiopian government to keep open for trade the route to Jibuti, and to allow French subjects and protected persons full liberty of entry into, trade in and service for the Ethiopian state.

[10] Here a word is illegible; possibly it has been exed out and is merely a typing error.

11 Japanese Imperialism and Aggression: Reconsiderations, II

Akira Iriye

Taiheiyō sensō e no michi: kaisen gaikō-shi [*The Road to the Pacific War: A Diplomatic History before the War*], edited by Nihon Kokusai Seiji Gakkai Taiheiyo Sensō Gen'in Kenkyūbu [The Japan Association of International Relations, the Committee to Study the Origins of the Pacific War] (Tokyo: Asahi Shimbun Sha, 1962–3):

Vol. I: *Manshū jihen zen'ya* [*The Eve of the Manchurian Incident*] xii, 498. Appendixes, Index. 650 yen.

Vol. II: *Manshū jihen* [*The Manchurian Incident*] viii, 435. Appendixes, Index. 650 yen.

Vol. III: *Nit-Chū sensō: jō* [*The Sino-Japanese War:* I] x, 404. Appendixes, Index. 650 yen.

Vol. IV: *Nit-Chū sensō: ge* [*The Sino-Japanese War:* II] viii, 426. Appendixes, Index. 650 yen.

Vol. V: *Sangoku dōmei, Nis-So chūritsu jyōyaku* [*The Axis Alliance, the Japanese–Soviet Neutrality Treaty*] vi, 393. Appendixes, Index. 650 yen.

Vol. VI: *Nampō shinshutsu* [*The Southward Advance*] x, 437. Appendixes, Index. 650 yen.

Vol. VII: *Nichi-Bei kaisen* [*The Outbreak of War between Japan and the United States*] x, 493. Appendixes, Index. 650 yen.

Reprinted from *The Journal of Asian Studies*, 23 (1963–4), by permission of the author and *The Journal of Asian Studies*. See also Introduction, pp. 20–1 and 27.

Review Editor's Note: In the last issue, *The Journal of Asian Studies* initiated a two-part review of samples of recent scholarship related to history and 'revisionism'. In the August issue, the argument of the review article centred on a book by an American scholar and Korean scholarly reaction; in this issue attention is turned to a series by Japanese scholars. In both cases, revisionist scholarship became the main topic of discussion in the Columbia University Seminar on Modern East Asia: Japan, which meets monthly in New York. During the discussions, Professor George Totten served as chairman of the Seminar; Don Thurston as rapporteur; and Dr Akira Iriye, who prepared the second review article, as member and speaker.

Here, at last, we have a multi-volume history of Japan's road to Pearl Harbor, written by Japanese historians after years of research. With this publication the days of almost sole dependence on Western works on the subject may be said to have come to an end.

Eighteen years after the war, Japanese historians seem to have gained a sense of confidence and perspective to venture on an ambitious project of writing a history of the pre-Pacific war period. Timing seems to have been opportune. Among Western scholars, there has been strong interest in re-examining the pre-war decade through Japanese sources. Writings by Professors Robert Butow, David Lu and James Crowley, among others, have attempted to dispute certain standard views of Japan's foreign relations, first popularised by the Far Eastern Military Tribunal and developed by Feis, Langer and Gleason, Jones, Storry and other historians. It was bound to happen, then, that Japanese scholars would try to liberate themselves from foreign writings and study the period on their own initiative.

There have, of course, been numerous other works by Japanese on the subject. But most of them have either been biographical writings or general accounts based on them, on Western publications or on questionable theories. Some biographical writings, such as the official biographies of Okada and Konoe, are well documented and useful, while some others, such as reminiscences by Morishima, Imamura and Hanaya are undocumented but filled with pertinent information.[1] All of them, however, necessarily present data from particular persons' points of view, and they need rigorous cross-checking, a task so many general histories of the period have failed to do. Japanese scholars, moreover, have primarily been interested in studying the road to war in terms of domestic affairs, as an unfolding drama of Japanese militarism, fascism, imperialism or emperor-absolutism, rather than in terms of an interaction between Japanese policies and those of foreign governments.[2] Scholars who have attempted this have tended simply to reiterate the findings of Western historians, orthodox and revisionist.[3]

It was only recently that there began to appear serious and informative monographs on Japanese foreign relations in general and during the 1930s in particular. Young scholars have been devouring unpublished documents and personal papers. Senior diplomatic historians never enjoyed such an opportunity before and during the war, and their works consequently tended to be legalistic analyses of given events or translations from Western sources. It is not surprising, then, that the most active students in the field have been a new crop of historians, deeply impressed with the works of their Western counterparts and eager to do their part to find out what actually happened. In 1955 Professor Hosoya Chihiro's study of the Siberian expedition heralded the coming of age of these historians, and in the same year Dr Kurihara Ken's documentary history of Showa diplomacy opened the door for serious research.[4] Since then young scholars such as Ōhata Tokushirō of Waseda and Seki Hiroharu of Tokyo University, and non-professional historians such as Usui Katsumi and Uno Shigeaki of the Foreign Ministry and Hata Ikuhiko of the Finance Ministry have turned out an impressive volume of monographs on pre-war diplomacy. It is difficult to characterise

their writings as revisionist, simply because there was
no standard history to be revised to begin with. It
would be more correct to say that they have endeav-
oured to accumulate basic data from which interpretations could be drawn. They have been interested in
questioning every point of fact which has been assumed by earlier writers.

The present publication draws on these works and
considerably expands them. The fourteen authors, representing the post-war generation of diplomatic historians, spent five years collecting data and writing out
their findings. Their investigation led them all over
Japan in search of private papers and in order to interview men active in the 1930s. They read not only
Foreign Ministry archival materials, which have begun
to be used by Western historians, but also archives of
the former military agencies as well as the Ministry of
Justice. The result of their labour is highly impressive.

The seven volumes are divided into nineteen parts
as follows:

Vol. i:

1. Naval Affairs (1921–36), by Kobayashi Tatsuo
2. Japanese Policy towards the Soviet Union (1917–
   27), by Kobayashi Yukio
3. The Manchurian Crisis (1927–31), by Seki Hiroharu

Vol. ii:

1. The Development of the Manchurian Crisis (1931
   –2), by Shimada Toshihiko
2. China's Response (1926–32), by Uno Shigeaki
3. Soviet Russia's Response (1926–33), by Hirai
   Tomoyoshi
4. The Responses of the United States, Britain and
   the League of Nations (1931–3), by Saito Takashi

Vol. III:

1. Sino-Japanese Relations (1933–7), by Shimada Toshihiko
1. China's Foreign Policy (1933–9), by Uno Shigeaki

Vol. IV:

1. The Sino-Japanese War (1937–41), by Hata Ikuhiko
2. Diplomatic Aspects of the Sino-Japanese War (1937–41), by Usui Katsumi
3. Soviet Russia's Response (1933–9), by Hirai Tomoyoshi

Vol. V:

1. The Anti-Comintern Pact (1935–9), by Ōhata Tokushirō
2. The Axis Alliance and the Soviet–Japanese Neutrality Pact (1939–41), by Hosoya Chihiro

Vol. VI:

1. Japanese Policy towards Southeast Asia (1937–41), by Nagaoka Shinjirō
2. The Southward Advance (1940–1), by Hata Ikuhiko
3. America's Response (1937–41), by Fukuda Shigeo

Vol. VII:

1. Japanese–American Relations (1940–1), by Tsunoda Jun
2. America's Response (1941), by Fukuda Shigeo

Compared with other multi-volume (*kōza*) publications in Japan, these nineteen parts are remarkably well knit and organised. Credit must be given to the editor, Tsunoda Jun, who must have taken pains to bring about more unity of style and coherence of con-

tent than is usually the case. Members of the project.
met from time to time to exchange ideas, and they
agreed to refrain from the use of terms such as militarism and imperialism. They did not intend to prove a
point, and they were intrinsically neither apologetic
for nor blindly critical of Japanese policy. These facts
account for the striking absence of contradictory information contained in these volumes. Even so, the
writers did not entirely succeed in integrating their
data and avoiding overlapping. The nineteen parts
can be divided between those dealing with Japan's
foreign policy and those discussing Japanese policies of
other Powers. The distinction is, however, at best
superficial and many identical stories are told twice.
Even with respect to the sections dealing with Japanese
policy, one wonders, as will be noted, if some of them
might not profitably have been combined to avoid
repetition.

Other complaints can be raised. Footnotes to cited
documents are often exceedingly simple, saying merely
'Foreign Ministry Archives' or 'Archives of the War
History Room'. The reader would wish for more pertinent information to locate some of these documents.
At one point an important document is mentioned
several times by name, but the author fails to describe
its content (III 112, 131, 207). One author, mentioning
another critical document, refers the reader to a documentary collection to obtain its content (IV 154). An
identical document is printed in full twice (V 204–5;
VII 60), but there are certain discrepancies in the texts.
Sometimes the authors fail to check Japanese statements against available foreign sources to ascertain
their accuracy. For instance, China's attitude towards
Britain in 1930 is deduced from two Japanese memoranda, but no attempt is made to study the published
British documents to see if the Japanese view was ten-
able (II 252).

These complaints are certainly outweighed by the
sense of gratitude one feels towards the authors for the
immense service they rendered in bringing out fresh
evidence. The parts dealing with foreign governments,

it is true, are on the whole less original than the rest, because of their primary dependence on Western works. Uno's discussion of Chinese policy, however, is extremely interesting. His main concern is with delineating factions in China and tracing their impact on Nationalist foreign policy. The Manchurian crisis, for instance, takes on a new meaning as the author relates it to the struggle for power between Chiang Kai-shek and Chang Hsüeh-liang. It is, nevertheless, the parts dealing with Japanese foreign policy which contribute most substantially to scholarship.

These parts may briefly be described with a view to highlighting some of their findings. In his discussion of naval affairs, Kobayashi Tatsuo makes it clear that during the upheaval following the London Naval Conference of 1939, Admiral Katō, chief of naval general staff, had initially acquiesced in the decision of the Navy Ministry to accept the Reed–Matsudaira compromise. Even after he changed his mind and decided to protest loudly against the treaty, he was opposed to the new naval ratio itself and not to the way it had beed decided upon. In other words, he did not dispute the Cabinet's right to determine the size of the armed forced. The alleged breach of the right of supreme command seems to have become a hot issue only when the opposition political party, the Seiyūkai, decided to take advantage of the naval discontent and embarrass the government.

Seki's discussion of the Manchurian crisis prior to 18 September 1931 is one of the most remarkable sections of this series. While historians have been vaguely aware of the complicity of the Tokyo supreme command in the Mukden plot, evidence for this has been limited to reminiscences by the participants written from memory. Now, thanks to research in the military archives and the papers of Ishiwara Kanji, the author succeeds in drawing a clear picture of personal ties between such key figures as Ishiwara, Nagata, Itagaki and Imamura. They seem to have been in close touch with one another after the mid-1920s and exchanged ideas about the future of Japan in Manchuria. Colonel

Nagata's role is for the first time fully delineated. As chief of the military administration section of the War Ministry after 1930, he was in a key position to devise means for an eventual control over Manchuria. By the fall of 1930 the general staff had drawn up a three-alternative plan for this purpose.

The first alternative was to press the Manchurian government of Chang Hsüeh-liang to concede further rights to Japan. If this proved ineffective, the second step, the replacement of Chang by a pro-Japanese régime, was to be carried out. When this failed, the final alternative was to resort to a military occupation of Manchuria. There is evidence that Nagata was in full accord with such a device and discussed it with Ishiwara's group when they met, in Mukden as well as in Tokyo. As Kwantung army officers proceeded with their plans, Nagata strove to bring his superiors to accept the inevitable in Manchuria. By the middle of 1931 they were willing to sanction drastic action in the spring of 1932. Actually, of course, the Kwantung army went ahead with its plans in September 1931, despite Tokyo's decision to postpone action until 1932. The mission of Major-General Tatekawa, sent from Tokyo to convey its decision, has remained obscure, but the present study shows not only that he revealed the nature of his mission to Hashimoto Kingorō of the general staff, so that the latter might forewarn the Ishiwara group of what was coming, but also that Tatekawa asked Okawa Shumei to send an emissary beforehand for the same purpose. Ishiwara, Itagaki and others were thus fully aware of the content of Tatekawa's message before his arrival, and after a heated discussion they decided to go ahead with their plot.

After the outbreak of the Mukden incident, there was a considerable discrepancy of views between the Kwantung army and the supreme command concerning the extent of action. Here the three-alternative plan, mentioned above, provided the basic framework of military thinking. Ishiwara had originally thought in terms of the third alternative, military occupation of Manchuria, but in time he was persuaded to take the second, namely establishment of a pro-Japanese régime. The military authorities in Tokyo, however, at first regarded action in Manchuria within the framework of the first alternative and sought to take advantage of it primarily in order to put an end to anti-Japanese trends in Manchurian policy. In his discussion of this episode, Shimada presents a most readable account of the irritation felt in both Tokyo and Manchuria over each other's lack of understanding. In order to curb the Kwantung army's northward advance, thereby inviting the danger of clash with the Soviet Union, the supreme command resorted to the rarely practised device of having the chief of staff issue directives directly to the Kwantung army. The acrimonious exchange between Manchuria and Tokyo provides a corrective to the generally accepted account of independent action by the military in the field, or of the Tokyo military's ready acceptance of *faits accomplis*. The author also offers fresh evidence for such episodes as the Korean army's crossing of the Manchurian border and the bombardment of the city of Chinchow.

Shimada continues his excellent discussion of Sino-Japanese relations after 1931 in volume III. The years of relative calm (1933–4), followed by a renewed thrust into North China, are discussed with a meticulous care for details. Fresh evidence is cited to show deliberate plans by the Kwantung army and the protocol force in Tientsin to frustrate the Tokyo government's efforts for a settlement of the Sino-Japanese crisis. These efforts, too, come under close scrutiny, and the data presented do not credit policy-makers with much imagination or courage. Foreign Minister Hirota, in particular, is pictured as a negative figure, intent on restoring friendly relations with China but unwilling to propose a fundamental change in the status quo. The author makes it clear that the notorious Amō (Amau) statement was taken almost verbatim from one of Hirota's instructions to the legation in Nanking. He was powerless, in drafting the 'three principles' as basis for negotiation with Chinese, to resist the military's demand for stiff terms. Ironically, by early 1937 when

Hirota resigned as prime minister, the military had come to regard their aggressive policy in North China as a failure. They were now more concerned with the menace from Soviet Russia.

Thus it happened that by mid-1937 the Japanese military and government had begun considering liquidating the North China puppet régimes and co-operating with China against the Soviet Union. This was in contrast to the trend within China, where moderate policy towards Japan had steadily been superseded by a more militant stand. The Marco Polo Bridge incident, therefore, took place just when Japan was in the process of retreat from China and the Nanking government was intent on extending its authority to that region. The story of the incident and its subsequent development into full-scale warfare is ably traced by Hata. It is regrettable that he does not discuss the incident as fully as he does in his own book.[5] In the present study, for instance, he does not attempt a close evaluation of various theses concerning the origin of the incident but instead is interested in giving a straight narrative of military affairs. For the extension of hostilities which neither side really wanted he blames several factors: a 'plot' by the pro-war faction in Japan, consisting primarily of the staff of the operations and the China sections of the general staff, the navy's opportunism in taking advantage of the incident to start action in the Shanghai area and independent action by the expeditionary forces.

Usui's account of Japanese policy in China between 1937 and 1941 might profitably have been combined with the above section. Together they form the most complete history to date of Sino-Japanese relations before the Pacific war. Such episodes as German mediation efforts, the establishment of the Wang Ching-wei régime and secret negotiations with the Chungking government have already been discussed in numerous memoirs and studies, but Usui brings them all together and correlates them with freshly uncovered documents. The author reveals the lack of real interest on the part of the Japanese military in a Wang Ching-wei project.

They were aware of the limitations of such a scheme and did not give up hope of a final accommodation with Chungking.

Volume v is complete in itself: a two-author discussion of Japanese–German relations. Ōhata develops a detailed textual analysis of the Anti-Comintern Pact and carried the story of its aftermath to the signing of the German–Soviet Non-Aggression Pact, at which point Hosoya continues the account to 1941. Here the author traces the unfolding drama of Japanese–German relations in terms of the struggle for supremacy between army and navy, and between the pro-Anglo-American and pro-German groups among Japan's policy-makers. The result is a highly comprehensive and stimulating narrative. Concerning the celebrated Ogikubo conference of 19 July 1940, attended by Prime Minister-designate Konoe, Matsuoka, Tōjō and Yoshida, the author has studied the Konoe papers and come to the conclusion that the conferees came to a basic agreement on the desirability of strengthening Japanese–German ties as a step towards establishing a new order in Asia, to include the British, French, Dutch and Portuguese colonies in southeast Asia. Navy Minister Yoshida, as is well known, was not totally convinced, and he had to be replaced by Oikawa to bring the navy to the acceptance of a tripartite alliance. Even then, the author disputes the general view that Oikawa was from the beginning in agreement with Matsuoka's conception of the contemplated alliance. The navy minister seems to have accepted the idea only after Matsuoka persuaded him that Japan had either to side with Germany and Italy or with the United States and Britain, and that the latter choice was out of the question so long as American policy in China remained stiff.

Such an argument was, of course, based on Matsuoka's famous formulation of bloc policy, viewing the world as divided into four major blocs under the leadership of Japan, the Soviet Union, the United States, and Germany and Italy, respectively. Here Hosoya clarifies the basic nature of the Axis alliance and says the participation of the Soviet Union in such a world division was essential and therefore that Germany's intention of using the alliance against the former, as well as against Britain and the United States, was fundamentally at odds with Matsuoka's. The author also traces the bloc idea in the Japanese Foreign Ministry and finds that most of Matsuoka's ideas had been presented by Shiratori Toshio, leader of the 'new bureaucrats', in 1939. Here Kobayashi Yukio's study of Japanese Soviet relations, contained in volume I, becomes relevant, as he carefully delineates arguments for a Soviet entente put forth by a number of influential Japanese during the 1920s.

At any rate, by the spring of 1940 some officials of the general staff had come to advocate rapprochement with the Soviet Union, and the navy also began pushing such a policy after the German victories in Europe, as a necessary prerequisite for its policy of southward advance. By the time their ideas were accepted and vigorously pushed by Matsuoka, they had to discover that the fundamental assumption of German–Russian peace had been mistaken. Upon the German invasion of Russia on 22 June 1941 Matsuoka, as is well known, strongly urged that Japan join Germany in attacking the Soviet neighbour. The author marshals evidence to show that the general staff, too, was now generally inclined to such a view. The Kwantung army was accordingly authorised in early August to bombard Soviet territory in case Russian planes attacked Manchuria, as seemed likely. By this time, however, the Japanese occupation of southern Indo-China and the critical relationship with the United States had come to preoccupy the attention of policy-makers, and the talks of war against Russia were allowed to peter out.

Japan's southward advance, rightly considered by many historians as the immediate cause of the Pacific war, is fully treated by Nagaoka and Hata in volume VI. Here again one feels that the two works might have been better combined. As it is, the former's description of Japanese negotiations with Dutch East Indies authorities is the best treatment of the subject in existence, and the latter's discussion of Japanese advance into French Indo-China is probably the most interesting part of the entire work. Hata discusses the Japanese navy's initial and consistent fear of involvement with the United States and its reluctance to undertake the southward advance because of such a fear. In closely analysing the drafting of the crucial 'principles of national policy' adopted by the Cabinet–supreme headquarters liaison conference on 27 July 1940, the author finds that the navy considerably toned-down the army's original draft, which called for preparation for war against the United States. The army–navy division of views on the southward advance resulted in chaos following the occupation of northern Indo-China in September 1940. Ironically, the army's insistence on positive action in southeast Asia, even at the risk of war with Britain and the United States, gave the navy a pretext to demand a greater share of strategic materials needed to prepare for such an eventuality. The causal relationship could be reversed, and in time there appeared within the navy a group of advocates for strong action. They dominated the 'first committee' organised in November 1940 by section chiefs of the Navy Ministry and the naval general staff. By mid-1941 they had come to regard war with the United States as inevitable, and their views had considerable influence on Admiral Nagano, chief of naval general staff.

Admiral Nagano is the villain in Tsunoda's account of Japanese–American relations. The author presents an absorbing story of the two nations' road to war, and his skilful use of Japanese and American sources and monographs makes this 390-page work the most up-to-date study on the subject. He treads mostly on familiar ground when dealing with last-minute negotiations in Washington, but he has uncovered fresh evidence concerning naval thinking. He relentlessly portrays Nagano as a man easily controlled by his subordinates, especially the staff of the first committee. Accepting its strong recommendations, Nagano began advocating war against the United States even before the latter put into effect its embargo on oil exports to Japan.

Strikingly enough, there was no thorough discussion between the army and the navy as to the feasibility of such a war. In fact, the author finds that the navy was actually well aware of its inferiority vis-à-vis the American navy and that even Nagano was not confident of victory in a drawn-out stuggle with the United States. But the navy was unwilling to acknowledge its inferiority, and the army based its stong stand on the assumption that the navy could win.

In the Tōjō Cabinet, too, the navy opposed Tōjō's effort for a last-minute understanding with the United States. The Hull note of 26 November 1941 was accepted by exponents of war as 'providential', and Tōjō realised the futility of further negotiation. Concerning the Pearl Harbor attack itself, however, the author makes it clear that all principal architects of Japanese policy were agreed that the attack should be preceded by the transmission of a note terminating negotiations.

In reading these volumes and comparing them with similar works, Japanese and Western, one becomes aware of certain characteristics of the present work. First, military affairs are emphasised to an unprecedented degree. This stems from the authors' research in the military archives. Memoranda by army and navy officials are taken very seriously, and their thinking is carefully analysed. This produces the second characteristic of these volumes, namely, their overriding concern with the question of decision-making. Important decisions on foreign policy are traced back to memoranda and minutes of conference by junior officials, and the process invariably leads to military documents. Divergence of views between army and navy, between a foreign minister and his staff, or between the War Ministry and the general staff is closely examined. As a result the third characteristic of the series emerges: the authors, well aware of the complexity of foreign-policy-making, do not attempt generalisations on the nature of Japan's foreign relations, leaving the reader with the task. It is possible, therefore, to regard the seven volumes as documentary collections, on the basis of which old theories could be revised and new interpretations drawn.

This latter task can be performed on at least three levels. One could, first of all, use these documents to test certain standard concepts of Japanese foreign policy. The concept of the role of junior officers in decision-making, for instance, would seem amply borne out by the present study. Their suggestions were not always accepted, and Usui's study of Foreign Minister Nomura and Ohata's account of Yonai, among others, indicate that strong leaders did from time to time suppress recommendations of their staffs. Nevertheless, the crucial importance of section chiefs in the supreme command and the service ministries cannot be disputed. The decision to fight the United States is a testimony to the tremendous influence of naval officials comprising the first committee. The concept of the civil–military dichotomy, on the other hand, would seem to evaporate in the light of the evidence presented. Foreign Ministers Hirota and Arita were as much interested as the military in a new order in Asia, and Foreign Ministry bureaucrats were in close touch with their army and navy counterparts.

Another concept may be examined in some detail. It is the idea that Japan and the United States were fated to clash in Asia. Historians have characterised Japanese–American relations before 1941 in terms of the conflict between Japan's particularistic diplomacy and America's open-door policy. Certainly these policies conflicted with each other in China. But does it necessarily follow that the two countries were destined to collide in the Far East? It cannot be denied that during the last stage of the Hull–Nomura negotiations the issue of Japanese troops in China proved a stumbling block. Evidence indicates, however, that at least until 1940 the Japanese did not think China would be the main issue of contest between Japan and the United States. The real issue seems to have been Japan's drive for imperial self-sufficiency. The idea of a national defence-state, where all resources and energies of the empire are geared to war preparation, was well

developed during the 1920s, and it was in time developed into a concept of imperial self-sufficiency. The
idea that future wars were unavoidable and therefore
that Japan should prepare for them by creating such
an empire was the driving force behind Ishiwara,
Nagata and other architects of the Manchurian incident. From this point of view, war with the United
States was inevitable simply because there was no end
to wars and the next war would be waged between the
giants of East and West. Thus Japanese action in
Manchuria was not an end in itself, nor a response to
Chinese nationalism, but only a first step towards
national mobilisation and self-sufficiency.

The picture further changed in the 1930s. The idea
of self-sufficiency was always there, and before 1938 it
meant predominance over Manchuria and China. The
costly war in China was justified only because it would
add to Japan's self-sufficiency. Until 1938, however, the
Soviet Union rather than the United States was
Japan's foremost imaginary enemy. One finds that even
Ishiwara was preoccupied with war with Russia. This
was due, on the one hand, to the Soviet military build-
up, and on the other hand to the realisation that the
United States had increased, rather than decreased, in
importance as supplier of raw materials. After 1938,
the supreme command became interested in procuring
mineral resources from southeast Asia, and this region
came to be considered an important part of the emerg-
ing self-sufficient empire. Until mid-1940, however, it
was Britain, not the United States, which was considered Japan's likely enemy as a result of its southward policy. In July 1938, for instance, War Minister
Itagaki presented a memorandum on foreign policy
and clearly distinguished Britain and the United
States. He advocated a strong policy towards the former, so as to induce it to give up its support of Chiang
Kai-shek. Towards the United States, however, he recommended that Japan should 'do as much as possible
to protect American interests in China' and consoli-
date economic ties between Japan and the United
States. This recommendation was derived from the

realisation that America's resources were essential even for Japanese self-sufficiency (v 62–7).

Towards the end of the year, the supreme command began considering the occupation of the offshore islands of South China as defence posts against Britain, in preparation for a future conflict with that country (IV 155). In July 1940, when the army formulated a policy outline advocating an Axis alliance and southward advance, it made it explicit that its primary target would be Britain and that war with the United States was to be avoided (v 175–6). The United States began to loom large again as a possible opponent only in September 1940, when the Foreign Ministry contemplated a military alliance with Germany against Britain and the United States. This, however, was objected to by the navy, and for some time thereafter the Japanese government and supreme command proceeded with the assumption that it would wage war against Britain but not against America. A statement of policy, drafted in preparation for Matsuoka's trip to Europe early in 1941, called for defeat of Britain but maintenance of peace with the United States (v 280–2). It was only in the spring and summer of the year that the army, navy and Cabinet came to accept an American war as unavoidable. Fundamentally this was because of the realisation that Britain and the United States could not be treated separately. The thrust into the French, Dutch and British colonies was considered so important that even the possibility of war with the United States had to be accepted. Even then, as Tsunoda's study fully reveals, the road to Pearl Harbor was by no means straightforward.

The documents presented in these volumes can also be used to trace the origins and developments of certain notions held by Japanese. The notion of self-sufficiency would be one example, and that of isolation another. The fear of diplomatic isolation is a theme cropping up again and again in Japanese documents. The authors of the present series on the whole accept Japan's isolation as a fact, but we cannot say that Japan was isolated simply because officials said so. A more penetrating study of the psychology of these men seems needed. At bottom is their image of their country and its relationship with the rest of the world. Underlying all their pronouncements is the fixed notion that Japan stood uneasily between East and West and that it should act quickly before it could be confronted with an overwhelming combination of Western Powers. Such an analysis would take us to the study of the mental development of the Japanese people after the mid-nineteenth century, and provide a meeting place between diplomatic history and domestic history.

Finally, the third level of analysis would be to study the 'structure' of international relations in the Far East. To understand why Japanese wanted an imperial self-sufficiency, to examine why they thought they were isolated, it would be imperative to study the degree to which other governments were committed in the Far East and to analyse their views of international relations. Between 1895 and 1914, for instance, Japanese leaders conducted their diplomacy under the assumption that their country was a respectable imperialist, just like any other Western Power. Under the prevailing 'diplomacy of imperialism', the Western Powers did allot Japan a role to play in the Far East, and the latter assumed that it need not fear isolation so long as it expanded its empire cautiously and did not infringe upon another empire's prerogatives. Such a structure, loosely defined as it was, was given a death-blow by the First World War. The peace found Germany, Russia and the United States defecting from the ranks of imperialists for various reasons, and an active movement in China began to restructure its own international relations. It is no wonder, then, that Japanese leaders lost sight of the basic patterns of diplomacy after 1918. The Washington Conference did not really create a new pattern, and Japanese diplomacy suffered from the lack of orientation. In this perspective, Japanese policy in the twenties and thirties was as much a function of other Powers' policies as of its own domestic factors.

It may be appropriate to conclude this review with a

plea for further collaboration between foreign and Japanese scholars. The foregoing remarks would indicate that Japan's foreign relations can be put in proper perspective only if they are related to the policies of other governments. Only a handful of Japanese historians have done more than perfunctory research in foreign archives, and only a fraction of Japanese monographs has been used by Western scholars. Now that the Japanese have presented their side of the picture, the time seems opportune for a really co-operative enterprise in multi-archival research.

Notes

¹ Okada Taishō Kiroku Hensankai (ed.), *Okada Keisuke* (Tokyo, 1956); Yabe Sadaji (ed.), *Konoe Fumimaro* (2 vols, Tokyo, 1952); Morishima Morito, *Imbō, ansatsu, gunto: ichi gaikōkan no kaisō* [*Conspiracies, Assassinations, Sabres: Reminiscences of a Diplomat*] (Tokyo, 1950); Imamura Hitoshi, *Kaisōroku* [*Memoirs*] (4 vols, Tokyo, 1960); Hanaya Tadashi, 'Manchu jihen wa kōshite keikaku sareta' ['Thus Was Planned the Manchurian Incident'], *Himerareta Shōwashi* [*Inside Stories of the Showa Era*] (Tokyo, 1956) pp. 40–50.
² E.g. Rekishigaku Kenyūkai (ed.), *Taiheiyō sensōshi* [*A History of the Pacific War*] (5 vols, 1954); Tanaka Sōgorō, *Nihon fascism-shi* [*History of Japanese Fascism*] (Tokyo, 1960).
³ E.g. Ōtaka Shōjirō, *Dainiji taisen sekinin-ron* [*On the Responsibility for the Second World War*] (Tokyo, 1958); Ashida Hitoshi, *Dainiji sekai taisen gaikō-shi* [*A Diplomatic History of the Second World War*] (Tokyo, 1959).
⁴ Hosoya Chihiro, *Siberia shuppei no shiteki kenkyū* [*A Historical Study of the Siberian Expedition*] (Tokyo, 1955); Kurihara Ken, *Tennō: Shōwa-shi oboegaki* [*The Emperor: A Memorandum on Showa History*] (Tokyo, 1955).
⁵ Hata Ikuhiko, *Nit-Chū sensō-shi* [*A History of the Sino-Japanese War*] (Tokyo, 1961).

Akira Iriye

Gendaishi shiryō [Documents on Contemporary History] (Tokyo: Misuzu Shobō, 1964–6):

Vol. VII: *Manshū jihen [The Manchurian Incident]* lxiv, 606. 2500 yen.
Vol. VIII: *Nit-Chū sensō:* I [*The Sino-Japanese War:* I] lxxv, 821. 3000 yen.
Vol. IX: *Nit-Chū sensō:* II [*The Sino-Japanese War:* II] lv, 798. 3000 yen.
Vol. X: *Nit-Chū sensō:* III [*The Sino-Japanese War:* III] ci, 705. 3000 yen.
Vol. XI: *Zoku Manshū jihen [The Manchurian Incident, continued]* xxxii, 991. 3500 yen.
Vol. XII: *Nit-Chū sensō:* IV [*The Sino-Japanese War:* IV] xxxiii, 596. 2500 yen.
Vol. XIII: *Nit-Chū sensō:* IV [*The Sino-Japanese War:* V] xxiii, 721. 2800 yen.

There seems to be no end to the publication of documents and monographs on Japan's foreign relations in the nineteen-thirties. It was only four years ago that the epoch-making *Taiheiyō sensō e no michi [Road to the Pacific War]* was published. Since then, additional memoirs have appeared, 'official biographies' have been written and several important studies have been made. Now comes probably the most formidable collection of Japanese source materials to date, covering

Reprinted from *The Journal of Asian Studies*, 26 (1966–7), by permission of the author and *The Journal of Asian Studies*. See also Introduction, pp. 25–7.

the 1931–41 period. Although these seven volumes are entitled either *The Manchurian Incident* or *The Sino-Japanese War*, they contain numerous documents relating to other topics. Among them are the London Naval Conference of 1930 (VII, XI) and of 1935 (XII), the Nomonhan incident (X) and the Axis alliance (X). By far the bulk of these 5000 pages of source material, however, is concerned with Chinese–Japanese relations of the nineteen-thirties. There are, for instance, documents on the establishment of Manchukuo (VII, XI), the Amau doctrine (VIII), military operations in China after 1937 (IX), the Wang Ching-wei scheme (XII) and the Shanghai and Tsingtao strikes of 1936 (XIII). In addition, some documents deal with the Japanese government's and military's plans for national mobilisation for the prosecution of the war with China. The compilers of these volumes – Tsunoda Jun, Inaba Masao and others – write that the seven-volume collection nearly exhausts the most basic available material on the subject. While new documents will undoubtedly be discovered from time to time, there is no question that students of pre-war Japanese history now have before them a treasure-house of genuine value.

Most of the documents here assembled have never before been printed. Because the compilers seem to have decided not to select documents that have been published elsewhere, these seven volumes cannot be used in isolation. The student must turn to other collections for certain key sources, in particular volume II of *Nihon gaikō nempyō narabi shuyō bunsho* [*A Chronology and Key Documents of Japanese Foreign Relations*] and volume VIII of *Taiheiyō sensō e no michi* (hereafter cited as *TSM*). Tsunoda, however, has prepared and appended to volume XIII a most useful index to all the documents in the present series plus the just mentioned supplementary volume to *TSM*.

A cursory comparison of *TSM* and the present volumes indicates that some documents now printed have already been consulted and fully utilised by the authors of *TSM*, a study noted for lengthy quotations from primary sources. These sources, however, were not always cited in their entirety by the authors of *TSM*. Most of the documents were very vaguely identified in the footnotes. The documentary supplement to *TSM* contained just a fraction of the available material. For these reasons, the series now published provides much-needed companion volumes to *TSM*. For instance, a considerable amount of writings by Ishihara Kanji is printed for the first time (VIII, IX). Kwantung army material relating to the Manchurian incident is reproduced in full (VII, XI). Many statements of fact and interpretation in *TSM* are amply corroborated by the evidence in the present series. There are numerous documents, however, that were unearthed only recently and made available now for the first time. Most of this new material was gathered by the War History Division of the Defence Agency and adds tremendously to existing knowledge. Particularly revealing are the newly discovered documents relating to the London Naval Conference, the North China operations (VIII, XII) and the policy of southern advance (X).

Japan's road to the Pacific war has been studied from various angles: civil–military relations, army factionalism, foreign policy and extra-Japanese factors. Any one of these topics can be researched more fully, thanks to the present publication. In this review Japanese military thinking in the nineteen-thirties will be taken as a focus, in order to illustrate the value of the documents.

First of all, there is much fresh evidence concerning the army's attitude towards the North China question shortly before the outbreak of the Sino-Japanese War. The documents now available do not fundamentally alter the generally accepted picture that the Japanese policy of separating North China and Inner Mongolia from Kuomintang control was the immediate cause of the war. However, there is now sufficient documentation to indicate some significant shifts in Japanese military thinking in the first months of 1937. Ishihara Kanji, who returned to Tokyo in mid-1935 as chief of the operations section of the general staff, began belatedly urging curtailment of anti-Kuomintang activities in North China. Judging from his numerous memoranda, he was strongly impressed with the strength of Chinese nationalism and the movement for Chinese unification, of which the Sian incident was a dramatic climax. Ishihara, and through him the general staff, came to the conclusion that the unification of China proper under the Nationalists was inevitable and should not be obstructed. Rather, the ideal of Japanese–Manchukuo–Chinese co-operation be 'the foundation stone of China's existence' and China would be induced to join 'the East Asian league' (VIII 378, 382). The idea was that only through working with Chiang Kai-shek could Japan reduce his reliance on Western help. More specifically, according to a general staff memorandum of 6 January 1937, 'We must purge ourselves of the idea that North China is a special region and revise the strategy of encouraging the independence of the five [northern] provinces. The area now under control of the Hopei-Chahar government naturally belongs to the Chinese Republic' (VIII 380). Naval authorities in Tokyo, too, recognised that the Sian incident had given impetus to China's reunification under the Kuomintang (XII 315, 321). While the naval general staff feared that Nanking would intensify its anti-Japanese policy, the Navy Ministry was ready to consider co-operation with the Kuomintang to reduce Western influence in China (VIII 397). Such ideas underlay the Hayashi Cabinet's moderate policy towards North China. The fact that the succeeding Konoe Cabinet brought about deterioration in Sino-Japanese relations does not lessen the significance of these developments in early 1937.

One factor in the army's revised attitude towards China was concern with preparedness against the Soviet Union. In this connection, too, Ishihara's writings, reproduced in full in these volumes, are very valuable. His strategic ideas had been neatly summed up in a paper he wrote in June 1933:

War will come when our national policy of estab-

lishing an East Asian league is obstructed by an
enemy. Whether the enemy be America, Russia or
Britain, the war will be a protracted one. We must,
therefore, expect to encounter their combined military force as well as China's resistance. The only way
to carry out our national defence plan is therefore to
establish control over China proper as speedily and
skilfully as possible, create a self-sufficient economic
bloc encompassing Japan, China and Manchukuo,
protect our position in the East Asian league by
force against the land force of the Soviet Union and
the naval force of the United States and Britain, and
then to devise ways to bring the enemy to his knees,
thus opening the way to victory (VIII 666).

Initially Ishihara was optimistic that an East Asian
league could be brought about militarily, through
quick and decisive military action in China. Soon he
came to emphasise the formation of a bloc knitting
together Japan, Manchukuo and North China. After
1936, however, he became so concerned with the Soviet
Union that he began advocating moral and peaceful
means for obtaining China's co-operation. From this
time on he actively interested himself in strategic planning vis-à-vis Russia. A memorandum drafted by his
section in the general staff on 29 July 1936 declared
that preparation against the Soviet Union must be
completed by 1941 (VIII 682).

The preoccupation with strategy towards Russia inevitably caused a slow-down of military planning towards China. As noted above, the general staff was inclined to reconsider policy towards North China. As
Kawabe Torashirō, who succeeded Ishihara as chief of
the operations section in the spring of 1937, recalled
three years later, the supreme headquarters favoured
the liquidation of the East Hopei régime. Before anything was done, however, war came – a war for which
'there had been absolutely no strategic plans' (XII 413).
The story about the reluctant involvement of the general staff in the China war is well known. The documents now made available do not significantly alter

existing interpretations, but provide more ample documentation for the dilemmas and frustrations of the military leaders after 1937. At bottom may have been the problem, in Ishihara's words, that 'we do not have the capacity to take a large view of policy and strategy and to pass judgements on the basis of the larger picture' (IX 310). An overall policy formulation was certainly needed if Japan were to be concerned with Russia, America and Britain, in addition to China. Earlier, the point had been to establish control over China as a necessary step in military preparedness against the big Powers. As the war in China began and dragged on, it tended to become an end in itself, and policies towards the Powers were reconsidered in the interest of prosecuting the war. Some continued to worry about the larger implications of the conflict, however, and persisted in the belief that the China war was a wasteful deviation from more fundamental policy needs of the nation. In August and September 1938, for instance, the general staff's operations section drafted a series of papers, advocating the termination of the war by the end of the year. The reason for this, explained a memorandum, was that the war's basic purpose lay in 'establishing a national defence zone and furthering co-operation among Japan, Manchukuo and China'. Preparedness against the Soviet Union must take precedence over the prosecution of the China war, and 'it will be unnecessary as well as impossible to turn China into another Manchukuo'. Japan should even be willing to reconsider its policy towards Chiang Kai-shek (IX 273–7).

That such a proposal was not carried through was fundamentally due to the concurrent rise of another view, calling for a diplomatic means of restraining the Soviet Union. From the middle of 1938 on, Japan's military leaders began to show an interest in an alliance with Germany in order to isolate Russia and at the same time to solve the war in China by neutralising other potential antagonists. The origins of the Axis alliance are given substantial documentation in these volumes. Most of the documents are taken from naval

archives but contain many memoranda drafted by the
army and the civilian agencies. What comes out clearly
is that both army and navy turned to Germany as a
way out of the predicament confronting Japan: if a
German alliance could restrain the Soviet Union,
Japan would be enabled to concentrate on the war in
China. Such a psychology explains the hardened attitude towards Britain in 1938. Both army and navy
strategists convinced themselves that Britain was a
major obstacle in the way of settling the China war (x
175, 339–43). Whereas the army was willing to purchase the German alliance by committing Japan to
fight against Britain, however, the navy refused to go
along, until conditions changed drastically in 1940. Before then naval authorities were unwilling to link explicitly the prosecution of the war in China to a German alliance directed against Britain.

In this connection, the question of Japanese–American relations may be raised. Usui Katsumi, in his
introduction to some of these documents, writes that
one of the fundamental questions facing Japan was
whether it should co-operate economically with the
United States in China or establish its own mono-
polistic position. The brutal fact was that even in the
Japan-occupied areas in China dependence on American goods was increasing. Under the circumstances, the
China question was the thorniest in the Japanese–
American crisis (ix xxxii–xxxiii). Any international
conflict, however, will have to be viewed in terms of
two aspects, 'real' and imagined. While there may have
been a fundamental conflict between America and
Japan in China, this was not always perceived by the
actors. In so far as one may judge from the military
documents, Japan's army leaders were extremely slow
in coming to the realisation that their action in China
might provoke war with the United States. A Kwantung army memorandum of 11 October 1937 noted,
'Concerning the United States we must respect its
rights in the Philippines and Kwangtung, promote economic and cultural co-operation, and if necessary bring
about an improved atmosphere by proposing a Pacific

defence agreement solely between the two countries' (IX 47). Throughout the rest of the year and in 1938, available evidence reveals that the Japanese army, both in China and in Tokyo, visualised normal, and at times even friendly, relations with the United States. On 18 November 1938, for instance, the supreme headquarters decided on maintaining good relations with America while doing the nation's utmost to conclude the war in China (IX 550). It is beside the point that the United States government would not have welcomed such an offer of friendship.

The navy, on the other hand, had, since 1917, considered the United States the most probable enemy. After the 1930 London Naval Conference, the imperial navy pushed vigorously for 'parity' with the United States. The reasons for this, however, were little connected with China. Basically, the Japanese navy argued that technological advances made the existing 10:6 ratio unrealistic (XII 60). Although the United States continued to be viewed as the imaginary enemy, this did not mean that an American war was foreseen in the immediate future. The 'first committee', organised in the spring of 1936 by section chiefs of the Navy Ministry and the naval general staff, studied specific plans for control of the western Pacific and an eventual advance southward, but no strategic connection was established between the prosecution of war in China and hostilities with the United States (VIII 351–6).

In 1939, the year of America's definite hardening towards Japan, the army leaders in Tokyo continued to profess their goal of achieving some understanding with America. A general staff memorandum drafted in May stated that it was 'particularly recommended to improve relations with the United States'. More specifically, the paper called for a trade and economic conference between the two countries, a negotiation for loans from the United States and a conclusion of an East Asian and Pacific agreement with America (IX 562–3). After Washington notified, in July, its intention of terminating the 1911 commercial treaty, the army supreme command decided 'to improve the situation so that ultimately the United States might be induced to contribute to the ending of the war in China' (IX 571). In an extremely interesting memorandum written on 28 August the operations section of the general staff considered three possible courses of action open to Japan, now that Germany had signed a non-aggression pact with Russia. These were: co-operation with Russia against Britain, co-operation with Britain against Russia and co-operation with all the Powers. The paper recommended that Japan should, for the time being, follow the third alternative while preparing for the second. The United States was mentioned only in the context of 'co-operation with all the Powers' (IX 574–5).

Actual conflict with the United States came to be visualised only in 1940, with the inception of the policy of southern advance. The idea of southern advance, of course, had originated much earlier. Ishihara, for instance, wrote in June 1933 that in order to establish an East Asian league, the Japanese army and navy should co-operate in attacking the Philippines, Hong Kong, Guam and Singapore (VIII 666). But such an eventuality was more hypothetical than real. It was when Japan tried expansion into southeast Asia to take advantage of the European war that war with America came to be considered a likelihood. This was because the United States was expected to retaliate against Japanese action by imposing a trade embargo. Even so, it is interesting to note that until mid-1941 Japan's army and navy strategists believed war with America could somehow be avoided even in the event of advance into the south seas. According to a series of papers written by General Koiso Kuniaki in the summer of 1940, the new Asian 'economic bloc', to be created in order to ensure Japan's self-sufficiency and expel Western influence from Asia, would initially exclude the Philippines. Japan would use force against the Dutch, French and British colonial possessions, but no war with the United States seemed inevitable so long as Japan respected the security of its territories in the Pacific. The Asian bloc would then promote economic interdepen-

dence with the European, Soviet and American economies (x 466–82).

As the authors of *TSM* have already amply demonstrated, such complacency in time gave way to a more
realistic appraisal of American policy, which in turn
produced an attitude of fatalism, driving the Japanese
to a hopeless Pacific war. Even so, in their minds the
decision for war against the United States was a by-
product, not of the China war, but of the advance into
southeast Asia. In policy statements and memoranda of
1940 and 1941, 'the solution of the China incident' and
'the solution of the southern problem' were always distinguished, and it was in connection with the latter
that the possibility of war with America, as well as with
the Netherlands, France and Britain, was considered (x
505). As late as July 1941, the Japanese army command
in China believed that there would be an American
war only in case Japan used force in southeast Asia
(XIII 424). Although there are relatively few documents
for 1941 in these volumes, all available evidence indicates that if there was a 'real' Japanese–American crisis
in China, it was not perceived by the Japanese.

Such observations will illustrate the pleasure that
awaits the user of these seven volumes. Together with
the eight volumes of *TSM* and the microfilmed documents of the Foreign Ministry, they enable the historian to raise more questions of detail and try to answer
them with more assurance and sophistication than has
been possible. At the same time, the more documentation we have for Japan, the greater grows the need for
comparative study. It is to be hoped that as more comes
to be known about Japanese foreign policy and
decision-making, these will be contrasted to ideas and
institutions in other countries. Only then will it become possible to view the international crisis of the
nineteen-thirties as it should be viewed, internation-
ally.

13 Pearl Harbor and the Revisionists

Robert H. Ferrell

It was perhaps inevitable that after the Second World War, as after the war of 1914–18, there should appear in the United States a school of historians questioning the purposes of the war and the motives of the wartime statesmen. The cost of both world wars, in human lives and in physical resources, was very high; and it was only natural that some individuals should question such expenditure. Yet the new school of 'revisionism' appearing after the Second World War has undertaken a line of investigation which, if successful, will force the rewriting of an entire era in American history. The revisionists hope to prove that in 1941 President Franklin D. Roosevelt purposely exposed the Pacific fleet at Pearl Harbor, and goaded the Japanese into attacking it, thus bringing the United States into the war on the side of the Allies. As Professor Harry Elmer Barnes has put the case, in rather plain English, 'The net result of revisionist scholarship applied to Pearl Harbor boils down essentially to this: In order to promote Roosevelt's political ambitions and his mendacious foreign policy some three thousand American boys were quite needlessly butchered....'[1]

In the years after the First World War there had probably been some need of historical revision. At any rate the general disillusionment of the American people with foreign affairs in the 1920s, blended as it was with pacifism, made the efforts of the revisionists take on an almost sensational appearance. Then too, the origins of the First World War lay tangled in de-

Reprinted from *The Historian*, xvii ii (spring 1955), by permission of the author and *The Historian*. See also Introduction, pp. 25–26.

cades of European international politics, in which a too-ardent nationalism in Berlin and Vienna and St Peters-burg had not always been countered by common sense in Paris and London. In the tragic events of the July crisis in 1914 there was a certain mechanical develop-ment, when diplomatic act brought counter-act, mobil-isation counter-mobilisation, and few military leaders really seemed at fault. The mechanistic events of July and the half-century of diplomatic manoeuvre which preceded them made it easy to forget the difference between Balfour's England and the Kaiser's Germany, between the gentle responsibility of Sir Edward Grey and the flashy diplomatics of Prince Bernhard von Bulow. For all these reasons the task of the revisionists after the First World War was not especially difficult; and a great many Americans came to believe that Germany had not been guilty in 1914.

The task of the revisionists after the Second World War has not been so easy. It is true that they can point to the results of the war, which are indeed heartily disagreeable: Russia has increased in stature, becom-ing a Super Power with only one rival, the United States; Europe has split into two areas, Communist-dominated and free; France is a shadow of her pre-war self, with chronic political instability; Germany is now rearming; the world's trade remains in an unsettled state, America constantly having to adjust the 'dollar shortage'; and in the Far East the Chinese have taken unto themselves a Communist government which gives every sign of stability and permanence, there is talk about the rearming of Japan, Korea is divided, Indo-China dubious, etc., etc. The picture is not a pretty one, and invites critical inquiry. Yet strangely enough the revisionists have been unable to convince the American people this time that participation in the Second World War was a mistake. Despite the alto-gether disquieting aftermath of the war, most Ameri-cans still believe that it was necessary to suppress by force the aggressive regimes in Berlin and Tokyo.

Certainly there has been no real *Kriegsschuldfrage* after the second war, and this has badly hindered the revisionist cause. The Hossbach Memorandum of November 1937, apparently genuine, recording the Berchtesgaden conference in which Hitler drew the pattern of his future conquests, has set at rest most speculation as to the primary authorship of the war.[2] For more remote antecedents of the conflict an inquiring student might still search back into the decade of the 1920s and the Depression period, and there is room for considerable investigation here; but the years prior to 1933 have thus far proved a relatively unprofitable area for revisionism. The revisionists have instead turned to what one of them has described as the 'back door' to war,[3] the crisis in American–Japanese relations in the summer and autumn of 1941 which came to a tragic end on 7 December with the military disaster at Pearl Harbor.

The revisionists after the Second World War are vitriolic and angry men, as any examination of their books and articles will clearly show. They have nothing but contempt for the so-called 'court historians' who write under the auspices of such organisations as the Council on Foreign Relations. Professor Barnes in several privately printed brochures has not hesitated to insult dozens of his most eminent colleagues.[4] In hotly setting forth their views, the revisionists have sometimes lapsed into downright misrepresentation.[5] They none the less are entirely within their rights in asking for a careful hearing, and it is only fair that one should read their writings, thoroughly and with an open mind before arriving at any conclusions, What can one conclude, then, about their scholarship? Fortunately in 1953 there appeared the symposium *Perpetual War for Perpetual Peace*, edited by Professor Barnes, which offers in a single volume the considered views of several of the leading revisionists. Moreover, two admirals who actually were with the Pacific Fleet at Hawaii on the disastrous Sunday morning in 1941 have very recently published books on the subject, and these 'non-professional' works of historical revision should also facilitate any necessary rewriting of the hitherto accepted version of the events at Pearl Harbor.

I

In *Perpetual War for Perpetual Peace* there are essays of varying length by Harry Elmer Barnes, William Henry Chamberlin, Percy L. Greaves, Jr, George A. Lundberg, George Morgenstern, William L. Neumann, Frederic R. Sanborn and Charles Callan Tansill. These individuals, all dedicated revisionists, are prominent in their respective fields of history, journalism, sociology and law. They have worked over much of the large body of literature now available on American foreign relations prior to entry into the Second World War.[6] From their investigations they firmly believe that, as Professor Barnes has put it, Roosevelt exposed the fleet at Hawaii to promote political ambitions and a mendacious foreign policy. They have none the less found no clear-cut documentary evidence of such a conspiracy.[7]

From a close reading of *Perpetual War for Perpetual Peace* it also becomes apparent that the contributions in the volume, despite their scholarly apparatus, are not as objective as a casual reader might assume. The chapters by Greaves, Tansill and Morgenstern, for example, have a disturbing way of proceeding along sedately, in a clear and able narrative style, and then rather suddenly moving to an illogical and unproved conclusion. The chapter by Greaves, dealing with the various official investigations of Pearl Harbor, marches in magisterial fashion and is writing of a very high order until it drops away at the end. Moreover, in some of the contributions there are other marks of partisan writing, such as a tendency to accept as American policy the contemporary or even later utterances of such outspoken American ambassadors as the ebullient William C. Bullitt in Paris.

One discovers surprising things in these essays. Professor Tansill in two chapters averaging at least three footnotes per page (36 pages and 131 notes; 90 pages and 334 notes) sketches the road to war in Europe and the 'Pacific back road' to war. In the former he relates

that Roosevelt made a most careful effort, including
very involved diplomatic manoeuvring, to encourage
'an Anglo-French-Polish stand which he knew meant war
in 1939'; and Roosevelt did this, rather than encourage
Germany to turn on Russia, because he believed that a
Russian–German war in 1939 would have been short
and victorious for Berlin, whereas an Anglo-French-
Polish war against Germany would be long and enable
him eventually to get into it. This is giving Roosevelt
credit for greater Machiavellian intelligence than his
worst enemies usually concede to him, but even so, he
required unexpected help from Hitler to make the
scheme work. 'No one at the time expected Hitler to
crush France and England as quickly as he did. Indeed,
but for Hitler's stupidity in playing soft with Britain
in 1940, the war would probably have ended so rapidly
in German victory that Mr Roosevelt could not have
found his way into the conflict.' Is this, indeed, saying
that it is too bad that Hitler did not conquer the British in 1940?

Perhaps the most thoughtful chapter in *Perpetual
War for Perpetual Peace* is by Professor Neumann, and
concerns general American–Japanese diplomatic relations before the outbreak of war at Pearl Harbor.
Written in a measured, careful manner, its entire argument at last comes to rest upon an interpretation of
Roosevelt's order in July 1941 freezing all Japanese
assets in the United States. This order served to stop
American trade with Japan, in particular cutting off
all oil supplies. After July 1941, according to Neumann, Japan 'had no alternative but to bow to American demands or fight for the resources by which her
economic and military strength was to be maintained'.
But here is the same sort of oversimplification which
the Japanese militarists themselves employed in 1941.
Did history in 1941 really turn on a dilemma? Is it not
instead one of the truths of history that choices seldom
are equally unsatisfactory? Was there not a dignified
alternative for Japan in 1941, other than humiliation
or war? The United States government was extraordinarily anxious that peace prevail in the Far East, so

long as it was a peace with honour. There were highly placed Japanese in 1941, including probably the emperor himself, who were not at all eager for war, and saw an alternative of honourable peace. Had the leaders of Japan in 1941 chosen a pacific role, and perhaps seen fit to aid the hard-pressed Allies, great benefits would have followed. Responsible Japanese statesmen today would certainly concede this point. Surely Professor Neumann, in his effort to prove the folly of American Far Eastern policy prior to Pearl Harbor, has oversimplified the facts of his subject.

In passing one should also remark the chapter entitled 'Roosevelt is Frustrated in Europe', by Frederic R. Sanborn. Here there is some curious documentation which brings into question the reliability of Sanborn's entire essay. On p. 198 he asserts flatly that prior to the Munich crisis the Russians delivered three hundred planes to Czechoslovakia, and that in addition several squadrons of Soviet warplanes were on the Czechoslovak airfields. For the three hundred planes delivered to the Czechoslovaks his source, in a footnote, is Louis Fischer's *Men and Politics*, an honest though not always correct book of reminiscence and surmise. Fischer himself says that 'Pierre Cot, the former French Minister of Air, tells me that ... the Soviet government delivered 300 military planes to Czechoslovakia. Mr Cot had this information from high Czech authorities.'[8] Hence a report of a report in an autobiography is treated by Sanborn as an established fact. As for the Russian warplanes on Czechoslovak fields at the time of Munich, Fischer remarks only that this 'is known now', and gives no source of his information.[9] Sanborn, moreover, accepts completely in his essay the authenticity of the so-called German White Paper, published by the Wilhelmstrasse in 1940, which purported to contain documents found in the Polish Foreign Office after the capture of Warsaw. The White Paper is at least of dubious provenance; the most one could safely say for it is that it was a careful selection of documents, and if one wished to be more doubtful there are a number of possibilities – fraudulent excerpting, outright composition, interlarding of material, etc.

In concluding this necessarily close look at the contributions to *Perpetual War for Perpetual Peace*, there remain the chapters by Professors Barnes and George A. Lundberg. One of Barnes's two essays is the book's summary; and the initial chapter on 'Revisionism and the Historical Blackout' may be described as rather similar to Barnes's recent anti-'court historian' brochures. Professor Lundberg, the eminent sociologist at the University of Washington, in his essay on 'American Foreign Policy in the Light of National Interest at the Mid-Century' undertakes to apply to international affairs the tools of social science. His investigation proves to him that 'the whole frame of reference within which current discussion of international policy is carried on is at best based on ignorance of the real issue and at worst on intellectual fraud'. He seeks to sweep away the confusion and dishonesty, but only plunges into a morass of sociological definitions. At least one reader was dismayed to be told that 'Security, to any person, usually means the absence of a felt threat of deprivation of any of the conditions which he highly values.' Such plain phrases as 'do not like', which may also be written as 'dislike', become 'negatively conditioned emotionally'. At one point Lundberg alludes to the principles of human ecology and sociology which govern all life on this earth. He hastily adds that 'This is not the place to discuss in detail what these principles are.' Readers, however, will be interested to know that in Professor Lundberg's essay they may discover what happened to the excess deer and pumas in the Kaibab Forest in Arizona. This, in turn, has more importance than one might at first think, for it indicates 'the *nature* and the *direction*' of the immutable principles of ecology and sociology, and 'the reason why neglect of them must result in disaster'.

In sum it is not unfair to say that *Perpetual War for Perpetual Peace* does not contribute anything new, other than impressionistic and occasionally tautological argument, towards the historiography of American entrance into the Second World War. The 'mystery' of

Pearl Harbor, if it is a mystery, remains. Instead of penetrating scholarship one finds a strange alliance of unexceptionable narrative joined together with unsupported statement, which at least in the case of Professor Lundberg's 'social science' approach allows him to rig arguments under the guise of science, and then to slip in his own conclusions which are logical only in the narrow 'context' of his argument. This, most historians would perhaps agree, will not advance the cause of historical revision.

And is there not a further question which begins to come to mind as one reads the revisionist interpretation of the Second World War? Is there not a certain uncritical partisanship in these revisionist arguments?

It is not a 'smear' (to use one of Professor Barnes's favourite words), nor is an individual a member of the 'smearbund', when he points to the way in which present-day historical revisionism has joined itself with a blind partisan hysteria and hatred for the late President Franklin D. Roosevelt. This personal animus of course marks another difference between the revisionists of the First and Second World Wars. Franklin D. Roosevelt was president longer than any other man in American history; his administrations introduced many social and economic reforms, some of which are not yet acceptable to certain sections of the American people; Mr Roosevelt in his public statements was sometimes lacking in candour, and in others ways it is possible that his actions on occasions left much to be desired. Yet it would be foolish to ascribe to a single man – whatever one's views of his character and policies – the woes of twenty years of American history.

II

There has been no convincing evidence produced to date that the disaster of 7 December 1941 was 'planned that way'. Despite the feverish activities of the revisionists there has been little real change in the diplomatic history of the events leading to Pearl Harbor. In another area, however, that of military history, it is possible to say that there is good reason for revision, especially of the hitherto accepted views on the responsibility for unreadiness in the fleet and at the airfields when the Japanese attacked. Rear Admiral Robert A. Theobald's *The Final Secret of Pearl Harbor: The Washington Contribution to the Japanese Attack*[10] has called attention to the military problems which prior to 7 December 1941 beset the fleet and base commanders at Hawaii. Admiral Husband E. Kimmel's own book, *Admiral Kimmel's Story*,[11] eloquently restates and enlarges the essential parts of Admiral Theobald's argument.

There is of course a fair-sized amount of balderdash in Theobald's book, and the allegations about President Roosevelt's 'secret plans' and his 'final secret' of exposing the fleet do not at all come off. But it is impossible to read this book and not feel friendly towards the bluff, honest soul who wrote it – an old sailor who entered at the beginning of the volume, for the guidance of readers, a 'Transcript of the Author's Naval Career'. It is an honourable and brilliant career, and if the admiral goes to sea in matters of high politics he still does a shipshape job of describing naval codes and code-breaking and the failure of the Pearl Harbor commanders to be included among the recipients of 'Magic', the Japanese diplomatic intercepts provided by the breaking of the highest Japanese cipher, the Purple code. The British and General MacArthur received Purple-decoding machines from Washington; why not the commanders at Pearl Harbor? This is a good question, and not as foolish as it might be made to appear by the usual answer that the authorities in Washington couldn't prevent the Pearl Harbor attack, even with the code, so what would Kimmel and his army opposite at Hawaii, Lieutenant-General Walter C. Short, have done with it.

This, together with other interesting matters, is further dealt with in *Admiral Kimmel's Story*. General Short died in 1949, but Kimmel has carried on the struggle to set the Pearl Harbor military record straight, and the result is the present volume. About half of Kimmel's book consists of his testimony before the joint congressional investigating committee in 1946, and this material is not identified in reprinting.[12] Yet the additional material, while it does not add greatly to the information in the congressional testimony, has been fitted neatly together with the old. The result is a readable and engrossing account of a man who, it seems almost certain, was made a scapegoat for a tragedy which he could not himself have prevented. This is not to say that President Roosevelt, rather than Kimmel, was responsible for the disaster, but only that unpreparedness at Hawaii derived from the belief and indeed conviction in Washington in November and early December 1941 that the Japanese would not strike at the Pacific Fleet. Siam was uppermost in the minds of Washington officials; how to deal with an attack on Siam was at the fore of all thoughts. It seemed only natural that the Japanese would proceed methodically with creation of their 'Greater East Asia Co-Prosperity Sphere', and move first to the areas south of China. They already were in Indo-China, by agreement with the Vichy French.[13] Siam was a logical next move. A relatively rich little country, it was independent and possessed a weak dynasty and a corrupt government. In some ways its plight in 1941 resembled that of Korea at the turn of the nineteenth century. Siam, so it seemed, would be the first Japanese victim. Malaya and the Dutch East Indies were secondary possibilities for Japanese attack. There was a bare chance that Japan might move against the Philippines. No one thought the attack would come at Hawaii.[14]

Even if Kimmel and Short had been on the watch for an attack, they possessed insufficient forces to ensure protection of the base. On this point *Admiral Kimmel's Story* is most convincing. It is true that the Pearl Harbor base, if compared to Panama, the Philippines and the American West Coast, was well equipped.[15] The difficulty of defending Hawaii remained, for to patrol adequately the surrounding waters would have required probably 250 planes, and maybe more. Kimmel

and Short had only 49 patrol planes, and no spare parts
or extra crews. Moreover, the Pearl Harbor commanders were constantly receiving new groups of personnel
to be trained in Hawaii and sent elsewhere. There was,
really, a pretty good argument for basing the fleet in
California, as the fleet commander in 1940, Admiral J.
O. Richardson, had argued with President Roosevelt.
In California the defence arc would have been only
180 degrees, just half that for Pearl Harbor. The West
Coast was two thousand miles more distant from
Japan. The fleet's supplies, especially fuel oil, would
have been readily available, for the long haul to
Hawaii would have become unnecessary. Fuel oil, in-
cidentally, had been very short at the time of the Pearl
Harbor attack, as there were neither sufficient tankers
nor storage facilities.[16] The only result of Admiral
Richardson's protests to the president, unfortunately,
was his being relieved of command early in 1941 and
succeeded by his subordinate, Admiral Kimmel.

Much has been made of the fact that on the fateful
Sunday morning at Pearl Harbor all the battleships
were at their moorings, rather than at sea; but even this
argument breaks down when one realises, as Admiral
Kimmel points out, that the fleet had only begun to
profit from the lessons of the war in Europe and that
installation of additional deck armour and anti-aircraft batteries was far from complete. The ships indeed
were so vulnerable to air bombing that it would have
been exceedingly dangerous to have taken them to sea
without carrier escort, as the British navy itself learned
when the *Prince of Wales* and *Repulse*, caught without
carrier protection, went down off Malaya three days
after the Pearl Harbor attack. Kimmel actually possessed only two carriers at the time of the attack – the
fleet's third carrier was refitting on the West Coast –
and the *Lexington* and *Enterprise* were both at sea on
7 December, ferrying planes to Wake and Midway on
instruction from the Navy Department in Washington.
When the Department advised sending the carriers in
two task forces to the outlying islands, it was in effect
telling Kimmel to keep his battleships in harbour.

There, at least, the big 'battle wagons' were surrounded by some of the base's anti-aircraft batteries.

Some writers have asked why Kimmel had not taken precautions against air torpedo attacks in the harbour, by installing steel baffle nets around the anchored ships.[17] The question had arisen early in 1941 in correspondence between Kimmel and the chiefs of naval operations, Admiral Harold R. Stark, and the latter had advised against baffles, because nets would have lessened the readiness of the fleet. In any event there seemed little possibility of an air torpedo attack. It is true that the British in 1940 had made a highly successful attack on the Italian fleet at Taranto, but there the torpedoes had been launched in about 84–90 feet of water. Pearl Harbor was much more shallow, with an average depth of 30 feet or less, and a channel depth of 40 feet. Military men considered that air torpedo attack in such shallow water would only have sent the torpedoes down uselessly into the mud.

Another point which deserves mention, and on the basis of which the Pearl Harbor commanders have been severely criticised, is the 'loss' of the Japanese carriers by fleet intelligence during the few days prior to the attack at Hawaii. Fleet intelligence had for years been following the common procedure of plotting the Japanese fleet by listening to the ships' radio call signals. This system had a certain usefulness, although it was subject to well-known uncertainties. When the Japanese navy, for example, changed its call signals, there followed a period of from one to two months before the new signals could be identified. The Japanese fleet in 1941 changed its signals on 1 May, 1 November and 1 December. Then, too, it was always possible for any vessel, even a fishing smack, to use a battleship or carrier call signal for purposes of deception. Moreover, vessels in harbour usually relied on shore-based radio and hence were temporarily 'lost' to the intelligence services of foreign fleets. It was therefore nothing unusual when in early December Kimmel had 'lost' the Japanese carriers. He had, in fact, lost most of the Japanese fleet because of the recent change

in call signals. There was no special reason why he
should have had to communicate this routine situation
to his army opposite in Hawaii, General Short; and
failure to tell Short certainly could not constitute any
dereliction of duty.[18]

There is, lastly, the already mentioned question of
'Magic'. It was the Roman philosopher Seneca who, as
Kimmel recalls, once said that 'It is better to have use-
less knowledge than to know nothing.' In retrospect it
appears that the contention of both Kimmel and his
friend Admiral Theobald, that Magic should have
been furnished to the Pearl Harbor command, is unexceptionable. True, the more individuals who were in
on this highly secret business of cracking the highest-
level Japanese diplomatic code, the more chance of a
leak and a consequent code change which would have
ruined the entire operation. None the less, if code
machines went to Manila and, especially, to London,
there is no convincing reason why a machine should
not have been shipped to Hawaii. The real tragedy of
the Magic episode is that this magnificent information
on Japanese intentions and diplomatic manoeuvring
was not properly evaluated in the War and Navy Departments; everybody's business (the intercepts went to
the top officials of the government and military) became nobody's business, and the careful evaluation of
the decoded intercepts was never accomplished.
Whether the intelligence officers in Hawaii could have
done this is naturally problematical, but it is almost
certain that such intercepts as those which instructed
the Japanese consul in Honolulu to divide the Pearl
Harbor anchorage into five sectors and report on each
twice a week would have received close and minute
attention. As Kimmel remarks, no other American base
was so carefully examined by the Japanese. In late
November the Honolulu consul received advices from
Tokyo to report on the base even when there were no
ship movements. Many other such straws in the wind
might well have caught the eye of fleet intelligence at
Hawaii. It is entirely possible, even probable, that had
Kimmel received proper intelligence prior to 7 De-

cember 1941 he could have 'ordered all fleet units in Pearl Harbor to sea, arranged a rendezvous with Halsey's task force returning from Wake, and been ready to intercept the Japanese force by the time fixed for the outbreak of war'.[19] There could have been a slaughter of the Japanese task force, and Kimmel immediately would have risen in stature to one of the great heroes of the Second World War.

Underlying the neglect to inform properly the Pearl Harbor commanders was, as we have seen, the almost complete unawareness of Washington officials, military and civil, that Japan might strike a blow at the American fleet. In 1894, 1904 and 1914 the Japanese had begun wars with sneak attacks, prior to declaration of hostilities. In 1941 the diplomatic negotiations in Washington had gone on for so long – Secretary Hull and Under-secretary Sumner Welles had conferred at length with the Japanese several dozen times between July and December[20] – that when the decisive hour came, no one would believe it. The hour, as is now well known, came at 1.00 p.m. Sunday afternoon, Washington time, when the two Japanese ambassadors were to present a detailed formal note to Secretary Hull. This note had followed the so-called American 'ultimatum' of 26 November in which the American government had proposed in a rather stiff communication that the Japanese, if they wished to come to an agreement with the United States, should do a number of things including evacuation of China.[21] The Japanese reply of 7 December, as had been apparent for several days from the Magic intercepts, was a most crucial one, and seemed obviously to be almost a breaking-off of diplomatic relations. The time of its delivery was most suspicious. Why should the two Japanese envoys insist upon seeing an elderly secretary of state at exactly 1.00 p.m. on a Sunday afternoon?

The deadline was known in the navy decoding room by 7.00 a.m., Washington time. What happened to this warning of disaster is, of course, common knowledge. Stark came to his office at 9.00 a.m. or thereabouts and refused to do anything until General Marshall arrived.

Marshall was taking his famous horseback ride, and
arrived at 11.15 or thereabouts. In the meantime subordinates in the Navy Department had compared the
Washington deadline, 1.00 p.m., with similar hours in
the various localities in the Far East where attack
might be expected. It would be 2.00 a.m. in Manila –
and 7.30 a.m. in Honolulu. Yet General Marshall at
about noon Washington time sent his warning to Pearl
Harbor by commercial cable, and the messenger boy
was pedalling his bicycle out to Fort Shafter when the
Japanese attack began.[22]

Admiral Kimmel, at the time of Pearl Harbor, had
been in the navy for more than forty years. He had
graduated from the Academy in 1904 and gone round
the world with the 'white fleet' in 1907–9, served
honourably during the First World War, and in the
inter-war years risen to a position of very high responsibility. On 8 December 1941 his court martial was
demanded on the floor of the House of Representatives. In following weeks and months, after summary
relief from his command, he was deluged with insult-
ing letters. In the spring of 1942 the chairman of the
military affairs committee of the House, Andrew Jackson May, suggested in at least one public speech that
Kimmel and Short should be shot. After having virtually been told to apply for retirement, the admiral
sought during the war to have his case reviewed. This
is not the place to evaluate the various inquiries, nor
the slipshod manner in which some of them were conducted.[23] Associate Justice Owen J. Roberts of the
Supreme Court told the joint congressional committee
after the war that, had he been given the Japanese
intercepts during his investigation in 1941–2, he would
not have taken the trouble to read them. Admiral King
in November 1944 reversed the findings of a naval
court of inquiry, and admitted to Kimmel a month
later that he had not even read the proceedings of the
court whose findings he had reversed.

Kimmel's predecessor at Hawaii, Admiral Richardson, said openly even during the war that much of the
responsibility for the Pearl Harbor disaster would have

to rest upon the occupant of 1600 Pennsylvania Avenue and the members of his Cabinet. Fleet Admiral William F. Halsey in the ten years since V-J Day has been echoing this opinion.[24] It is not difficult to agree with Halsey and Richardson, and Kimmel and Theobald, that in 1941 the Administration, including the Washington military leaders, badly misestimated the power and intentions of Japan. Yet one must be very careful to add that Pearl Harbor was essentially a military error; and that there has been no clear proof yet brought forward to show that the tragic disaster of 7 December 1941 was – as revisionist historians such as Professor Barnes have asserted – a matter of diplomatic planning.

Notes

[1] 'Of course, they were only a drop in the bucket compared to those who were ultimately slain in the war that resulted, which was as needless, in terms of vital American interests, as the surprise attack on Pearl Harbor.' H. E. Barnes (ed.), *Perpetual War for Perpetual Peace* (Caldwell, Idaho, 1953) ch. 10, 'Summary and Conclusions', p. 651. See also George Morgenstern, *Pearl Harbor: The Story of the Secret War* (New York, 1947); and Charles A. Beard, *President Roosevelt and the Coming of the War, 1941: A Study in Appearances and Realities* (New Haven, 1948). There is a trenchant criticism of the Morgenstern book in Samuel Flagg Bemis's 'First Gun of a Revisionist Historiography for the Second World War', *Journal of Modern History*, XIX (March 1947) 55–9. For an adverse view of Beard's book, see Samuel Eliot Morison, *By Land and By Sea* (New York, 1953) ch. 15, 'History through a Beard', pp. 328–45.

[2] Department of State, *Documents on German Foreign Policy: 1914–45*, series D, I (Washington, 1949) 29–39.

[3] Charles Callan Tansill, *Back Door to War* (Chicago, 1952).

⁴ *The Chickens of the Interventionist Liberals Have Come Home to Roost: The Bitter Fruits of Globaloney; Rauch on Roosevelt; The Struggle Against the Historical Blackout; The Court Historians versus Revisionism.*

⁵ See the letter by Samuel Flagg Bemis to the editor of the *Journal of Modern History*, xxvi (June 1954) 206.

⁶ *Pearl Harbor Attack: Hearings before the Joint Committee on the Investigation of the Pearl Harbor Attack* (39 vols, Washington, 1946); *Report on the Investigation of the Pearl Harbor Attack* (Washington, 1946). The archives of the Department of State, with certain restrictions, are open to qualified scholars for all material up to the date of 7 Dec 1941. The Grew papers and diary are open to students upon application to the curator of manuscripts of the Houghton Library at Harvard. Herbert Feis in his *Road to Pearl Harbor* (Princeton, 1950) and Professors William L. Langer and S. Everett Gleason in their *The Undeclared War: 1940–41* (New York, 1953) have used the Stimson and Morgenthau diaries. The Roosevelt papers at Hyde Park are available to the public, and are under the administration of the National Archives.

Frederic R. Sanborn in his essay in *Perpetual War for Perpetual Peace* dwells on the inaccessibility of the wartime Roosevelt–Churchill correspondence, some 1700 missives which have been 'kept secret to this day'. Historians, of course, would like to see such material. Yet the practices of opening archives, public and personal, at least in the United States, have been extraordinarily liberal in recent years. If the most private correspondence of statesmen is to be published within a decade or so of its writing, there is no question but that statesmen in the future will feel themselves severely circumscribed in communicating with each other. The result, indeed, has already been a severe deterioration of communication through regular diplomatic channels, for diplomats and their superiors no longer can be certain as to the confidential handling of their dispatches. The Roosevelt–Churchill correspondence beyond doubt would contain a considerable amount of day-to-day speculation and wonderment, which, if taken out of context by inexperienced or unfriendly readers, would look very compromising.

[7] A frequently cited remark in proof of a Rooseveltian conspiracy is a certain passage in the diary of Secretary of War Stimson. At a White House meeting in November 1941 Stimson had said that it was all a matter of 'how we should manoeuvre them [the Japanese] into the position of firing the first shot'. A peacefully inclined democracy, as Stimson well knew, was at great disadvantage when it had to await a blow by an aggressor. Washington leaders in late November 1941 knew that Japan was planning a large-scale aggressive military movement in the Far East, and everyone supposed that the Japanese would be intelligent enough to move on Siam, or perhaps Malaya or the Dutch East Indies, but not American territory – thus avoiding an open *casus belli* with the United States and, in view of the divided state of public opinion at the time, making it extremely difficult for the Roosevelt administration to convince the country that vital American interests were imperilled. Stimson hoped that, somehow, perhaps by presidential announcement, Japan (and the American people) could be informed that the then-impending Japanese move would traverse vital American interests; that the move could then be made to appear as a case of 'firing the first shot'; and that the president could thereby go before Congress and ask for war. See Richard N. Current, 'How Stimson Meant to "Maneuver" the Japanese', *Mississippi Valley Historical Review*, XL (June 1953) 67–74. The revisionists have certainly not been fair to Secretary Stimson in the interpretations put upon this 'manoeuvre' statement since the time when it first appeared in the record of the congressional investigation of 1945–6. Stimson usually recorded from four to ten doublespace typescript pages of diary each day, dictating the previous day's occurrences into a machine on the following morning while shaving.

[8] *Men and Politics: An Autobiography* (New York, 1941) pp. 555–6.

[9] Ibid., p. 570.

[10] New York, 1954.

[11] Chicago, 1955.

[12] See the review by Commander Walter Muir Whitehall in the *New York Times* (30 Jan 1955).

[13] On 30 Aug 1940 Vichy had conceded to Japan the use of three airfields and several ports in northern Indo-China. The Japanese foreign minister on 25 July 1941 informed Ambassador Joseph C. Grew in Tokyo that Vichy had consented to admit Japan to a joint protectorate of all Indo-China.

[14] See the testimony of Major-General Sherman Miles, head of army intelligence in Washington at the time of Pearl Harbor, in his 'Pearl Harbor in Retrospect', *Atlantic Monthly*, CLXXXII (July 1948) 65–72. Rear-Admiral Theodore Stark Wilkinson, director of naval intelligence, likewise minimised the possibility of a Hawaii attack: S. E. Morison, *Rising Sun in the Pacific* (Boston, 1948) pp. 134–5. See also Langer and Gleason, *The Undeclared War: 1940–41*, chs 27, 28. Even Henry L. Stimson and McGeorge Bundy, *On Active Service in Peace and War* (New York, 1948), who state firmly a belief in the negligence of Kimmel and Short, admit that the men in Washington did not foresee the attack at Pearl Harbor and were astonished by it (pp. 389–93). For Stimson's surprise at the attack, and his subsequent reactions in the matter of responsibility, see Richard N. Current, *Secretary Stimson: A Study in Statecraft* (New Brunswick, N.J., 1954) ch. 8, 'The Old Army Game'.

[15] Miles, in *Atlantic Monthly*, CLXXXII 68.

[16] According to Morison, the Pearl Harbor attack was 'wrongly concentrated on ships rather than permanent installations and oil tanks': *Rising Sun in the Pacific*, p. 132.

[17] See, for example, Morison, *Rising Sun in the Pacific*, pp. 138–9.

[18] But see Walter Millis, *This Is Pearl!*, p. 298, where the author feels that liaison between Kimmel and Short was poor, and that Kimmel should have in-

formed Short that fleet intelligence officers had lost the Japanese carriers.

Another warning, which Morison believes (*Rising Sun in the Pacific*, p. 138) should have roused the Hawaiian command, was the discovery and sinking of a Japanese midget submarine off the fleet entrance to Pearl Harbor by the destroyer *Ward*, in the early morning of 7 December. Actually, it is not easy to know when a ship has sunk a submarine, and in preceding weeks and months various vessels of the Pacific Fleet had had a number of suspicious contacts. A contact by destroyer *Ward* in the early hours of 7 December was hardly, in itself, sufficient basis for ordering a general fleet alarm. Sensing his responsibility, the commander of *Ward* must have felt much like a passenger on a train, about to pull the emergency cord.

[19] *Admiral Kimmel's Story*, p. 111.

[20] Langer and Gleason, *The Undeclared War, passim.* See also Cordell Hull, *Memoirs* (2 vols, New York, 1948) II 982–1037, 1054–1105.

[21] For the complete text of the 'oral statement' handed by Hull to the Japanese ambassadors, see *Foreign Relations of the United States: Japan, 1931–41* (2 vols, Washington, 1943) II 766–70. The statement contained an 'Outline of Proposed Basis for Agreement between the United States and Japan', labelled 'Tentative and without Commitment'. This was hardly an ultimatum, for apart from its tentative and unofficial character it had no attached time limit. See Bemis, in *Journal of Modern History*, XIX 57. On the other hand, Langer and Gleason, *The Undeclared War*, p. 906, believe that 'in substance if not in form the ... note did constitute America's final terms for the indefinite future, and this was recognised by those who formulated it. In this very real sense it was an ultimatum and it is understandable that the Japanese should have generally regarded it as America's "last word", a "sort of ultimatum"....'

[22] Apart from the warnings given by the ordinary Magic traffic, there was the special 'winds' broadcast. A prearranged phrase about the weather, inserted in a

daily short-wave Japanese-language news broadcast from Tokyo, was to warn Japanese consulates in soon-to-be belligerent countries that they should destroy their remaining secret papers. The message was to be varied in such a way as to reveal the countries which would be entering the war: *higashi no kaze ame* (east wind, rain: war between Japan and the United States), *kitano kaze kumori* (north wind, cloudy: war between Japan and the U.S.S.R.), *nishi no kaze hare* (west wind, clear: war between Japan and Britain). There is still confusion over whether any 'winds' message was ever received in Washington. The revisionist historians hold that a message was received prior to 7 Dec, suppressed and later removed from Pentagon files.

[23] There were eight different investigations.

[24] As Halsey wrote to Kimmel on 20 July 1953, '... you know I have always thought and have not hesitated to say on any and all occasions, that I believe you and Short were the greatest military martyrs this country has ever produced, and that your treatment was outrageous.' (*Admiral Kimmel's Story*, p. 168.) See also his foreword to Theobald's *Final Secret of Pearl Harbor*.

Notes on Contributors

ALAN BULLOCK, Master of St Catherine's College, Oxford, and author of *Hitler, a Study in Tyranny* (1952), *The Liberal Tradition* (1956), *The Life and Times of Ernest Bevin* (2 vols, 1960, 1967), and general editor (with F. W. Deakin) of the *Oxford History of Modern Europe*.

C. ROBERT COLE teaches History at the Pamona College, Claremont, California.

ROBERT H. FERRELL, Professor of History at Indiana University, and author of *Peace in Their Time: Origins of the Kellogg–Briand Pact* (1952) and *American Diplomacy in the Great Depression* (1963).

AKIRA IRIYE, Professor of History at the University of Rochester, and author of *After Imperialism: The Search for a New Order in the Far East* (1965) and *Across The Pacific: An Inner History of American–Asian Relations* (1967).

JAMES JOLL, Professor of International History at the London School of Economics, and author of *The Second International* (1955) and *Intellectuals in Politics* (1960).

H. W. KOCH, Lecturer in History at the University of York.

T. W. MASON, Research Fellow at St Antony's College, Oxford.

E. M. ROBERTSON, Lecturer in History at the University of London, and author of *Hitler's Pre-War Policy and Military Plans 1933–39* (1963).

A. J. P. TAYLOR, formerly Fellow of Magdalen College, Oxford; Librarian, Beaverbrook Library, and author of *The Struggle for Mastery in Europe 1848–1914* (1954), *The Origins of the Second World War* (1961), *The Course of German History* (1945), *English History 1914–45* (1965), *Sarajevo to Potsdam* (1966), etc.

H. R. TREVOR-ROPER, Regius Professor of History at the University of Oxford, and author of *The Last Days of Hitler* (1947), editor of *Hitler's Table Talk* (1953) and *Hitler's War Directives 1939–45* (1964), etc.

D. C. WATT, Reader at the London School of Economics, and author of *Personalities and Policies* (1965) and (with others) *A History of the World in the Twentieth Century* (1967).

T. DESMOND WILLIAMS, Professor of History at University College, Dublin.

Select Bibliography

(An asterisk denotes books with comprehensive
bibliographies.)

Books

BAER, G. W., *The Coming of the Italian–Ethiopian War* (Cambridge, Mass., 1957).

BEASLEY, W. G., *The Modern History of Japan* (London, 1963).

BELOFF, MAX, *Foreign Policy of Soviet Russia, 1929–1941* (2 vols) (Oxford, 1947–9).

BRENAN, G., *The Spanish Labyrinth* (London, 1960).

BULLOCK, ALAN, *Hitler: A Study in Tyranny,* new ed. (London, 1942).

BUTOW, R. J., *Tojo and the Coming of War* (Princeton, 1961).

CARR, E. H., *Ambassadors at Large: A Study of Foreign Policy from Versailles to the Outbreak of War,* with an introduction by Lord Halifax (London, 1940).

CARR, E. H., *Twenty Years' Crisis* (London, 1958).

CARR, E. H., *German–Soviet Relations between Two Wars* (Baltimore, 1951).

CARROLL, B. A., *Design for Total War – Arms and Economics in the Third Reich* (The Hague, 1968).

CELOVSKY, B., *Das Münchener Abkommen* (Stuttgart, 1958).

CHURCHILL, W. S., *The Second World War,* I: *The Gathering Storm* (London, 1948).

COLLIER, B., *Barren Victories: Versailles to Suez, The Failure of the Western Alliance, 1918–1956* (New York, 1964).

COLLIER, B., *A Short History of the Second World War* (London, 1969).

COMPTON, J. V., *The Swastika and the Eagle: Hitler, the United States, and the Origins of the Second World War* (London, 1968).

CRAIG, G. A., and GILBERT, F., *The Diplomats* (Princeton, 1953).

DEAKIN, F. W., and STORRY, G. R., *The Case of Richard Sorge* (London, 1966).

DIVINE, R. A., *The Illusion of Neutrality* (Chicago, 1962).

DRESCHLER, KARL, *Deutschland–China–Japan 1933–1939: Das Dilemma der deutschen Fernostpolitik* (Berlin, 1964).

ERICKSON, J., *The Soviet High Command, 1918–1941* (London, 1962).

FEILING, KEITH, *The Life of Neville Chamberlain* (London, 1946).

FEIS, H., *The Road to Pearl Harbor* (Princeton, 1950).

GATHORNE-HARDY, A. M., *Short History of International Affairs 1920–1939* (London, 1950).

GEHL, J., *Austria, Germany and the Anschluss 1931–1938* (Oxford, 1963).

GILBERT, M., *The Roots of Appeasement* (London, 1964).

GILBERT, M., and GOTT, R., *The Appeasers* (London, 1963).

GRAML, H., *Europa zwischen den Kriegen* (Munich, 1969).

HEINRICHS, W. H., *American Ambassador Joseph Grew and the Development of the United States Diplomatic Tradition* (New York, 1966).

HILGER, G., and MEYER, A. G., *The Incompatible Allies: A Memoir History of German–Soviet Relations 1918–1941* (New York, 1953).

HINSLEY, F. H., *Power and the Pursuit of Peace* (London, 1963).

HOFER, W. J., *War Premeditated* (London, 1954).

IRIYE, AKIRA, *After Imperialism: The Search for a New Order in the Far East* (Cambridge, Mass., 1965).

*IRIYE, AKIRA, *Across the Pacific: An Inner History of American–East Asian Relations* (New York, 1967).

IRVING, D., *Breach of Security: The German Intelligence File on Events Leading to the Second World War*, with an introduction by D. C. Watt (London, 1968).

*Jacobsen, H. A., *Nationalsozialistische Aussenpolitik 1933–1939* (Frankfurt, 1969).

Jonas, M., *Isolationism in America 1935–1941* (Ithaca, N.Y., 1966).

Jones, F. C., *Japan's New Order in Eastern Asia, 1937–1945* (London, 1954).

Kirby, S. W., *The War against Japan* (London, 1957 onwards).

Kirkpatrick, I., *Mussolini, A Study of Power* (New York, 1964).

Klein, B., *Germany's Economic Preparations for War* (Harvard, 1959).

Kochan, L., *The Struggle for Germany* (Edinburgh, 1963).

Kordt, E., *Wahn und Wirklichkeit* (Stuttgart, 1948).

Krausnick, H., Buchheim, H., Broszat, M., and Jacobsen, H. A., *The Anatomy of the S.S. State*, trans. R. Barry, M. Jackson and D. Long, with an introduction by Elizabeth Wiskemann (London, 1968).

Laqueur, W., *Russia and Germany, A Century of Conflict* (London, 1965).

Langer, L., and Gleason, S. E., *The Challenge of Isolation* (New York, 1952).

Langer, L., and Gleason, S. E., *Undeclared War* (New York, 1953).

Macleod, I., *Neville Chamberlain* (London, 1961).

Marwick, A., *Britain in the Century of Total War* (London, 1968).

Medlicott, W. N., *Contemporary England* (London, 1967).

Meinck, G., *Hitler und die deutsche Aufrüstung 1933–1939* (Wiesbaden, 1959).

Milward, A., *The German War Economy* (London, 1965).

Namier, L. B., *Diplomatic Prelude, 1938–1939* (London, 1948).

Namier, L. B., *Europe in Decay: A Study of Disintegration 1936–1940* (London, 1950).

Namier, L. B., *In the Nazi Era* (London, 1952).

Nolte, E., *The Three Faces of Fascism* (London, 1965).

Northedge, F. S., *The Troubled Giant* (London, 1966).

O'NEILL, R. J., *The German Army and the Nazi Party 1933–1939* (London, 1966).

PARKER, R. A. C., *Europe, 1919–1945* (London, 1969).

PLAYFAIR, I. S. O., *History of the Second World War: The Mediterranean and the Middle East* (U.K. series, London, 1956).

ROBBINS, K., *Munich 1938* (London, 1968).

ROBERTSON, E. M., *Hitler's Pre-War Policy and Military Plans* (London, 1963).

ROSSINI, G. (ed.), *L'Europa fra le due Guerre* (Turin, 1966).

SADAKO, N. OGATA, *Defiance in Manchuria; the Making of Japanese Foreign Policy* (Berkeley, 1964).

SCHROEDER, P., *The Axis Alliance and Japanese–American Relations* (Ithaca, N.Y., 1958).

SCOTT, W. E., *Alliance against Hitler: The Origins of the Franco-Russian Pact* (Durham, N.C., 1962).

SELVEMINI, G., *Prelude to World War II* (London, 1953).

SOMMER, T., *Deutschland und Japan zwischen den Mächten* (Tübingen, 1962).

STORRY, G. R., *The Double Patriots: A Study of Japanese Nationalism* (London, 1957).

STORRY, G. R., *A History of Modern Japan* (London, 1960).

TAYLOR, A. J. P., *The Origins of the Second World War* (London, 1963).

TAYLOR, A. J. P., *English History, 1914–1945* (London, 1965).

THEOBOLD, R. A., *The Final Secret of Pearl Harbor* (New York, 1954).

THOMAS, H., *The Spanish Civil War* (Penguin ed., 1965).

THORNE, C., *The Approach of War 1938–1939* (London, 1967).

*TOSCANO, M., *The History of Treaties and International Politics* (Baltimore, 1966).

TOSCANO, M., *The Origins of the Pact of Steel* (Baltimore, 1967).

WAITE, R. G. L. (ed.), *Hitler and Nazi Germany* (New York, 1965).

WALTERS, F. P., *History of the League of Nations*, 2 vols (1954).

WARNER, G., *Pierre Laval and the Eclipse of France* (London, 1968).

WATT, D. C., *Personalities and Policies: Studies in the Formulation of British Foreign Policy in the Twentieth Century* (London, 1965).

*WATT, D. C. (ed.), *Contemporary History in Europe: Problems and Perspectives*, with an introduction by Alan Bullock (London, 1969).

WEINBERG, G. L., *Germany and the Soviet Union, 1939–41* (The Hague, 1954).

WHEELER-BENNET, J. W., *The Nemesis of Power* (London, 1954).

WHEELER-BENNET, J. W., *Munich: Prologue to Tragedy* (London, 1966).

WISKEMANN, ELIZABETH, *Europe of the Dictators, 1919–1945* (London, 1966).

WISKEMANN, ELIZABETH, *The Rome–Berlin Axis* (London, 1966).

WISKEMANN, ELIZABETH, *The Europe I Saw* (London, 1968).

WISKEMANN, ELIZABETH, *Undeclared War*, 2nd ed. (New York, 1967).

WOHLSTETTER, R., *Pearl Harbor: Warning and Decision* (Stanford, 1962).

Articles and Essays

CARR, E. H., 'Britain as a Mediterranean Power', *The Gust Lecture* (University College, Nottingham, 1937).

CRAIG, G. A., 'Totalitarian Approaches to Diplomatic Negotiations', in A. O. Sarkissian, *Studies in Diplomatic History and Historiography in Honour of G. P. Gooch* (London, 1961).

CROWLEY, J. B., 'A Reconsideration of the Marco Polo Bridge Incident', *Journal of Asian Studies*, 22 (1962–3).

DELZELL, L., 'Pius XII, Italy and the Outbreak of War', *Journal of Contemporary History*, 4 (1967).

HILL, L., 'Three Crises 1938–1939', *Journal of Contemporary History*, 1 (1968).

MEDLICOTT, W. N., 'Britain and Germany: The Search for an Agreement 1930–1937', *The Creighton Lecture in History, 1968* (London, 1969).

MEDLICOTT, W. N., *The Coming of World War II* (Historical Association pamphlet, London, 1963).

ROBERTSON, E. M., 'Die diplomatische Vorbereitung der Rheinlandbesetzung 1936', *Vierteljahrshefte für Zeitgeschichte*, 2 (1962).

ROBERTSON, E. M., 'L'Europa e l'avvento di Hitler (1933–1939)', in *L'Europa fra le due Guerre*, ed. G. Rossini (Turin, 1966).

TOSCANO, M., 'Eden's Mission to Rome on the Eve of the Italo-Ethiopian Conflict', in A. O. Sarkissian, *Studies in Diplomatic History and Historiography in Honour of G. P. Gooch* (London, 1961).

TREUE, W., 'Hitlers Rede vor der deutschen Presse, 10. November 1938', *Vierteljahrshefte für Zeitgeschichte*, VI (Oct 1958).

TREVOR-ROPER, H. R., 'Hitlers Kriegsziele', *Vierteljahrshefte für Zeitgeschichte* (April 1962).

VITAL, D., 'Czechoslovakia and the Powers, September 1938', *Journal of Contemporary History*, 1 iv (1966).

VOGELSANG, T., *Vierteljahrshefte für Zeitgeschichte*, Beilage (Bibliography) (1953).

WATT, D. C., 'Anglo-German Naval Negotiations on the Eve of the Second World War', *Journal of the Royal United Services Institute* (May–Aug 1958).

WATT, D. C., 'Appeasement: The Emergence of a Revisionist School', *Political Quarterly* (April–June 1965).

WATT, D. C., 'The Anglo-German Naval Agreement of 1935: An Interim Judgement', *Journal of Modern History*, XXVII ii (1956).

WATT, D. C., 'The Reoccupation of the Rhineland: The Myth of the Orders to Withdraw', *Journal of Contemporary History*, 4 (1966).

WEINBERG, G. L., 'The May Crisis of 1938', *Journal of Modern History* (1957).

WILLIAMS, T. DESMOND, 'Negotiations Leading to the

Anglo-Polish Alliance', *Irish Historical Studies*, 10 (1956).

Memoirs and Diaries

ALOISI, P., *Journal (25 Juillet 1932–14 Juin 1936)*, trans. Vaussard (Paris, 1957).

AVON, THE RT HON. EARL OF, *The Eden Memoirs: Facing the Dictators* (London, 1962).

CIANO, G., *Diary 1937–1938* (London, 1952) and *Diary 1939–1943* (London, 1947).

CIANO, G., *Diplomatic Papers* (London, 1948).

COULONDRE, R., *De Stalin à Hitler* (Paris, 1950).

FOERSTER, W., *General Oberst Ludwig Beck, sein Kampf gegen den Krieg* (Munich, 1953).

FRANÇOIS-PONCET, A., *Souvenir d'une Ambassade à Berlin* (Paris, 1946).

HASSELL, U. VON, *Diary 1938–1943* (London, 1948).

HENDERSON, N., *Failure of a Mission* (London, 1940).

HITLER, ADOLF, *Mein Kampf*, with an introduction by D. C. Watt (London, 1969).

HITLER, ADOLF, *Hitler's Secret Book* (London, 1963).

HITLER, ADOLF, *Hitler's Table Talk*, with an introduction by H. R. Trevor-Roper (London, 1953).

HITLER, ADOLF, *Hitler's War Directives*, with an introduction by H. R. Trevor-Roper (London, 1964).

HOSSBACH, F., *Zwischen Wehrmacht und Hitler* (Hanover, 1949).

HULL, C., *Memoirs*, 2 vols (London, 1948).

ROSENBERG, A., *Das Politische Tagebuch*, ed. H. G. Seraphim (Göttingen, 1965).

TEMPLEWOOD, VISCOUNT, *Nine Troubled Years* (London, 1954).

Documents

DEGRAS, J., *Soviet Documents on Foreign Policy, 1917–1941*, 3 vols (London, 1951–3).

Documents on British Foreign Policy, 1919–1939, ed. Rohan Butler and Sir E. L. Woodward (London, 1946).

Documents diplomatiques francais 1932–1939, 1st series, vols I–III: July 1932–Nov 1933; 2nd series, vols I–III: Jan–Nov 1936 (Paris, 1962–).

Documents on German Foreign Policy 1918–1945 (London, 1948–).

Documenti Diplomatici Italiani, 8th series, ed. M. Toscano, vols XII–XIII (Rome, 1952–).

Documents and Materials relating to the Eve of the Second World War, 2 vols (Moscow, 1947).

Foreign Relations of the United States: Diplomatic Papers 1939 (Washington, 1955).

International Affairs (Moscow, 1963–).

International Military Tribunal Far East (Tokyo, 1946–8).

International Military Tribunal Nuremberg: Nazi Conspiracy and Aggression, 8 vols (1946).

Trial of Major War Criminals, 42 vols (1947–9).

Royal Institute of International Affairs, Documents 1928–; Surveys 1924–.

Index

References to World War II are shown as WWII